Seeking Compliance

Contributors

Franklin J. Boster, Professor, Department of Communication, Michigan State University, East Lansing, MI.

Judee K. Burgoon, Professor, Department of Communication, University of Arizona, Tucson, AZ.

Michael H. Burgoon, Professor, Department of Communication, University of Arizona, Tucson, AZ.

James Price Dillard, Professor, Department of Communication Arts, University of Wisconsin, Madison, WI.

Timothy Edgar, Professor, Department of Communication, University of Maryland, College Park, MD.

Mary Anne Fitzpatrick, Professor, Department of Communication Arts, University of Wisconsin, Madison, WI.

Claire Dzur Harkness, Professor, Department of Communication Arts, University of Wisconsin, Madison, WI.

Beth Haslett, Professor, Department of Communication, University of Delaware, Newark, DE.

Kathleen J. Krone, Professor, Department of Communication, The Ohio State University, Columbus, OH.

Tae-Seop Lim, Professor, Department of Communication, University of Colorado, Boulder, CO.

John Ludlum, Department of Communication, The Ohio State University, Columbus, OH.

Gerald Marwell, Professor, Department of Sociology, University of Wisconsin, Madison, WI.

Janet R. Meyer, Professor, Department of Communication, University of Wyoming, Laramie, WY.

Gerald R. Miller, Chair, Department of Communication, Michigan State University, East Lansing, MI.

Barbara J. O'Keefe, Professor, Department of Communication, University of Illinois, Urbana-Champaign, Urbana, IL.

David R. Schmitt, Professor, Department of Sociology, University of Washington, Seattle, WA.

Seeking Compliance

The Production of
Interpersonal Influence Messages

Edited by

James Price Dillard

ඟP
Gorsuch Scarisbrick, Publishers
Scottsdale, Arizona

Editor	John W. Gorsuch
Consulting Editor	Gerald R. Miller
Production Manager	Carol Hunter
Manuscript Editor	Sally Scott
Cover Design	Cynthia Maliwauki
Typesetting	Publication Services

Gorsuch Scarisbrick, Publishers
8233 Via Paseo del Norte, Suite F-400
Scottsdale, Arizona 85258

10 9 8 7 6 5 4 3 2 1

ISBN 0-89787-340-8

Printed in the United States of America.

For Ione Stroup and Evelyn Dillard

Contents

viii   *Contents*

Preface

T he study of interpersonal influence is about how individuals use messages to affect behavioral change in others. This book is narrowly focused on one aspect of that process: the production of influence messages. This topic has piqued the interest of researchers in many of the diverse disciplines that together comprise the social sciences, but nowhere have these production processes been studied with such sustained vigor as they have been studied in the field of communication during the 1980s.

Many communication scholars have commented on the rapid growth in the area now known as compliance-gaining. Some have expressed enthusiasm about this development, saying that it provides better balance to a field that has, as a matter of tradition, over-emphasized message effects. Others, speaking with equal or even greater ardor, have condemned compliance-gaining, pointing to the absence of a broad theoretical vision and a seeming insistence on a limited set of methodological tools. It is true that inquiry in compliance-gaining has proceeded unevenly despite the fervor of its proponents, a demonstration, perhaps, of the not-so-profound revelation that interest alone is insufficient to guide research in any meaningful way.

Nonetheless, a body of research now exists that warrants attention and consideration. This book represents an attempt to develop several vantage points on the message-production literature. One vantage point is retrospective; its purpose is to provide a sense of the brief history of this emergent area. From a second vantage point, we can see clearly that distinct theoretical positions are evolving. Although these positions are not fully articulated, they may provide the basis for the theoretical jousting essential to the maturation of an area of inquiry. By moving to yet another vantage point, we can see the implications that compliance-gaining has for applied issues and the connections that might be established with other fields; using messages to change behavior is a concern that transcends disciplinary boundaries. Finally, taking a step back from this trio of perspectives demonstrates that compliance-gaining is beginning to make a significant contribution to the study of interpersonal influence. With time and further research, we can expect the importance of that contribution to grow.

Beginnings

An Introduction

Gerald Marwell
University of Wisconsin, Madison

David R. Schmitt
University of Washington

W | hen we began working on compliance-gaining behavior as a theoretical and research problem, neither of us had given any thought to the process of communication. Although we are both social psychologists, we come from very different traditions and are interested in different issues. Marwell was trained in "small groups." As a research assistant to Edgar F. Borgatta, he learned both factor analysis and how to code behavior in terms of R. F. Bales's Interaction Process Analysis. Bales's system is based on coding the intention behind behavior, and one of its most frequently used categories is "attempts to influence." For a sociologist, Schmitt was trained in an even more unusual graduate program. Led most directly by Keith Miller at Washington University, the program was highly influenced by the ideas of B. F. Skinner. Patterns of behavior (including compliance gaining) are "selected" because of their effects on a person's environment.

In 1964, both of us were new Assistant Professors of Sociology at the University of Wisconsin, Madison. We had recently completed our Ph.D.s and were looking for a new project. At that time, the country was experiencing a newly awakened concern over the problems of the poor and disadvantaged, and both of us were teaching courses in social problems. We speculated that one of the problems faced by the disadvantaged might be their lack of the compliance-gaining skills possessed by their middle-class counterparts—skills that are needed to deal successfully with employers and teachers. Given our experimental and observational backgrounds, we both preferred to use laboratory-based research styles. When we started thinking about compliance-gaining behavior, however, we realized that we had a difficult conceptual reconnaissance task to complete before we could operationalize any research in laboratory terms.

Perhaps the key new insight that we brought to this topic was the idea of a behavioral repertoire. Several pieces of research limited to specific forms of compliance-gaining behavior had already been published. For example, French and Raven's (1960) bases of social power had been very influential, Jones (1964) had recently introduced the notion of "ingratiation" and Weinstein (Weinstein & Deutchberger, 1963) had described the effects of "altercasting" in interaction. The powerful effects of reward and punishment, of course, were well-known in the dominant learning theories of the time.

Our first paper on this subject began as the theoretical "front end" of our N.S.F. research proposal. "Compliance-Gaining Behavior: A Synthesis and Model" (Marwell & Schmitt, 1967a) has not had the visibility of "Dimensions of Compliance-Gaining Behavior: An Empirical Analysis" (Marwell & Schmitt, 1967b) in part because the *Sociological Quarterly* was not as widely read as *Sociometry*, and in part because of the time required to get the piece published—journals were and are less likely to accept "think pieces" than research efforts (Marwell, now editor of the *American Sociological Review*, suspects that he is behaving in much the same way).

Perhaps more important in setting the difference in visibility between the two papers is the fact that the empirical analysis contained an instrument and methodology that others could use. Our list of sixteen compliance-gaining tactics, together with what is now called the "vignette" method, could be applied in a variety of settings, providing a vehicle for further research. To tell the truth, that particular number of tactics was not derived from "theory." Rather, it represented the limits of our imagination and the literature at the time. This list has proved to be the part of our work most consistently reproduced by others (beginning with Ed Fink, whom we suspect is the starting point for interest in the topic within the area of communication).

For our purposes, the factor analyses we reported were intended to reduce this list of techniques to a smaller core that could be operationalized as options in the field or laboratory. We did pursue several applied studies of compliance-gaining using questionnaires and vignettes (e.g., Marwell & Schmitt, 1967c). However, our major thrust was toward a line of work in the laboratory. Our Skinnerean impulse re-emerged. Communication and influence seemed too complex to catch on the fly. We selected a specific context in which people often seek to gain the compliance of others—actions that involve cooperation. Hence, our first laboratory study: "Reward and Punishment as Influence Techniques for the Achievement of Cooperation under Inequity" (Schmitt & Marwell, 1970).

Gradually, the thrust of our collaborative work veered toward the determinants of the initiation and disruption of cooperation rather than compliance gaining. In part, this alteration of emphasis resulted from what we perceived as a luke-warm reception of our compliance-gaining work within sociology. The notions of power and influence had long-standing traditions, but our expansion of these topics to include a variety of more subtle techniques did not find a ready audience. We were young and did not appreciate how long it usually takes (about a decade) for ideas to make an impact. On the other hand, issues surrounding cooperation in the prisoner's dilemma and elsewhere were achieving real prominence in social psychology—and we decided to bring our somewhat different perspective to the emerging debate.

Only recently have we become aware of the vigorous work on compliance gaining that has been going on in communication. It is a bit like having a long-lost child reappear with a family in tow. Since the family is interesting and admirable, the experience is a pleasure, but it is nonetheless strange. We are grateful to the authors of the articles in this volume, and their colleagues, for giving life to a useful idea.

REFERENCES

French, J. R. P., & Raven, B. (1960). The bases of social power. In D. Cartwright & A. Zander (Eds.), *Group Dynamics* (2nd ed.) (pp. 607-623). New York: Harper & Row.

Jones, E. E. (1964). *Integration.* New York: Harper & Row.

Marwell, G., & Schmitt, D. R. (1967a). Compliance-gaining behavior: A synthesis and model. *Sociological Quarterly, 8*, 317-328.

Marwell, G., & Schmitt, D. R. (1967b). Dimensions of compliance-gaining behavior: An empirical analysis. *Sociometry, 30*, 350-364.

Marwell, G., & Schmitt, D. R. (1967c). Attitudes toward parental use of promised rewards to control adolescent behavior. *Journal of Marriage & the Family, 29*, 500-504.

Schmitt, D. R., & Marwell, G. (1970). Reward and punishment as influence techniques for the achievement of cooperation under inequity. *Human Relations, 23*, 37-45.

Weinstein, E. A., & Deutchberger, P. (1963). Some dimensions of altercasting. *Sociometry, 26*, 454-466.

An Examination of the State of Compliance-Gaining Message Behavior Research

Franklin J. Boster
Michigan State University

I n a recent check of my compliance-gaining message behavior bibliography I noticed that there were more than one hundred entries, the majority of which are published articles. That number is especially impressive in view of the fact that most have been written since 1980.

With the aid of hindsight it is easy to understand the emergence of this large literature. The ability to generate and transmit a message that gains the compliance of others, especially if in so doing one can keep the agent-target relationship intact, is a skill that is useful in many contexts. For instance, elementary school teachers can be more effective if they can control their pupils without destroying the students' love of learning (for example, see Kearney et al., 1984, 1985), supervisors can enhance organizational goals by motivating workers without alienating them (see Kipnis & Cosentino, 1969; Kipnis, Schmidt, & Wilkinson, 1980; Richmond et al., 1984), and spouses can maximize relational goals by exerting some control over each other's behavior without producing resentment (see Dillard & Fitzpatrick, 1985; Fitzpatrick & Winke, 1979).

Just as it is not surprising that communication scholars are interested in compliance-gaining message behavior, the specific features of compliance-gaining message behavior that are chosen for study are also understandable. Many of us working in the area were trained in programs that emphasized the importance of generating and testing hypotheses, as opposed to doing purely observational, descriptive work, and this emphasis shows in the types of studies that have been conducted.

One way in which this predilection for hypothesis testing has been manifested is in the search for situational determinants of compliance-gaining message behavior. To provide some personal history as an example, Michael Roloff, David Seibold, and I were students in a Gerald Miller interpersonal seminar in the summer of 1974. A draft of *Between People* by Miller and Steinberg (1975) had been recently reviewed, and the reviews suggested that there were a number of interesting ideas in the book but that it would be nice if some data bearing on these ideas were available. In the seminar Miller suggested that it would be in our best interests if we transformed these ideas into specific hypotheses and collected some data to test them. We complied.

Having just read a paper by Marwell and Schmitt (1967b) for an Ed Fink seminar, I suggested that compliance-gaining behavior might differ in interpersonal and noninterpersonal situations. Miller, Roloff, Seibold, and I fleshed out the idea, constructed both interpersonal and noninterpersonal scenarios, crossed these descriptions with scenarios that differed in the duration of relational consequences, and collected some data. These results were first presented at the International Communication Association conference in 1976, and were subsequently published in *Communication Monographs* (Miller et al., 1977).

Since that time, others have examined the impact of these situational variables (Cody, McLaughlin, & Schneider, 1981; Lustig & King, 1980). For example, communication scholars have studied the effect of context (Burgoon, Dillard, Koper, & Duran, 1984), other-benefit (Boster & Stiff, 1984), power (Miller, 1982), and self-interest (Boster & Stiff, 1984; Clark, 1979) on compliance-gaining. Moreover, Cody et al. (1986) have measured the effects of all these factors on compliance-gaining behavior (see also Dillard & Burgoon, 1985).

A second way in which the hypothesis generating and testing training has been expressed is in the study of individual difference correlates of compliance-gaining message behavior. For example, communication scholars have studied the impact of cognitive complexity on compliance-gaining behavior (O'Keefe & Delia, 1979), communication apprehension (Koper & Boster, 1988; Lustig & King, 1980), dogmatism (Boster & Stiff, 1984; Neuliep, 1986; Roloff & Barnicott,

1979), and Machiavellianism (Boster & Stiff, 1984; Pandy & Rastogi, 1979; Roloff & Barnicott, 1978).

Scholars have employed the hypothesis generating and testing approach in a third area as well. They have generated and tested hypotheses concerning the effects of demographic characteristics, such as age (Clark & Delia, 1976; Clark, O'Dell, & Willihnganz, 1986; Delia, Kline, & Burleson, 1979; Finley & Humphreys, 1974), culture (Hirokawa & Miyahara, 1986; Neuliep & Hazelton, 1985), and sex (Andrews, 1987; Bisanz & Rule, 1989; Burgoon et al., 1984; deTurck, 1985; Falbo, 1977a; Falbo & Peplau, 1980; Instone, Major, & Bunker, 1983; Offerman & Schrier, 1985), on compliance-gaining message behavior.

Taken together, these studies provide a large and diverse collection of data. Unfortunately, few reviews have attempted to summarize and synthesize this rapidly growing archive (see, however, Boster, 1985; Wheeless, Barraclough, & Stewart, 1983). One of the difficulties facing the scholar who is attempting to write such a review is the diversity of methods that have been employed to examine compliance-gaining message behavior. It is to this issue that I now turn.

There are three major ways in which compliance-gaining has been measured. In *message selection* procedures, respondents are provided with a compliance-gaining scenario and a list of messages, and are then asked how likely they would be to use each message in the particular situation. These message lists are generated either by the investigator or by respondents. The former method is occasionally referred to as the deductive method, and the latter as the inductive method (see Wiseman & Schenck-Hamlin, 1981). These terms carry a considerable amount of additional conceptual baggage, and, therefore, are likely to be confusing. Consequently, they will not be employed in subsequent discussion.

When the investigator develops a list of message strategies, the strategy definitions are used to construct specific compliance-gaining messages (e.g., see Marwell & Schmitt, 1967a, 1967b). A respondent-generated list, however, requires a pilot study in which persons are given a compliance-gaining scenario, and are asked to write as many messages as they can. These messages are then analyzed to form a set of strategies. It is this set of strategies that is used to generate compliance-gaining messages in the subsequent experiment (e.g., Falbo, 1977b).

Some scholars have claimed that the latter approach is superior to the former approach (Wiseman & Schenck-Hamlin, 1981), although I find it difficult to imagine that undergraduate students, the usual respondents in these studies, can generate a substantial number of strategies of which social scientists, at least those who have made a career out of studying compliance, are unaware. Consistent with my skepticism, research has found that the two kinds of lists are similar in content, and that responses to them are correlated almost perfectly (Boster, Stiff, & Reynolds, 1985).

Regardless of the method used to derive the list, responses to them are generally treated in one of two ways (cf., Dillard, 1988). The data are analyzed either with each strategy considered as a separate variable, or with some data reduction algorithm, such as factor analysis (e.g., Roloff & Barnicott, 1978, 1979), or scholars employ multidimensional scaling (e.g., Cody, McLaughlin, & Jordan, 1980) to create strategy factors.

Recently, Hunter and Boster (1987) developed a scaling model of message selection responses, which showed them to be unidimensional and that the relationship of each strategy to the underlying factor is nonlinear. This nonlinearity, in turn, produces the spurious multidimensional factor solutions found by others (e.g., Marwell & Schmitt, 1967b). Thus, compliance-gaining message selection responses are to be summed to create a single variable, although the substantive character of this variable has remained elusive in spite of a spate of construct validation work (e.g., Boster & Levine, 1988).

In *message generation* procedures, the second way in which compliance-gaining message behavior is measured, scholars provide respondents with a description of a compliance-gaining situation, and ask them to report orally or in writing what they would say in order to gain the target's compliance. These responses are then coded into categories, rating scales, or both. The categories and rating criteria can be developed either a priori or a posteriori. For example, Clark (1979) rated compliance-gaining messages on even criteria, which had from two to ten levels. Alternatively, Delia, Kline, and Burleson (1979) coded the extent to which each message was adapted to the listener.

The relative merits of the message-selection and message-generation procedures have been debated extensively, and I shall not review those arguments (see Boster, 1988; Burleson et al., 1988; Burleson & Wilson, 1988; Hunter, 1988; Seibold, 1988). Nevertheless, the purpose of both methods is to collect data from which one can make an inference about compliance-gaining message behavior. The necessity of this inferential process can be questioned when it is possible to observe compliance-gaining message behavior directly, and several studies have made these direct observations.

By *message behavior* I mean those compliance-gaining messages uttered in situations in which the speaker and the target are engaged in message exchange (e.g., Dillard & Fitzpatrick, 1985). Unlike self-report techniques, these situations often have important consequences for the speaker. For example, Boster and Stiff (1984) observed the messages transmitted by experimental participants when negotiating the allocation of rewards following an anagram task, Boster and Lofthouse

(1986) noted the compliance-gaining messages employed by experimental participants given the task of soliciting persons to complete a survey, Lofthouse (1985) examined the message behavior of students arguing about a grade with their professor, and Scudder (1986) studied the types of threats employed by participants engaged in a simulated bargaining situation.

As mentioned above, the diversity of topics and methods presents the reviewer with a formidable task. In several instances there are relatively few studies that have examined the same variables measured in the same manner, and their findings are not always consistent. Thus, this literature is a striking contrast to a phenomenon such as the choice shift, in which the data are relatively consistent, and controversy surrounds the way in which data are explained (Isenberg, 1986). Here the nature and strength of important bivariate relationships are unknown, and the much desired synthesis of the literature, especially if employing quantitative reviewing techniques, may have to await the publication of many more studies. It is indeed ironic that although a surfeit of data have been collected, they may be insufficient to draw firm conclusions.

Of course, an alternative way in which data are synthesized is the development of theory. For example, Zajonc's (1965) drive theory rendered a paradoxical social facilitation literature understandable (temporarily), and Petty and Cacioppo's (1981) elaboration-likelihood model helped to organize a number of persuasion findings that previously appeared irreconcilable. It is interesting to note that both social-facilitation experiments and attitude-change experiments waned prior to the development of these explanations, and that both areas boomed after the introduction of the new models.

These examples suggest the hypothesis that without some principle(s) to organize the facts, or at least some quantitative literature review to tell us what we do and do not know, areas of study are likely to become fallow. I fear that the study of compliance-gaining message behavior is susceptible to such a fate. The problems of review have been mentioned previously, and in spite of the development of several theories (Baxter, 1984; Chmielewski, 1982; Smith, 1984), none has been able to integrate the baffling set of empirical findings.

Lest I be perceived as a Jeremiah, I hasten to add that I am not advocating the inevitability of the decline of compliance-gaining message behavior theory and research. Moreover, I should also make one of my attitudes clear: I hope that this line of inquiry advances because it is my hunch that certain characteristics of compliance-gaining messages are pertinent to understanding some very important features of human behavior. I merely wish to point out some of the difficulties in realizing this goal.

Unfortunately, I have no specific remedy in mind. I cannot advance a new theory at the moment, and I do not plan to undertake a comprehensive review of the subject. Rather, I shall set the more modest goal of suggesting two ways in which this area of research might become focused more clearly.

First, in the second paragraph of this essay I provided several examples to illustrate the importance of studying compliance-gaining message behavior. In each of these examples, the choice of a compliance-gaining message is said to have an effect on whether or not the target complies with the request and on certain sentiments that the target might develop. To review one example, our hypothetical elementary educator wants to transmit compliance-gaining messages that control the students, to get them to stop talking in class, for example, without having them hate school. This is the type of situation that Miller, Roloff, Seibold, and I had in mind when we performed our first experiment, but interestingly enough it differs in a key way from that experiment. The educator's problem is one in which the compliance-gaining message is the antecedent, or independent, variable, and in our experiment the compliance-gaining message was the consequent, or dependent, variable.

Our thought was to begin by finding those factors that would allow us to predict the compliance-gaining messages that persons would use, and then examine the consequences of those choices. We were optimistic that it would be a relatively simple task to find the antecedents of message selection, but, as the spate of subsequent work showed, our optimism was unwarranted.

Thus, our original goal has not been pursued to a great degree. It is my suspicion that a detailed consideration of compliance-gaining message *effects* may be profitable, as a paper by O'Keefe and Shepherd (1987) also indicates. One benefit of initiating research programs to address this issue, aside from the obvious importance of the phenomenon, is that if dimensions of compliance-gaining message behavior can be found to predict important interaction outcomes, then we will know which are the important variables to predict when examining the antecedents of compliance-gaining message behavior. Conversely, if compliance-gaining message behavior has no impact on such outcomes, then perhaps studying the antecedents of message choice is not such a critical enterprise.

I hasten to add that this point is not merely pedantic. When attempting to find antecedents of compliance-gaining message behavior, one looks in different places to find predictors of the amount of perspective taking in the message and the degree of persistence in the compliance-gaining attempt.

A second research program that may serve to advance the study of compliance-gaining message behavior requires that some descriptive work be initiated. For instance, we do not know with any reasonable degree of certainty that compliance-gaining message behavior is something that people often do. Compliance-gaining messages result from an internal conflict: Person A is doing, or failing to do, something that Person B wishes her to do, or refrain from doing. More importantly, these messages may signal the initiation of interpersonal conflict. Given good reasons to be reluctant about initiating conflict (Axelrod, 1981), it would not be surprising to find that compliance-gaining messages are rare in naturally occurring interactions.

Although tempting, it is unwarranted to equate frequency and importance of behavior. For example, punishment may have its strongest effect when it is used sparingly, and similarly, compliance-gaining messages may be effective when employed infrequently.

Nevertheless, it would be instructive to know what kinds of people use compliance-gaining messages, in what kinds of situations, and with what outcomes. Although it is particularly difficult to distinguish causal forces from spurious correlations in naturalistic inquiry, such data provide important clues for the construction of subsequent controlled investigations. Stated differently, these data suggest which situational and individual difference constructs have an impact on compliance-gaining message behavior, and they inform us as to the consequences of varying compliance-gaining messages.

It bears repeating that following my two suggestions will not ensure the advance of the study of compliance-gaining message behavior. Replication and synthesis of past research, as well as the development of theory, are at least as critical. But, if ten years hence I am able to peruse a bibliography of two hundred entries, and these entries include studies that examine the consequents of compliance-gaining messages and studies that describe basic features of the compliance-gaining environment, then I suspect that the advance in our knowledge of this phenomenon will be substantial.

REFERENCES

Andrews, P. H. (1987). Gender differences in persuasive communication and attribution of success and failure. *Human Communication Research, 13,* 372–385.

Axelrod, R. (1981). The emergence of cooperation among egoists. *American Political Science Review, 75,* 306–318.

Baxter, L. A. (1984). An investigation of compliance-gaining as politeness. *Human Communication Research, 10,* 427–456.

14   Beginnings

Bisanz, G. L., & Rule, B. G. (1989). Gender and the persuasion schema: A search for cognitive invariants. *Personality and Social Psychology Bulletin, 15,* 4–18.

Boster, F. J. (1985). Argumentation, interpersonal communication, persuasion, and the process(es) of compliance gaining message use. In J. R. Cox, M. O. Sillars, & G. B. Walker (Eds.), *Argument and social practice: Proceedings of the fourth SCA/AFA conference on argumentation* (pp. 578–591). Annandale, VA: Speech Communication Association.

Boster, F. J. (1988). Comments on the utility of compliance gaining message selection tasks. *Human Communication Research, 15,* 166–177.

Boster, F. J., & Levine, T. (1988). Individual differences and compliance gaining message selection: The effects of verbal aggressiveness, argumentativeness, dogmatism, and negativism. *Communication Research Reports, 5,* 114–119.

Boster, F. J., & Lofthouse, L. J. (1986, May). *Situational and individual difference determinants of the persistence and content of compliance gaining behavior: A test of the generalizability of some compliance gaining message choice findings.* Paper presented at the annual meeting of the International Communication Association, Chicago.

Boster, F. J., & Stiff, J. B. (1984). Compliance gaining message selection behavior. *Human Communication Research, 10,* 539–556.

Boster, F. J., Stiff, J. B., & Reynolds, R. A. (1985). Do persons respond differently to inductively-derived and deductively-derived lists of compliance gaining message strategies? A reply to Wiseman and Schenck-Hamlin. *Western Journal of Speech Communication, 49,* 177–187.

Burgoon, M., Dillard, J. P., Koper, R., & Doran, N. (1984). The impact of communication context and persuader gender on persuasive message selection. *Women's Studies in Communication, 7,* 1–12.

Burleson, B. R., & Wilson, S. R. (1988). On the continued undesirability of item desirability: A reply to Boster, Hunter, & Seibold. *Human Communication Research, 15,* 178–191.

Burleson, B. R., Wilson, S. R., Waltman, M. S., Goering, E. M., Ely, T. K., & Whaley, B. B. (1988). Item desirability effects in compliance-gaining research: Seven studies documenting artifacts in the strategy selection procedure. *Human Communication Research, 14,* 429–486.

Chmielewski, T. L. (1982). A test of a model for predicting strategy choice. *Central States Speech Journal, 33,* 505–518.

Clark, R. A. (1979). The impact of self interest and desire for liking on the selection of communicative strategies. *Communication Monographs, 46,* 257–273.

Clark, R. A., & Delia, J. G. (1976). The development of functional persuasive skills in childhood and early adolescence. *Child Development, 47,* 1008–1014.

Clark, R. A., O'Dell, L. L., & Willihnganz, S. (1986). The development of compromising as an alternative to persuasion. *Central States Speech Journal, 37,* 220–224.

Cody, M. J., Greene, J. O., Marston, P. J., O'Hair, H. D., Baaske, K. T., & Schneider, M. J. (1986). Situation perception and message strategy selection. In M. L. McLaughlin (Ed.), *Communication yearbook, vol. 9* (pp. 390–420). Beverly Hills, CA: Sage.

Cody, M. J., McLaughlin, M. L., & Jordan, W. J. (1980). A multidimensional scaling of three sets of compliance-gaining strategies. *Communication Quarterly, 28,* 34–46.

Cody, M. J., McLaughlin, M. L., & Schneider, M. J. (1981). The impact of relational consequences and intimacy on the selection of interpersonal persuasion tactics: A reanalysis. *Communication Quarterly, 29,* 91–106.

Delia, J. G., Kline, S. L., & Burleson, B. R. (1979). The development of persuasive communication strategies in kindergarteners through twelfth-graders. *Communication Monographs, 46,* 241–256.

deTurck, M. A. (1985). A transactional analysis of compliance-gaining behavior: Effects of noncompliance, relational contexts, and actor's gender. *Human Communication Research, 12,* 54–78.

Dillard, J. P. (1988). Compliance-gaining message-selection: What is our dependent variable? *Communication Monographs, 55,* 162–183.

Dillard, J. P., & Burgoon, M. (1985). Situational influences on the selection of compliance-gaining messages: Two tests of the predictive utility of the Cody-McLaughlin typology. *Communication Monographs, 52,* 289–304.

Dillard, J. P., & Fitzpatrick, M. A. (1985). Compliance-gaining in marital interaction. *Personality and Social Psychology Bulletin, 11,* 419–433.

Falbo, T. (1977a). Relationship between sex, sex-role, and social influence. *Psychology of Women Quarterly, 2,* 41–52.

Falbo, T. (1977b). Multidimensional scaling of power strategies. *Journal of Personality and Social Psychology, 35,* 537–547.

Falbo, T., & Peplau, L. A. (1980). Power strategies in intimate relationships. *Journal of Personality and Social Psychology, 38,* 618–628.

Finley, G. E., & Humphreys, C. A. (1974). A naive psychology and the development of persuasive appeals in girls. *Canadian Journal of Behavioral Science, 6,* 75–80.

Fitzpatrick, M. A., & Winke, J. (1979). You always hurt the one you love: Strategies and tactics in interpersonal conflict. *Communication Quarterly, 27,* 3–11.

Hirokawa, R. Y., & Miyahara, A. (1986). A comparison of influence strategies utilized by managers in American and Japanese organizations. *Communication Quarterly, 34,* 250–265.

Hunter, J. E. (1988). Failure of the social desirability response set hypothesis. *Human Communication Research, 15,* 162–168.

Hunter, J. E., & Boster, F. J. (1987). A model of compliance gaining message selection. *Communication Monographs, 54,* 63–84.

Instone, D., Major, B., & Bunker, B. B. (1983). Gender, self confidence and social influence strategies: An organizational simulation. *Journal of Personality and Social Psychology, 44,* 322–333.

Isenberg, D. J. (1986). Group polarization: A critical review and meta-analysis. *Journal of Personality and Social Psychology, 50,* 1141–1151.

Kearney, P., Plax, T. G., Richmond, V. P., & McCroskey, J. C. (1984). Power in the classroom IV: Alternatives to discipline. In R. N. Bostrom (Ed.), *Communication yearbook, vol. 8* (pp. 724–746). Beverly Hills, CA: Sage.

Kearney, P., Plax, T. G., Richmond, V. P., & McCroskey, J. C. (1985). Power in the classroom III: Teacher communication techniques and messages. *Communication Education, 34,* 19–28.

Kipnis, D., & Cosentino, J. (1969). Use of leadership powers in industry. *Journal of Applied Psychology, 53,* 460–466.

Kipnis, D., Schmidt, S. M., & Wilkinson, I. (1980). Intraorganizational influence tactics: Explorations in getting one's way. *Journal of Applied Psychology, 65,* 440–452.

Koper, R. J., & Boster, F. J. (1988). Factors affecting verbal aggressiveness and compliance gaining effectiveness: The relationship between communication rewards, communication approach/avoidance, and compliance gaining messages. In D. O'Hair & B. R. Patterson (Eds.), *Advances in Interpersonal Communication Research* (pp. 129–146). Las Cruces, NM: CRC.

Lofthouse, L. J. (1985). *An empirical investigation of individual and situational differences in compliance gaining.* Unpublished thesis, Arizona State University, Tempe.

Lustig, M. W., & King, S. W. (1980). The effect of communication apprehension and situation on communication strategy choices. *Human Communication Research, 7,* 74–82.

Marwell, G., & Schmitt, D. R. (1967a). Compliance-gaining behavior: A synthesis and model. *Sociological Quarterly, 8,* 317–328.

Marwell, G., & Schmitt, D. R. (1967b). Dimensions of compliance-gaining behavior: An empirical analysis. *Sociometry, 30,* 350–364.

Miller, G. R., Boster, F. J., Roloff, M. E., & Seibold, D. R. (1977). Compliance-gaining message strategies: A typology and some findings concerning effects of situational differences. *Communication Monographs, 44,* 37–51.

Miller, G. R., & Steinberg, M. (1975). *Between people.* Chicago: Science Research Associates.

Miller, M. D. (1982). Power and relationship type as predictors of compliance-gaining strategy use. *Journal of Language and Social Psychology, 1,* 111–121.

Neulip, J. W. (1986). Self-report vs. actual use of persuasive messages by high and low dogmatics. *Journal of Social Behavior and Personality, 1,* 213–222.

Neuliep, J. W., & Hazelton, V. (1985). A cross cultural comparison of Japanese and American persuasive strategy selection. *International Journal of Intercultural Relations, 9,* 389–404.

Offermann, L. R., & Schrier, P. E. (1985). Social influence strategies: The impact of sex, role, and attitudes toward power. *Personality and Social Psychology Bulletin, 11,* 286–300.

O'Keefe, B. J., & Delia, J. G. (1979). Construct comprehensiveness and cognitive complexity as predictors of the number and strategic adaptation of arguments and appeals in a persuasive message. *Communication Monographs, 46,* 231–240.

O'Keefe, B. J., & Shepherd, G. J. (1987). The pursuit of multiple objectives in face-to-face persuasive interaction: Effects of construct differentiation on message organization. *Communication Monographs, 54,* 396–419.

Pandy, J., & Rastogi, R. (1979). Machiavellianism and ingratiation.

The Journal of Social Psychology, 108, 221–225.

Petty, R. E., & Cacioppo, J. T. (1981). *Attitudes and persuasion: Classic and contemporary approaches.* Dubuque, IA: Brown.

Richmond, V. P., Davis, L. M., Saylor, K., & McCroskey, J. C. (1984). Power strategies in organizations: Communication techniques and messages. *Human Communication Research, 11,* 85–108.

Roloff, M., & Barnicott, Jr., E. F. (1978). The situational use of pro- and antisocial compliance-gaining strategies by high and low machiavellians. In B. D. Ruben (Ed.), *Communication yearbook vol. 2* (pp. 193–205). New Brunswick, NJ: Transaction Books.

Roloff, M., & Barnicott, Jr., E. F. (1979). The influence of dogmatism on the situational use of pro- and anti-social compliance-gaining strategies. *Southern Speech Communication Journal, 45,* 37–54.

Scudder, J. (1986, November). *Power, threat use, and the formation of agree-ments: An alternative compliance gaining approach.* Paper presented to the annual meeting of the Speech Communication Association, Chicago.

Seibold, D. R. (1988). A response to "Item desirability in compliance-gaining research." *Human Communication Research, 15,* 152–161.

Smith, M. J. (1984). Contingency rules theory, context, and compliance behaviors. *Human Communication Research, 10,* 489–512.

Wheeless, L. R., Barraclough, R., & Stewart, R. (1983). Compliance-gaining and power in persuasion. In R. N. Bostrom (Ed.), *Communication yearbook, vol. 7* (pp. 105–145). Beverly Hills, CA: Sage.

Wiseman, R. L., & Schenck-Hamlin, W. (1981). A multidimensional scaling validation of an inductively-derived set of compliance-gaining strategies. *Communication Monographs, 48,* 251–270.

Zajonc, R. B. (1965). Social facilitation. *Science, 149,* 269–274.

Orientations to Interpersonal Influence

Competition for Resources and the Origins of Manipulative Language

Claire Dzur Harkness
University of Wisconsin, Madison

LANGUAGE AND SOCIAL INFLUENCE

W|hat do children acquire when they acquire a language? One way to answer this question is to say that they have learned to use a system of symbols to refer to things in the world. This answer highlights the codelike relationship between language and the world, and it places an emphasis on the child's acquisition of that code. Another way to answer the question, however, is to say that in acquiring a language children become able to perform different sorts of actions in the world. This answer highlights children's acquisition of a new mode of social behavior containing potentialities for influence that did not exist in the modes that were previously available. Several researchers who have viewed language acquisition in this way have delineated the different functions that language serves for children and adults (Jakobson, 1960; Halliday, 1975; Rees, 1978;

Author's Note: I am very grateful to William Charlesworth, James Dillard, Carolyn Dzur, and Allan Harkness for helpful comments on earlier drafts of this paper.

Schacter et al., 1974). Most of these have built upon the work of Jakobson (1960) who divided the functions of language into six categories:

Expressive: language that directly reveals speakers' feelings.
Poetic: language that is structural, so as to achieve the illuminative or exhibitive effects of an art form.
Conative: language used to produce desired behavior in the listener.
Phatic: language used to make and maintain social contact.
Metalinguistic: language used to refer to itself.
Referential: language used to identify referents in the world.

It is important to note that these different functions do not occur independently in natural language use but exist to differing degrees in different utterances (thus, for example, expressive or referential functions are usually a part of any utterance but may be weighted differently in different utterances). While this is the case, the use of each of these motives or functions in linguistic expression appears to be a gradual acquisition in children's language, with some functions appearing early in children's speech and others only later (Halliday, 1975).

The language children acquire in the first years of life, then, is not acquired merely to encode things in the world. It also functions to link children in multiple ways to the world. Although some functions are originally mediated nonlinguistically, as the child's linguistic skills develop, these different functions are served linguistically and in turn have a shaping impact on the child's developing language. While each of the functions, individually, should have a special impact on the substance as well as on the style of what is learned by children, the impact of the conative function may be singularly profound. Why might this be? What reason is there to suspect that this function in particular has a critical shaping influence on language?

The Evolutionary Origins of Complex Language

Burling (1986) provides us with an answer to this question by taking a fresh look at the elusive issue of the evolutionary origins of complex language. He asks what could have made our complex language, with its characteristic ambiguity, functional redundancies, and enormous vocabulary of near synonyms, selectively advantageous. He rules out the possibility that these selective advantages were obtained through use of complex language in cooperative pursuits such as group hunting or foraging. The planning and coordination required by such group tasks do not require the multiple and subtle forms that language can take. Rather, for such tasks, simple, clear, and stereotyped communicative signals would best serve the hunters or foragers. He also rejects the possibility that educating young children requires sophisticated language. Teaching others requires active demonstration rather than subtle speech. Instead, he proposes that the selective advantage of complex language lies in its contribution to aspects of social influence and manipulation in the individual's search for social power and control of resources.

> Language in its delicately nuanced forms is used, not so much for basic subsistence tasks, as for establishing, maintaining, and refining social relationships . . . it is in defining ourselves in relation to others, in conducting interpersonal negotiations, in competing, in manipulating, in scheming to get our own way, that the most subtle aspects of language become important (Burling, 1986, pp. 7–8).

While certainly not solely responsible for the form of modern languages, the conative function may thus have had an especially important role in effecting the richness of our linguistic system. Social interactions requiring persuasion, manipulation, and self-presentation, among others, made linguistic subtlety, afforded by linguistic complexity, important.

Linguistic complexity is doubtless multiply determined. Other factors could also conspire to produce complexity. What I suggest here, in line with Burling as well as with current thinking by animal ethologists on signalling (see p. 24), is that intra-specific competition in particular was served by an increasingly sophisticated syntactic, semantic, and pragmatic linguistic system. In ontogenesis, where competitive goals continue to exist, but where the potential for linguistic complexity is already inherent in the genome, its "unfolding" may occur in response to the requirements of competition over resources.

In the following section, I will try to show how the subtle linguistic forms that children acquire during ontogeny to influence the behavior of others are related to the requirements of resource acquisition. I will make the argument that children acquiring language should be, among other things, acquiring elements of the linguistic symbol system that will allow them to be persuasive in those social contexts in which resources are available. This implies that the contexts of competition for resources are contexts of linguistic acquisition and modification, and, additionally, that such contexts provide an excellent source for data on children's acquisition of language.

Current theorizing and research on children's acquisition of directives has not been influenced by the implications of Burling's theorizing or by recent advances in the sociobiology of animal social interactions. As a result, there is a theoretical gap in the area of child language since a more competitive view of social interaction has not made an impact. Thus we must turn first to the recent literature on animal signals to get an idea of what we might expect children to be acquiring as a result of competing for resources. In this literature, rather than in the literature on linguistic pragmatics, resource competition has been linked explicitly to signal development and modification.

Animal Signals: Manipulative Devices for Resource Acquisition

Earlier research on animal signals, such as Smith (1977), suggested that signals evolved from nonsignals as a result of the benefits that accrued from intraspecific cooperation. For example, individuals who were more capable of clearly advertising their capabilities or intentions (e.g., their strength or their intention to fight) were more successful in avoiding dangerous aggression or unexpected responses from members of the same species.

The signal behaviors that evolved from nonsignals were believed to be more clear, more communicative, and hence more cooperative. Smith (1977) argued that

> during evolution, signal acts become differentiated from their precursors as they are increasingly formalized—that is, modified specifically to serve as useful sources of information. They may become stereotyped, exaggerated, simplified, iterated, or have their performances extended in time and space (p. 461).

In recent years, additional descriptive work as well as theoretical modelling of the selective mechanisms operating on signals have considerably broadened our perspectives (Dawkins & Krebs, 1978; Krebs & Dawkins, 1984; Caryl, 1979, 1982; Whiten & Byrne, 1988). Kaplan (1987) has written an excellent review of the recent signalling literature. He suggests that as social interaction among animals frequently involves competition rather than cooperation, information given by signals should not necessarily be honest and nor should signals be designed to be maximally informative: "Why should any organism wish to provide another organism with information, especially if this information aids the receiver at some expense to the sender?" (p. 103). Caryl (1979) has also challenged the assumption that broadcast information in contexts such as fights ("I'm mad enough to charge!") should allow clear predictions about what an animal will do next. His analysis of earlier data shows that frequently this is not the case (in some birds the probability that an animal will attack following an agonistic display is less than chance).

Instead of viewing signalling as a behavior that enhances intra-specific cooperation, recent research suggests that it ought to be viewed as an extension of the organism's repertoire of manipulative abilities used to influence the psyche of the receiver and make use of their "muscle power"; the resulting action benefits the sender, but not necessarily the receiver (Dawkins & Krebs, 1978). The evolution of manipulative signals has brought about the coevolution of "mind reading" by receivers in order not to be duped (Krebs & Dawkins, 1984). This development, in turn, has led to further sophistication of signalling to take advantage of mind reading. (See Whiten and Byrne [1988] who discuss tactical deception in primates and argue that deceivers take advantage of the tendency of receivers to mind read.)

These advances in a theory of signal evolution yield at least one important perspective for thinking about child language acquisition: Intraspecific competition has influenced the evolution of both the production and interpretation of manipulative signals in other animals; should we expect that competition for resources influences human language development as well? As discussed previously, Burling has proposed that the requirements of resource competition and social influence provided a selection pressure for complex language in evolution. If resources are obtained via social influence with the help of directives in humans, the child's language development should reflect changes occurring in response to early contexts of resource competition. Let us now turn to what we know about directives and how they change during development.

Linguistic Means of Resource Acquisition: Directives

Types of Directives

Researchers have used different terms to refer to utterances used to obtain resources, but I prefer *directive* (following Ervin-Tripp, 1976). "Directive" generally refers to a word or string of words used to influence a listener to give or to do something. Directives come in many forms, but the most typical is the command form, as in "Give that to me." Other forms of directives include questions ("Can I have that?" "Isn't it my turn?" "Won't you give me that?") and statements ("It's mine," "I want that," "I'll have that now," "It's my turn"). This tripartite distinction between commands, questions, and statements within the class of directives is a formal one, based upon the syntactic structure of the utterances.

The Psychology of Directive Differences

The existence of alternative forms of speech for performing the same type of social act (for example, to obtain an action or an object from a listener) suggests that alternative forms have different effects. How are the different forms related to the different effects? The most prominent view is that directives differ in the degree to which they encode what the speaker wants the listener to do. This aspect of directives, called *explicitness*, alters the psychological effect that a directive has. The less explicit a directive is, the more polite it is felt to be by listeners (Ervin-Tripp, 1976, 1977; Becker, 1981; Garvey, 1975; Read & Cherry, 1978; Wilkinson, Calculator, & Dollaghan, 1982).

Variation in directive explicitness has been linked with how directives are used in social interaction. Ervin-Tripp (1976, 1977) has suggested that the more explicit a directive is, the more commonly it is used in an interactional context in which speakers have greater status than listeners (age, power, sex, and role are all considered status-indicating variables). In contrast, implicit directives tend to be used when speakers have lower status than listeners and in cases in which the speaker wants the listener to do something that is difficult or outside his or her typical role. This descriptive work led Ervin-Tripp to suggest that speakers depart from the stereotyped, explicit form under conditions in which they need to be polite or to display subservience.

A Theory of Politeness

The link between explicitness and politeness is further supported by a theory of linguistic politeness developed by Brown and Levinson (1987) based on their cross-cultural data on adults' directives. According to them, a directive is polite if it attends to listener "face" (a concept brought to the attention of social scientists by Goffman in 1955). In many different cultures, explicit forms of directives are regarded as "face-threatening," and in most situations speakers will wish to avoid making such a threat and will use various types of implicit forms of directives instead.

According to Brown and Levinson, the reason implicit forms are considered polite is because they allow the directive recipient *not to comply* with the directive. And although speakers who use the more implicit form may therefore be less likely to gain compliance, they have not jeopardized their relationship with the listener by putting him or her "on the spot." Linguistic politeness comes in many forms, but they all involve minimization of the impact of the directive, maximization of deference shown to the listener, and/or maximization of the opportunity for the listener to decline to comply. Implicitness, then, is the linguistic means for performing these face-saving acts.

Development of Politeness

In developing the conative function of language through acquisition of directive forms, the child begins by using exclusively explicit directives, a phase that Forbes and Lubin (1984) term the "mechanistic phase." During this time, children apparently believe that directives act like Aladdin's "Open sesame!" and function automatically. Gradually, however, they become aware of the psychological net that words can cast over the motives and emotions of others. This can be seen when children start adding politeness markers such as "please" or forming directives as questions (such as "Can I?" "Can you?" "Will you?"). According to politeness researchers, the use of such directives is an important turning point: It represents the awareness that to get others to do what you want, you have to make them feel that they have an alternative to compliance or that they want to comply. At this point, the child has entered a new realm in understanding the pragmatics of his or her language, and begins to choose words for their psychological effect. Researchers have agreed that politeness is the best solution to the problem of social influence, and that the linguistic means for expressing politeness is to make an explicit directive implicit.

Work on children's perception of the politeness of different directive forms supports the view that children understand the psychological impact that different forms have on listeners. Becker (1981) has suggested that children distinguish between the politeness of directives according to their differing explicitness. She found that even young children consider more explicit directives "bossy" (or rude) and standard implicit forms (e.g., "Can I?") "nice" (or polite).

Problems with Politeness

The research on animal signals leads one to suspect that linguistic politeness may not be the only strategy available to children honing their resource-acquisition skills. Although it is clearly part of the child's task to learn ways to maintain social relationships by relinquishing strong claims to resources (something that politeness does), it must also be part of the child's task to learn *more* effective ways to get things from others; that is, the child should not only want to give others a way to say "no," but he or she should also want a way to make them feel they have to say "yes." Nevertheless, research on young children's directives has not provided us with sufficient data supporting two tracks of directive development (e.g., politeness and coerciveness).

Problems with the Study of Directives

A factor that has limited the investigation of children's directives has been the contexts in which researchers have collected these directives. Frequently, this context has been the preschool classroom during a free-play period when children have the opportunity to change from teacher-directed to self-chosen activity. In the typical preschool, resources are abundant and children spread themselves relatively evenly across the resources, encountering few restrictions. In this context of unnatural abundance, the constraints of resource scarcity do not operate on children's language. As a result, the very factors that could be hypothesized reasonably to have shaped directive form do not exist.

Let us consider for a moment a different context. In this one resources are scarce, and in order to obtain them a child must use directives. Compliance to directives here will represent a genuine sacrifice. Two factors affecting directives in this context are, one, the child's strong motive to obtain resources, and two, his or her strong motive to retain resources. The task the child faces in such a context in obtaining resources from peers is quite complex, and there is no single strategy that resolves the problem entirely. The problem facing the child can be conceptualized roughly as follows: How do you get someone to do something you want that does not benefit the other person? I suggest that contexts such as this one may have as important an influence on children's directive acquisition as the less competitive contexts utilized and observed by previous researchers.

RESEARCH ON DIRECTIVES AND COMPETITION FOR RESOURCES

In what follows, I will describe my research on children's directives. In order to obtain a more complete understanding of how young children solve this problem with directives, children were videotaped in a context in which a desirable resource was scarce and the children had to use directives to obtain the resource from other children. The directives children used in the experimental setting were the data for this study (Harkness, 1988), which is just one of a series of studies, conducted by William Charlesworth and myself, investigating young children's competitive abilities in contexts of scarce resources.

The Experimental Context

One hundred and twenty preschool-aged children were divided into thirty groups of four previously acquainted classmates. Each of these thirty tetrads was brought to a playroom in which they were video-taped while playing with a movie viewer apparatus (designed by Charlesworth & La Freniere, 1983). This apparatus is constructed in such a way that one child can view a cartoon movie through a peep-hole, provided that one other child turns a crank (causing a filmstrip to move) and one other child presses a light button (illuminating the cartoon strip). Since the movie viewer apparatus has only three po-sitions (viewing, cranking, and pressing the light button) the fourth child in the tetrad is forced into a bystanding position. Children were allowed to play with the movie viewer with no adult present until they either lost interest or indicated a desire to leave the room.

This setting is a rich context for the study of directives for two reasons. First, it restricts children's behavior by making the goals of obtaining positions and others' cooperation salient. This is important, since in naturalistic contexts it is frequently the case that children's goals in interaction are not clear. Because of the scarcity of resources in this experimental setting, children's behaviors were directed to-wards the resources almost exclusively and the level of competition was intense. Second, since the viewing-position resource was so de-sirable and difficult to obtain, it was expected that this would en-courage use of a wider range of directive types than would occur in a context of relative plenty.

Results

Directives

I created twenty-one low inference, descriptive categories of directives on the basis of exhaustive examination of the 1,522 directives found in the transcripts made from the videotaped sessions (see Table 1). These ranged dramatically from categories that were quite implicit (e.g., "How come you're taking all the turns?") to those that were more standard, explicit forms (such as "Let me see it!"). For the pur-pose of statistical analysis, categories with fewer than twenty in-stances were dropped (as were directives for which no single recipient was indicated). The eleven categories for which there were sufficient data are starred in Table 1. There was a total of 1,210 directives in the final sample.

Table 1   **Twenty-One Syntactic/Semantic Categories of Directives Used by 120 Preschool-Aged Children**

Questions

1.   Ask others to say if they are willing to do x.
      "Would you like to push the button?"
      "Laura, would you crank?"

2.   Ask others to say if they are able to do x.
      "Can you press the button?"

3.   Ask others to say what the rules are pertaining to x.
      "Everybody gets a turn?"

4.   Ask others to say how/when/what S should do about x.*
      "When do I get a turn?"
      "What can I do?"

5.   Ask others to say that S has permission to do x.*
      "Can I push the button?"
      "Now, can I look through?"

6.   Ask others to explain their behavior.
      "How come you're taking all the turns?"

7.   Ask others to give information about x.
      "What do you see?"
      "Is the movie done?"

8.   Ask others to give reasons for not doing x.
      "Ok, why don't you stop?"
      "Why don't you turn the crank?"

Assertions

9.   Assert that S is unable to do x.*
      "I don't see anything."
      "I can't see in there."

10.   Assert that S wants/needs x.*
      "I wanna do that."
      "I want to see the ghosts."

11.   Assert S's intentions to do x.*
      "I'm gonna do it now!"
      "I'll look through that!"

12.   Assert that S will do something bad to L.
      "I won't be your friend anymore."

13.   Assert a negative fact about S's activities.*
      "I only got a little turn!"
      "I can't even get one view of the picture!"

(continued)

14.   Assert that rules pertain to S, L, x.[*]

15.   Assert a negative fact about x.
     "It keeps going blop, blop!"

16.   Assert a negative fact about L.[*]
     "You got to do this and not me!"

Commands

17.   Tell others to act or to stop acting.[*]
     "Push it on, Jenny!"
     "Don't go so fast!"

18.   Tell others to give S the opportunity to act.[*]
     "Let me see it!"

19.   Tell others they have S's permission to act/have an object.
     "Now you can do this."

20.   Tell others to give information about x, L.
     "Tell me if it starts over again."
     "Tell me when it's over."

21.   Urgency Ellipsis[*]
     "Hey!"
     "Joanna!"

Note: S=Speaker, L=Listener, x=Object (i.e., the movie viewer), [*] =Directives that are used for further analysis.

Gauging the Meaning of Directives

Recall that in previous analyses of directive meaning, researchers (notably Brown & Levinson, 1987; Ervin-Tripp, 1976) connected form (such as degree of explicitness) with meaning or function (such as showing rudeness or powerfulness). I have suggested that the unidimensional framework for interpreting children's directives that was yielded by this form-function connection may have limited our understanding of children's early capabilities. It is critical to possess a method for making appropriate inferences about the meaning of the directives children use in order to construct a theory about children's manipulative abilities. An assumption that knowing the form of a behavior inevitably tells us about the meaning or function of that behavior may be mistaken. Blurton-Jones (1972) gives an example of this in his discussion of "rough and tumble" behavior. He found that this category was made up of behaviors such as laugh, run, jump, hit at, and wrestle. "Rough and tumble," then, is an active behavior, frequently involving rough body contact. As such, it shares formal elements with "aggressive" behavior. And yet his analyses showed that these two categories are distributed quite differently across actors and contexts. If he had grouped behaviors solely on the basis of form (for example, behavior involving rough body contact or high activity), he would have obfuscated the different functions such behaviors have for children. As Parkhurst and Gottman (1986) stated about linguistic categories: "It cannot be overemphasized that similarly structured linguistic forms may represent different tactics and serve different strategies, whereas widely different structures and devices may serve the same strategy" (p. 73).

Concern for these issues led to the use of a two-step procedure to further categorize and define the eleven descriptive categories of directives. First, the eleven categories were cluster analyzed. Table 2 gives the eight categories that were produced by the data reduction of the clustering procedure and their frequency of occurrence.

To gain an understanding of the psychological dimensions underlying differences between the eight clustered categories, I used a multidimensional scaling procedure. I chose a two-dimensional solution to reflect the best balance between parsimony, goodness-of-fit, and substantive interpretability (Shepard, 1980). Examination of the two-

Table 2   Clustered Directives and Their Frequency of Use by 120 Preschool-Aged Children

Directive	Frequency

ASK PERMISSION
    "Can I push the button?"
    "When can I do it?"
	125

ASSERT NEED
    "I don't see anything."
    "I wanna do that!"
	182

ASSERT INTENT/URGENCY
    "I'm gonna do it now!"
    "Hey!"
	140

COMPLAIN "I can't even get one view of the picture!"	38
ASSERT RULE "It's my turn to do it."	117
ACCUSE "You got to do this and not me!"	43
COMMAND ACTION "Push it on!"	476
COMMAND PERMISSION "Let me see it!"	89

Table 3 **Dimensional Quadrants and the Directives Contained in Them**

Quadrant 1: Implicit & Authoritative

ASSERT RULE	"It's my turn to do it."
ASSERT INTENT/URGENCY	"I'm gonna do it now!"
ACCUSE	"You got to do this and not me!"

Quadrant 2: Explicit & Authoritative

COMMAND ACTION	"Push it on!"
ASSERT NEED	"I wanna do that!"

Quadrant 3: Explicit & Supplicating

COMMAND PERMISSION	"Let me see it!"

Quadrant 4: Implicit & Supplicating

ASK PERMISSION	"Can I push the button?"
COMPLAIN	"I can't even get one view of the picture!"

---

dimensional layout of directive categories yielded two interpretable dimensions that were labeled "Implicit-Explicit" and "Supplicating-Authoritative." The two dimensions together define four quadrants that can be used to further clarify the categories conceptually. These four quadrants and the directive categories located within them can be seen in Table 3. Location in one of the four quadrants suggests that the directives occurring within it should be viewed as possessing attributes indicated by the two ends of the dimensions forming the quadrant.

Use of the dimension-defined quadrants to group the categories should be viewed as only a rough indicator of similarity between items within a quadrant. The quadrants are used to gain additional depth of understanding of the psychology of directives. Despite formal disparity, directives such as those in the implicit/authoritative quadrant may share similar meanings and functions for children who use them.

Interpretation of Children's Directives

The appearance of the Authoritativeness-Supplicating dimension in addition to the Explicitness-Implicitness dimension creates a two-dimensional psychological and motivational space considerably more complex than that described by other researchers (as mentioned above) for interpreting children's directive meaning. The clusters and maps yielded by these procedures suggest that children's developing psychology of competition allows them to create directives with co-ercive as well as cooperative force.

What makes a directive coercive? It appears to be the result of an interaction between the semantic content of directives and listener socialization. A directive that makes certain types of claims or com-mands leaves listeners with little room for resistance, or at least the listener must comply or strongly resist, and thus options are reduced. In such directives, words are used that serve the same purpose as a push or a trap. This can be done both implicitly—where the trap is laid by asserting a state of affairs that implicates compliance ("It's my turn, you know."), as well as explicitly—where the words are more like a physical push ("You do x!"). The reason a listener feels compelled may have to do with the limitations of the imagination, but it more likely has to do with the social rules and the attendant fears of transgression that govern interpersonal behavior.

If we look at the frequency with which children used each of the directives in the four quadrants, it is interesting to see that the ste-reotypic "polite" forms so frequently studied in other research are underrepresented here in this competitive context. Instead, children's directive use in this setting reveals a reliance both on the traditional "bossy" forms (explicit, authoritative), and also on the implicit yet coercive forms (implicit, authoritative).

		Frequency
Quadrant 1:	Implicit/Authoritative	300
Quadrant 2:	Explicit/Authoritative	658
Quadrant 3:	Explicit/Supplicating	89
Quadrant 4:	Implicit/Supplicating	163

The reason for the difference between these findings and those of other researchers may lie in the use of an experimental context that differs strikingly from other contexts that have been used to in-vestigate young children's directives. The dictates of the cooperative view of social interaction led previous researchers to investigate the acquisition of linguistic politeness in settings where children would be likely to exhibit its acquisition. A competitive view of social inter-action (one in which interactions are seen as frequently involving re-source acquisition at the expense of one participant) suggests that the finding of resources and the discovery of the best means of obtaining them are equally critical to young children.

These data suggest that even young children are acquiring lin-guistic devices for manipulating others in resource acquisition con-texts. Their linguistic tool boxes are filled with implements that a cooperative view of social interaction might not have predicted. Further, the clustering and scaling procedure suggests that these linguistic tools are not employed randomly, but that functionally isomorphic forms tend to be used with matching proportions. Although the majority (54 percent) of the children's directives were explicit and authoritative forms, a large minority were implicit and authoritative (26 percent). Thus, many of the children's directives were neither stereotyped command forms nor standard polite forms. It is also important to note that despite an age range of approximately three years (subjects ranged in age from 3 to 6 years), younger children were as able to use these implicit/authoritative forms as were older children.

Earlier research on children's directives depicted essentially half of the story. Children are capable of both comprehending and producing polite directives in response to the status differentials in some interactive contexts. In the context of competitive peer interaction, however, obtaining resources becomes more critical than leaving the listener with a way to say "no." Children in the present setting showed considerable versatility in linguistic manipulation.

CULTURAL DIFFERENCES IN RESOURCE COMPETITION

The child learning to use language is learning to use a tool for influencing the behavior of others. The greater the child's appreciation for the cultural rules governing interpersonal behavior, the more effective his or her directives will be. Eventually, a person's language becomes uniquely suited to the constraints governing the social behavior of the particular group to which he or she belongs.

The research that was discussed in this chapter was based on English-speaking, United States samples exclusively, with the exception of Brown and Levinson's work on adults. What implications does this sample limitation have for the findings I have presented here? To answer this question we need to ask another: What features of social life influence this aspect of language acquisition?

I have suggested that competition for resources early in life may be one important influence on children's acquisition of directives and, more generally, on manipulative language. Thus we can say that the area of social life influencing this aspect of language acquisition is resource competition. Do societies differ in resource competition? One way societies may differ that could influence resource competition is in how individualistic members of a society are expected to be.

The child who is reared to strike out on his or her own will have different expectations about resource availability than the child who is reared to fulfill a clear-cut, interlocking role in a social group. Whereas in some groups grown children are on their own, in other groups grown children remain integrated, contributing, and contributed-to members of their families. Thus, although competition may in fact lie at the heart of much of social interaction, in some societies the degree to which competition is expressed will be tempered by the structure of the society itself. Full-blown competitive acquisitiveness would surely run counter to the goals of many cooperative, co-dependent societies.

Let us now return to the question posed: How might differences in societies (with respect to resource competition) influence the acquisition of manipulative language? Broadly speaking, I would hypothesize that in societies in which members are mutually dependent, directives would be framed so as to maintain the close-knit fabric of the group. It could be said that in such societies politeness is considered more important than effectiveness obtained through use of coercion. The potential benefit of short-term gain carries less weight than the long-term maintenance of the social matrix. Hence, linguistically, children's directives should aim toward leaving listeners with room to say "no," rather than the reverse. Children in such a society, in recognition of the constraints of co-dependence, might be less likely than children in American society to make a directive that does not acknowledge the burden it places on the listener. Nor would children in such a society frame a directive without considering the indirect cost to themselves resulting from taking resources from other group members. Conventional politeness (as represented by Quadrant 4—Implicit/Supplicating) as opposed to coercive indirectness (Quadrant 1—Implicit/Authoritative) might be expected to predominate in such societies.

A good example comes from Patricia Clancy's work (1986) in which she contrasts the communicative style of the Japanese child learning directives with that of the American child. Her data show that the greater use of indirect (implicit) speech in Japanese society, as well as the reluctance to say "no," is a way of avoiding overt expression of conflict, a response to life in a more closely knit society. "Japanese society is, in fact, extremely homogeneous, and more group-oriented than American society, which has much greater ethnic diversity and places a much higher value on individualism." (p. 216)

While these broadly defined linguistic differences may characterize the manipulative language use of societies differing in the value they place on individualism, it would still be expected that within any given society there exists the potential for use of a broad array of directives. I am suggesting here that the proportion of use of these four basically different types may differ from group to group.

SUMMARY

This view of the relationship between resource competition and the acquisition of directives places language squarely at the center of human social interactions. The superabundance of forms of directives and the relative absence of stereotyped, direct forms used by adults may be related to a more general characteristic of modern human languages. Burling's (1986) theorizing has provided some clues as to why this might be the case. The aspect of language that contributed to its proposed evolution from simple to complex was the power it gave its possessors in complex social interaction involving resource acquisition.

In ontogenesis, children acquire complex and functionally redundant forms of language in the context of competition over resources. Such acquisition may be supported by various psychological mechanisms including those that are specifically linguistic, as suggested above. Work on children's directives suggests that, as early as three years of age, children begin to substitute implicit forms of directives for some of the explicit forms they had earlier used. Their use of these alternative forms for both polite and coercive purposes points to their appreciation for the differential psychological impact that alternative forms have. Thus young children begin to add to their repertoire of competitive strategies some psychological ploys that will aid in resource acquisition, especially as they look for these from others besides their parents. We need further studies to supply detailed information about how differences between social groups, in terms of resource availability and the methods of resource distribution, affect linguistic development.

REFERENCES

Becker, J. (1981). The development of the abilities to produce and identify nice and bossy requests. Unpublished doctoral dissertation, University of Minnesota, Minneapolis.

Blurton-Jones, N. (1972). Categories of child-child interaction. In N. Blurton-Jones (Ed.) *Ethological studies of child behavior.* Cambridge, England: Cambridge University Press.

Brown, P., & Levinson, S. (1987). *Politeness: Some universals in language*

usage. Cambridge, England: Cambridge University Press.

Burling, R. (1986). The selective advantage of complex language. *Ethology and Sociobiology, 7,* 1–16.

Caryl, P. (1979). Communication by agonistic displays: What can game theory contribute to ethology? *Behavior, 68,* 136–169.

Caryl, P. (1982). Animal signals: A reply to Hinde. *Animal Behavior, 30,* 240–244.

Charlesworth, W., & La Freniere, P. (1983). Dominance, friendship and resource utilization in preschool children's groups. *Ethology and Sociobiology, 4,* 175–186.

Clancy, P. (1986). The acquisition of communicative style in Japanese. In B. Schieffelin & E. Ochs (Eds.), *Language socialization across cultures.* Cambridge, England: Cambridge University Press.

Dawkins, R., & Krebs, J. (1978). Animal signals: Information or manipulation? In J. Krebs & N. Davies (Eds.), *Behavioral ecology.* Oxford: Blackwell Scientific Publications.

Ervin-Tripp, S. (1976). "Is Sybil there?" The structure of some American English directives. *Language in Society, 5,* 25–66.

Ervin-Tripp, S. (1977). "Wait for me roller skate!" In S. Ervin-Tripp & C. Mitchell-Kernan (Eds.), *Child Discourse.* New York: Academic Press.

Forbes, D., & Lubin, D. (1984). Verbal social reasoning and observed persuasion strategies. In H. Sypher & J. Applegate (Eds.), *Communication by children and adults: Social cognitive and strategic processes.* Beverly Hills, CA: Sage.

Garvey, C. (1975). Requests and responses in children's speech. *Journal of Child Language, 2,* 41–63.

Goffman, E. (1955). On face-work: An analysis of ritual elements in social interaction. *Psychiatry: Journal for the Study of Interpersonal Processes, 18,* (#3), 213–231.

Halliday, M. (1975). *Learning to how to mean: Explorations in the development of language.* Oxford: Elsevier North-Holland, Inc.

Harkness, C. (1988). The form and function of directives young children use in competition. Unpublished doctoral dissertation, University of Minnesota, Minneapolis.

Jakobson, R. (1960). Linguistics and poetics. In T. A. Sebeok (Ed.), *Style in language.* Cambridge, MA: MIT Press.

Kaplan, H. (1987). Human communication and contemporary evolutionary theory. In S. Sigman (Ed.), *Research on language and social interaction, 20,* 79–139.

Krebs, J., & Dawkins, R. (1984). Animal signals: Mindreading and manipulation. In J. Krebs & N. Davies (Eds.), *Behavioral ecology, 2nd ed.* (pp. 380–402) Oxford: Blackwell Scientific Publications.

Parkhurst, J., & Gottman, J. (1986). How young children get what they want. In J. Gottman & J. Parker (Eds.), *Conversations of friends.* New York: Wiley.

Read, B., & Cherry, L. (1978). Preschool children's production of directive forms. *Discourse Processes, 1,* 233–245.

Rees, N. (1978). Pragmatics in language. In R. Schiefelbusch (Ed.), *Bases of language intervention.* (pp. 191–268) Baltimore: University Park Press.

Schacter, F., Kirshner, K., Klips, B., Friedricks, M., & Sanders, K. (1974). Everyday preschool interpersonal speech usage. *Monographs of the Society for Research on Child Development, 39* (#145).

Shepard, R. N. (1980). Multi-dimensional scaling, tree-fitting, and clustering. *Science, 210,* 390–398.

Smith, W. J. (1977). *The Behavior of communicating.* Cambridge, MA: Harvard University Press.

Whiten, A., & Byrne, R. (1988). Tactical deception in primates. *Behavioral and Brain Sciences, 11*, 233–274.

Wilkinson, L., Calculator, S., & Dollaghan, C. (1982). "Ya wanna trade—just for awhile": Children's requests and responses to peers. *Discourse Processes, 5*, 161–176.

A Goal-Driven Model of Interpersonal Influence

James Price Dillard
University of Wisconsin, Madison

K urt Lewin is often remembered for his claim that there is nothing so practical as a good theory. He meant, I believe, that theory is valuable because it both points the way to a destination and provides some advice on how to get there. In this sense, theories are maps. Even when maps are poorly drawn or when they distort what they are supposed to represent, they may still prove useful if they stimulate more accurate renditions of the subject under scrutiny.

What follows is an exercise in theoretical cartography. It is an attempt to outline the processes that underlie the production of interpersonal influence messages. I begin by sketching the assumptions and general outline of a theory of interpersonal influence. In the sections that follow, I elaborate on the parts of the model, and finally I examine the processes that connect them. In the spirit of Lewin's dictum, my aim is to provide something that might be of practical use to students of communication.

Author's Note: I would like to thank Joe Cappella and David Ritchie for their comments on an earlier version of this chapter.

ASSUMPTIVE GROUND: LIMITED ACTION AND LIMITED CAPACITY

Broadly construed, action is purposeful behavior. Attempting to gain the compliance of another person is obviously one sort of purposeful behavior. To claim that compliance seeking is purposeful implies both agency and awareness. Having made that statement, it is immediately necessary to qualify it.

Although agency denotes free will, it need not be taken to mean that *all* behavior is directed by the act of choosing. One study of purposeful behavior found that people who decide to eat peanuts do in fact eat more peanuts than people who resolve not to consume the nuts (Howard & Conway, 1986). Obvious? Yes, but the study also showed that some of the people who decided against ingesting peanuts nonetheless ate them. Certainly, choice shapes some behaviors some of the time, but it is apparent that other forces are also at work. To the extent that this point is in doubt, an even more compelling case is made by the large numbers of people who resolve to maintain their diets or to quit smoking but do neither.

Further, although awareness implies conscious appreciation of one's own behaviors, it should not be interpreted to mean total awareness of all aspects of the message production process (cf., Seibold, Cantrill, & Meyers's (1985) Strategic Choice Model). Many aspects of message production are well learned, perhaps scripted (Schank & Abelson, 1977), and can be executed without awareness (Greene, 1984). Minimally, however, awareness of an influence goal is needed before compliance-seeking behaviors can be construed as action.

At the confluence of these two action assumptions is a conclusion that bears on research strategy. If actors possess agency and awareness, then their own perceptions and interpretations of their behavior constitute an invaluable source of data. Because agency and awareness are limited, however, that data alone will be insufficient for a thorough account of behavior. A phenomenologically grounded explanation will tell only a portion of the theoretical tale. Consequently, it must be fused with concepts derived from other sources.

It will also be taken as axiomatic that humans are limited and conservative information processors. They are limited in the sense that there is an upper boundary or limit to the amount of information that may be operated upon by any given individual. That boundary may vary with the state of the individual, for example, with fatigue or anxiety.

The conservative aspect of humans as information processors is neatly encapsulated in Chaiken, Liberman, and Eagly's (in press) principles of least effort and sufficiency. The least-effort principle asserts that individuals attempt to meet their information-processing goals in the manner perceived to be most efficient. The sufficiency principle takes note of the fact that deliberative processing is effortful, and it makes the claim that people will exert cognitive effort commensurate with their perception of the importance of the task.

INFRASTRUCTURE

Like any attempt at explanation, the present one requires a set of constructs as a foundation upon which a theoretical account can be erected. The present formulation relies on goals, plans, and action for its conceptual underpinnings (Miller, Galanter, & Pribram, 1960). Goals are defined as future states of affairs which an individual is committed to achieving or maintaining (cf., Hobbs & Evans, 1980; Klinger, 1985). Of course, people have multiple goals that vary in degree of abstraction (hierarchy) and importance over time and at any given point in time, and therefore, different goals will be dominant at different times.

Goals serve several functions. For example, they initiate action and act as a standard against which the outcomes resulting from that action may be compared (Hacker, 1985). They also impart meaning to human action and interaction. Appreciation of this second aspect of goals is crucial because it is the ability to understand that enables other important processes. First, a goal aids in one's comprehension of an action by saying what it is about (Bruce, 1980). Lines of research as different as attribution theory, artificial intelligence, and story comprehension focus on people's efforts to understand their own goals and those of others. Second, knowledge of goals allows people to segment the stream of behavior into meaningful units (von Cranach, Machler, & Steiner, 1985). Third, through understanding, goals determine what aspects of behavior are attended to, encoded, and retrieved (Cohen 1981).

Plans follow from goals. A plan is that which specifies the set of actions necessary to achieve a goal (see Berger, 1988a). Plans may be differentiated on three dimensions: hierarchy, complexity, and completeness. Plans vary in hierarchy in proportion to the level of goal abstraction. For example, an abstract goal such as "to be happy" might invoke an equally abstract plan such as "to work less." Initially at least, planning takes place at a level of abstraction that corresponds to the level of abstraction at which the goal was conceptualized (Dillard, 1990).

Plan complexity refers to the number of elements and contingencies in a plan and to the sequence in which those elements must be executed (cf., Berger, 1988b). For example, an ingratiation tactic is more complex than a direct request because it requires two steps (butter up, then request) rather than one, and because those two steps must be carried in a specific sequence.

The concept of plan completeness refers to the extent to which the elements of a plan are fleshed out. Plans may be horizontally incomplete when they lack contingencies at the level of the original goal; for example, "If he does X, then I don't know what I'll do." Plans may be vertically incomplete when the subcomponents of a plan are not developed prior to the influence attempt. For instance, an individual may approach an influence attempt planning to use a bargaining strategy, but may have no well-specified notion concerning exactly what will be bartered. In accordance with their desire for efficiency, it is assumed that actors typically approach social influence situations armed only with a general idea about how the interaction will proceed. Because of the potentially vast complexity of any interaction, the details are filled out as the communication episode unfolds (Hayes-Roth & Hayes-Roth, 1979; Hobbs & Agar, 1985).

Although plans exist as psychological entities, they flow into the empirical world as action. For the most part, action is the result of plans that have been put into effect. The process of translating plans into action is not completely straightforward, however; rather, it is subject to the demands and limitations of other aspects of the goals-planning-action (GPA) sequence. For instance, one or more of an individual's other goals may displace the goal-plan that is currently being translated into action. Features of the situation or interaction may come to light that make it apparent that pursuing a particular goal is fruitless, thereby terminating plan execution. In addition, translating a plan into action may require cognitive capacity that is available only in limited quantities. This latter problem should be particularly acute when plans are complex or largely incomplete. Finally, individuals may find that they neither possess nor are able to create the behaviors necessary to flesh out incomplete plans.

A MODEL OF INTERPERSONAL INFLUENCE

Goals

Given the framework described above, it is readily apparent that influence attempts are goal driven. Two general classes of goals are specified: influence, or primary, goals and secondary goals. These two types of goals can be distinguished by their centrality to the influence attempt and by their causal relations to one another. Influence goals are primary because they bracket the attempt and provide the explanation for the interaction. Influence goals also instigate consideration of secondary goals.

Influence Goals

Awareness of an influence goal occurs when the actor perceives some discrepancy or potential discrepancy between the current state of affairs and the desired state of affairs. The phrase "state-of-affairs" is intended to refer to the behaviors of the target person. Both the magnitude of that discrepancy and the importance of the desired state of affairs contribute to the importance of the influence goal, probably in a multiplicative fashion. If the goal is of sufficient importance that it exceeds an individually determined threshold, then it initializes the GPA sequence.

Earlier, I claimed that one of the functions of a goal is to explain. If true, then it seems reasonable to expect some commonality of goals within a given culture. Although the body of research on influence goals is small and is limited to samples of North Americans, it supports this expectation. The top half of Table 4 summarizes the overlap

Table 4   **A Comparison of Three Influence-Goal-Classification Studies**

Study			
	Cody et al. (in press)	Dillard (1989)	Rule et al. (1985)
Goal Types Common to Close Relationships			
	Gain Assistance	Gain Assistance	Agency/ Assist
	Share Activity	Share Activity	Activity
	Give Advice (Friend)	Give Advice (Lifestyle)/ (Health)	Habit
	Escalate/ De-escalate Relationship	Change Relationship	Change Relationship
Points of Contrast			
Method: Quantitative		Quantitative	Qualitative
Stimuli: Situations		Recalled Goals	Hypothetical Goals

among the findings of three studies the purpose of which was to explore and classify types of influence goals. Because one of the studies (Dillard, 1989) restricted its focus to influence goals in close relationships, comparison among the studies is possible only in that context. Nonetheless, the comparison is instructive and reveals considerable convergence of results. This level of agreement is all the more encouraging because of the variations in method and stimuli.

It is important to emphasize that these investigations are not simply exercises in list making. Rather, illumination of the substance of goals provides some clues as to what constitutes culturally viable explanation and to the ways in which compliance seekers conceive their own actions. What is more important for students of interpersonal influence is the identification of a variety of different phenomenologically grounded goal types that suggests that researchers should not presuppose that all influence goals are equal. There is reason to believe that influence goal type affects planning (Berger, Mann, & Jordan, 1988) and message output (Blum-Kukla, Danet, & Gherson, 1985; Cody, Canary, & Smith, in press; Dillard, 1989). Considered collectively, these studies argue strongly against influence research predicated on the notion of *one* influence goal. Instead, each goal defines separate persuasive domains and should be investigated as such. Failure to attend to variations at the beginning of the GPA sequence (i.e., to different goal types) is bound to obfuscate potentially important variations in later stages of the sequence (i.e., planning and action).

Secondary Goals

This second category of goals springs from a set of concerns that are common across individuals and situations. Rather than driving the influence episode, as does the primary goal, secondary goals act as a counterforce to it and as a set of dynamics that help to shape planning and message output.

With regard to the latter, Hample and Dallinger's (1987b) intriguing work on cognitive editing is relevant. They propose the existence of three standards that are used to reject possible compliance-gaining messages: (in)effectiveness, person-centered issues, and discourse-competence issues. In a similar vein, an investigation by Dillard, Segrin, and Harden (1989) suggests an expanded set of secondary goals. *Identity goals* are objectives related to the self concept. They derive from one's moral standards, principles for living, and personal preferences concerning one's own conduct. *Interaction goals* are concerned with social appropriateness. They represent one's desire to manage impressions successfully, to ensure a smooth flow to the communication event, to avoid threatening the face of the other actor, and to produce messages that are relevant and coherent. The focus of *relational resource goals* is on increasing or maintaining valued relational assets such as attention, positive stimulation, emotional support, and social comparison (Hill, 1987). *Personal resource goals* are concerned with maintaining or improving all of those physical, material, mental, and temporal assets that a person may have. Finally, by positing the existence of *arousal management goals*, it is assumed that people have a desire to maintain a state of arousal that falls within certain idiosyncratically preferred boundaries. Usually this will mean that people attempt to dampen their apprehension induced by participation or anticipation of making an interpersonal influence attempt.

The Decision to Engage

Although the relationships among primary and secondary goals may be complex at the microscopic level, in the broader view the goals can be seen as composing sets of approach and avoidance forces oriented toward securing compliance. The influence goal obviously constitutes the major approach dynamic. The secondary goals will typically act to inhibit the approach force, and, when they act together, they may overwhelm it. When this occurs the source will choose not to engage the target, or, if the attempt is in progress, will choose to exit the interaction either physically or topically.

Thus, for any given compliance-gaining attempt each goal may be assigned a weight with respect to the decision to engage. The sign of the influence goal will always be positive, indicating a desire to achieve compliance. The more important the influence goal is, the more likely that the source will instigate and persist in the influence attempt (cf., Emmons & Diener, 1986). The signs of the secondary goals' weights will be negative, indicating that the goal contributes to the avoidance dynamic, or zero, indicating that the goal is irrelevant to this particular attempt. Since humans are limited information processors, only a small number of goals are likely to be operative at any given moment in an interaction.

To help clarify the plausibility of this formula, it is necessary to backtrack to the notion of hierarchy. Assume a three-tiered system composed of motives at the highest level, followed by goals, and followed finally by subgoals. Motives are broad, abstract orientations that may be instantiated as goals. For the moment, assume further that each type of secondary goal has a corresponding motive. I now add the additional restriction that influence goals must have empirical referents. Consequently, to go from motive to influence goal is to move in two directions simultaneously: down the hierarchy and from the conceptual to the empirical.

Imagine a situation in which I want to convince you to sell me a bottle of wine that you hold dear. Obtaining the wine could be thought of as augmenting my personal resources. My motive-level orientation toward enhancing my material assets has been instantiated as a more specific desire to improve my enological lot. In this instance, a personal resource motive has been instantiated as an influence goal. Other instantiations of the same motive may produce secondary goals. In this example, one obvious personal resource goal is the maintenance of my bank account. I want the wine, but only at a reasonable price. Thus it is possible for a single motive to generate both an influence goal and a secondary goal.

Of Plans and Planning

Planning consists of producing one or more schemes for goal attainment, evaluating their overall effectiveness, and choosing among them. In the sphere of interpersonal influence, planning becomes more serviceable by treating it as two relatively independent activities; tactic plan generation and tactic plan selection. Before turning to those processes, however, it is necessary to further explicate the meaning of tactic plan.

The Nature and Substance of Tactic Plans

A tactic plan is a representation of a set of verbal and nonverbal actions that might modify the behavior of the target. Tactic plans differ from tactics as cognitions differ from behavior (Seibold et al., 1985). Because tactic plans are simply plans of a special type, they vary in terms of hierarchy, complexity, and completeness. Together, these concepts are sufficient to describe the nature of tactic plans.

Equally important, however, is the *substance* of tactic plans. Cumulatively, the exploratory investigations of the perception of influence tactics suggest that at least three dimensions are relevant to this issue (Cody, McLaughlin, & Jordan, 1980; Falbo, 1977; Falbo & Peplau, 1980; Tenney, 1988; Wiseman & Schenck-Hamlin, 1981). Tactics, and by implication, tactic plans, are *direct* to the extent that they specify a set of behaviors that makes the influence goal explicit. *Positivity* refers to the degree to which positive (or negative) outcomes for the target are linked with compliance (or noncompliance). Tactics and tactic plans also exhibit *logic* to the extent that they incorporate evidence and reason. Finally, there is some evidence that the degree of source *control* over the outcomes associated with compliance also figures into the substance of tactic plans (Wiseman & Schenck-Hamlin, 1981).

Tactic Plan Generation

Tactic plan generation encompasses all of those processes that underlie the retrieval and creation of a tactic plan. People possess repertoires of "boilerplate" tactic plans that they may draw upon to generate plans suited to the occasion. These plans exist in long-term memory (Greene, Smith, & Lindsey, 1988; Meyer, this volume), but must be adapted to the specifics of any given influence attempt.

Despite the diversity of influence tactics shown to exist *across* persons (Falbo, 1977; Kipnis, Schmidt, & Wilkinson, 1980; Rule, Bisanz, & Kohn, 1985; Wiseman & Schenk-Hamlin, 1981), individuals' repertoires of tactic plans are far more limited (Kipnis, 1984; Vroom & Yetton, 1973). Clark and Delia (1979), remarking on the extent of individual differences in their data state that, "[a] striking feature of the results was the consistency in types of tactic employed by any one individual. That is, if an individual used bribery in one persuasive situation, he was likely to use it in another as well" (p. 1013). The number of tactic plans and variations generated in any given influence attempt is a joint function of the importance of the influence goal and the size of the actor's repertoire.

Tactic Plan Selection

One of the most common assumptions in the study of compliance-gaining has been that there is a preferred order of tactic usage. Several studies that show that tactics tend to increase in directness and decrease in positivity when the source is confronted with resistance attest to this ordering (deTurck, 1985; Lim, 1988). In addition, numerous studies in which people were provided with a set of tactics and asked to indicate their preference for each reveal a fairly consistent pattern of endorsement (see Burleson et al., 1988; and Wheeless, Barraclough, & Stewart, 1983 for reviews).

Several variables, including empathy (Hunter & Boster, 1985) and moral development (Rule et al., 1985), have been proposed as candidates to account for ordering. The current formulation views these variables as remote from the selection process. It focuses instead on the source's goals in a particular influence attempt, and suggests that there are multiple bases on which the ordering of tactic plans is undertaken, that is, the primary and secondary goals. A growing body of research indicates that reliance on different secondary goals varies as a joint function of situational and individual difference variables including self-monitoring (Hample & Dallinger, 1987a), gender, argumentativeness, and interpersonal orientation (Hample & Dallinger, 1988).

The Planning Process

Planning may be a highly organized and methodical activity, a relatively effortless utilization of simple decision rules, or a mixture of the two (Chaiken et al., in press). Deliberative or systematic planning is a process that utilizes considerable quantities of cognitive capacity and is concerned with generating plans, filling out incomplete plans both vertically and horizontally, and estimating the impact and desirability of alternative plans. Heuristic planning is characterized by the use of simple decision rules such as "Use the most positive tactic first" or "Begin with the least costly tactic." Any influence interaction probably involves some of both kinds of planning, but it seems reasonable to expect that as the importance of the influence goal increases so does the willingness to engage in systematic planning. Evidence from one recent investigation supports this claim and shows that variations in the importance of the influence goal have an impact not only on the amount of thought that goes into planning but also on the degree to which the tactic incorporates evidence and reason (Dillard et al., 1989). The magnitude of these relationships was only moderate. Given the principles of least effort and sufficiency, however, moderate correlations are all that should be expected. The desire to be effective in the influence attempt may be satisfied by an original and carefully constructed plan or by the same well-practiced routine that has been successful many times in the past.

Implementing Plans as Action

The final stage of the GPA sequence requires putting the plan into effect. Because of the nature of plans, however, the plan-action link is susceptible to at least two general sorts of problems. One is the matter of having the requisite materials to complete the plan. Despite the fact that people almost universally report that they prefer the use of rational, logic-based tactics (see Kipnis, et al., 1980), such a persuasive approach requires sound evidence and compelling reasons. Similarly, power-based tactics such as threats are impossible in the absence of the ability to follow through. Without the necessary personal and situational ingredients, the preferred tactic plan cannot be enacted.

Cognitive capacity also plays an important role in plan instantiation. Although some tactic plans, such as direct request, are short and to the point, others, such as explanation and deceit, are inherently more complex. These complex plans require greater cognitive effort to put into effect, and thus should be adversely affected by the numerous forces that may cause decrements in cognitive capacity. Along the general line of this claim, Berger, Mann, and Jordan (1988) provide evidence that plan complexity is negatively related to verbal fluency. In a more specific vein, Dillard et al. (1989) report that arousal has a negative impact on the use of logic.

Moving Through the Model

The model in Figure 1 provides an illustration of the parts and processes of the goal-driven model. As the figure shows, the source may go first to the engagement decision point or to the tactic generation process. It is suggested that only one of two contingent paths will operate at any given time. As indicated by the dashed lines, goal awareness may cause the decision to engage, which in turn brings about tactic generation and selection. Such a process would occur when the source is convinced that an influence attempt must be made. The task, then, is one of determining the best method. Alternatively, the source may become aware of an influence goal, but may reserve the decision to actually make the influence attempt until a satisfactory means is discerned. Which path is followed should be determined by

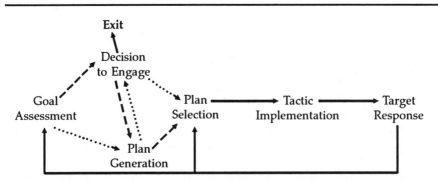

Note: The dashed lines show one of two possible pathways to plan selection while the dotted lines indicate the alternative. Solid lines show noncontingent, sequenced stages in the model.

Figure 1   **A Goal-Driven Model of Interpersonal Influence**

the relative weight of the approach and avoidance dynamics. In cases where the approach forces greatly outweigh the avoidance dynamic, the awareness-decision-generation sequence should obtain. When engagement is absolutely required (in the mind of the source), tactic generation should follow.

Of course, there may be instances in which the approach and avoidance dynamics are fairly closely matched. The influence goal is a motivating one, but the potential costs in terms of damage to the relationship, interaction mismanagement, or anxiety are considerable. The decision to engage is contingent upon finding a means of obtaining compliance that minimizes the avoidance factors. In these instances, tactic generation will precede the decision to engage. In the absence of the requisite persuasive materials, the influence goal may enter into a state of "top spin" (Heckhausen & Kuhl, 1985), in which it affects perception (search for the needed materials), but not action.

From Action to Interaction

One additional concept is needed to make the fledgling theory interactive, and that is some type of response from the target. On the basis of that response, the source may adapt a plan, select a new plan, re-evaluate goals, or seek additional information to assist with those processes.

Basically, there are three sorts of responses that the target might make to an influence attempt: compliance, resistance, or exit (topically or physically). If the target complies with the request the process stops, that is, the influence episode is over. Similarly, if the target exits physically, then the influence attempt has reached an end. Topical exit is conceptually messier since the definition of the communication event itself may become the goal of a substantively different influence attempt.

As the term is used here (simplistically), resistance means nonacquiescence. Thus, many forms of response, including avoidance, negotiation, and information-seeking, as well as flat-out refusal, are considered to be resistance. If the target resists, the model iterates until compliance is achieved or the decision to engage is reversed. Like influence tactics, resistance messages may vary along the dimensions of directness, positivity, logic, and perhaps control.

Two feedback loops are specified. First, the source may return to the goal awareness stage and move through the complete model again. In such a sequence, goals are reevaluated in light of the degree of resistance observed each time the target makes a response. Alternately, the source may store a number of tactics in a buffer and iterate only as far back as the tactic selection stage.

It is reasonable to suppose that both loops may operate at different times in a single interaction. People may use the shorter and more efficient route until the current store of tactic plans is depleted, and may then engage in goal reevaluation and a new round of tactic generation, or they may reconsider the decision to engage.

Interaction as Interdependent Action

Up to this point, analysis of the interpersonal influence process has emphasized the perspective of the source, but the proposed model can also be used to account for the actions of the target. To do so requires a brief reconsideration of the relationship between primary and secondary goals.

The notion of influence is troublesome since it says nothing about the behavior that is being influenced. It is insufficient to say "I intend to influence him" without at least implicitly making reference to the targeted behavior, such as "I intend to influence him regarding X." In this sense, a category of goals called influence goals is an empty vessel that must be filled before the interaction can be made sensible. The category is meaningfully filled by the reification of an abstract orientation, a motive, in a specific setting. That is, motives are instantiated as goals. Influence goals make sense because they exist in order to satisfy some higher-level desire.

In terms of the model being developed here, the essential difference between source and target is the deletion of the influence goal and its replacement with a resistance goal. The crucial distinction between influence and resistance goals lies in the manner in which the motive is instantiated. Influence goals are *offensive* instantiations in that the source seeks to control the behavior of the target (Swann, Pelham, & Roberts, 1987; see also Arkin, 1981, on acquisitive and protective modes of self-presentation). A *defensive* instantiation results in a resistance goal. Awareness of a source's influence goal should be sufficient to trigger in the target the instantiation of one or more motives in the form of a resistance goal.

CONCLUSION

The GPA (goals, planning, action) formula casts the process of interpersonal influence in a new light. Although it is a crude map, it does fit well with what is now known, and it offers a perspective from which to structure further inquiry. To the extent that this formula stimulates research that permits us to draft the theoretical map with bolder strokes and greater confidence, then it may be judged practical.

REFERENCES

Arkin, R. M. (1981). Self-presentation styles. In J. T. Tedeschi (Ed.), *Impression management theory and social psychological research* (pp. 311–334). New York: Academic Press.

Berger, C. R. (1988a). Planning, action, and social action generation. In L. Donohew, H. Sypher, & E. T. Higgins (Eds.), *Communication, social cognition and affect*. Hillsdale, NJ: Lawrence Erlbaum.

Berger, C. R. (1988b, May). *Communication plans and communicative performance*. Paper presented at the annual meeting of the International Communication Association, New Orleans.

Berger, C. R., Mann, S. K., & Jordan, J. M. (1989). When a lot of knowledge is a dangerous thing: The debilitating effects of plan complexity on verbal fluency. *Human Communication Research, 16,* 91–119.

Blum-Kukla, S., Danet, B., & Gherson, R. (1985). The language of requesting in Israeli society. In J.P. Forgas (Ed.), *Language and social situations* (pp. 113–139). New York: Springer-Verlag.

Bruce, B. C. (1980). Plans and social action. In R. J. Spiro, B. C. Bruce, & Brewer, W. F. (Eds.), *Theoretical issues in reading comprehension* (pp. 367–384). Hillsdale, NJ: Lawrence Erlbaum.

Burleson, B., Wilson, S., Waltman, M.S., Goering, E. M., Ely, T. K., & Whaley, B. B. (1988). Item desirability effects in compliance-gaining research: Seven studies documenting artifacts in the strategy selection procedure. *Human Communication Research, 14,* 429–486.

Canary, D. J., Cody, M. J., & Marston, P. J. (1987). Goal types, compliance-gaining and locus of control. *Journal of Language and Social Psychology, 5,* 249–269.

Chaiken, S., Liberman, A., & Eagly, A. H. (in press). Heuristic and systematic information processing within and beyond the persuasion context. In J. S. Uleman & J. A. Bargh (Eds.), *Unintended thought: Limits of awareness, intention, and control.* New York: Guilford.

Clark, R. A., & Delia, J. C. (1979). Topoi and rhetorical competence. *Quarterly Journal of Speech, 65,* 187–206.

Cody, M. J., Canary, D. J., & Smith, S. W. (in press). Compliance-gaining goals: An inductive analysis of actors' goal types, strategies, and successes. In J. Daly & J. Wiemann (Eds.). *Communicating strategically.* Hillsdale, NJ: Lawrence Erlbaum.

Cody, M. J., McLaughlin, M. L., & Jordan, W. J. (1980). A multi-dimensional scaling of three sets of compliance-gaining strategies. *Communication Quarterly, 28,* 34–46.

Cohen, C. E. (1981). Goals and schemata in person perception: Making sense from the stream of behavior. In N. Cantor & J. F. Kihlstrom (Eds.), *Personality, cognition, and social interaction* (pp. 45–68). Hillsdale, NJ: Lawrence Erlbaum.

deTurck, M. (1985). A transactional analysis of compliance-gaining behavior. *Human Communication Research, 12,* 54–78.

Dillard, J. P. (1990). The nature and substance of plans in tactical communication. In M. Cody & M. McLaughlin (Eds.), *The psychology of tactical communication.* (pp. 70–90) Clevedon, England: Multilingual Matters.

Dillard, J. P. (1989). Types of influence goals in close relationships. *Journal of Social and Personal Relationships, 6,* 293–308.

Dillard, J. P., Segrin, C., & Harden, J. (1989). Primary and secondary goals in the interpersonal influence process. *Communication Monographs, 56,* 19–39.

Emmons, R. A., & Diener, E. (1986). A goal-affect analysis of everyday situational choices. *Journal of Research in Personality, 20,* 309–326.

Falbo, T. (1977). Multidimensional scaling of power strategies. *Journal of Personality and Social Psychology, 35,* 537–547.

Falbo, T, & Peplau, L. A. (1980). Power strategies in intimate relationships. *Journal of Personality and Social Psychology, 38,* 618–628.

Greene, J. O. (1984). A cognitive approach to human communication: An action assembly theory. *Communication Monographs, 51,* 289–306.

Greene, J. O., Smith, S. W., & Lindsey, A. E. (1988, May). *Memory representations of compliance-gaining strategies and tactics.* Paper presented at the annual meeting of the International Communication Association, New Orleans.

Hacker, W. (1985). On some fundamentals of action regulation. In G. P. Ginsburg, M. Brenner, & M. von Cranach (Eds.), *Discovery strategies in the psychology of action* (pp. 63–84). London: Academic Press.

Hample, D., & Dallinger, J. M. (1987a, March). Cognitive editing of argument strategies. *Human Communication Research, 14,* 123–144.

Hample, D., & Dallinger, J. M. (1987b). Self-monitoring and the cognitive editing of arguments. *Central States Speech Journal, 38,* 152–165.

Hample, D., & Dallinger, J. M. (1988). *The use of multiple goals in cognitive editing of arguments.* Paper presented at the Temple University Discourse Conference, Philadelphia.

Hayes-Roth, B., & Hayes-Roth, F. (1979). A cognitive model of planning. *Cognitive Science, 3,* 275–310.

Heckhausen, H., & Kuhl, J. (1985). From wishes to action: The dead ends and shorts cuts on the long way to action. In M. Frese & J. Sabini (Eds.). *Goal directed behavior.* Hillsdale, NJ: Lawrence Erlbaum.

Hill, C. A. (1987). Affiliation motivation: People who need people. . . but in different ways. *Journal of Personality and Social Psychology, 52,* 1008–1018.

Hobbs, J. R., & Agar, M. H. (1985). The coherence of incoherent discourse. *Journal of Language and Social Psychology, 4,* 213–232.

Hobbs, J. R., & Evans, D. A. (1980). Conversation as planned behavior. *Cognitive Science, 4,* 349–377.

Howard, G. S., & Conway, C. G. (1986). Can there be an empirical science of volition? *American Psychologist, 41,* 1241–1251.

Hunter, J. E., & Boster, F. J. (1987). A model of compliance-gaining messages selection. *Communication Monographs, 54,* 63–84.

Kipnis, D. (1984). The use of power in interpersonal settings. In S. Oskamp (Ed.), *Applied social psychology annual 5: Applications in organizational settings* (pp. 179–210). Beverly Hills, CA: Sage.

Kipnis, D., Schmidt, S. M., & Wilkinson, I. (1980). Intraorganizational influence tactics: Explorations in getting one's way. *Journal of Applied Psychology, 65,* 440–452.

Klinger, E. (1985). Missing links in action theory. In M. Frese & J. Sabini (Eds.), *Goal directed behavior* (pp. 311–321). Hillsdale, NJ: Lawrence Erlbaum.

Lim, T. S. (1988, May). *Influences of receiver's resistance on persuaders' verbal aggressiveness.* Paper presented at the annual meeting of the International Communication Association, New Orleans.

Miller, G. A., Galanter, E., & Pribram, K. H. (1960). *Plans and the structure of behavior.* New York: Holt, Rinehart, & Winston.

Rule, B. G., Bisanz, G. L., & Kohn, M. (1985). Anatomy of a persuasion schema: Target, goals, and strategies. *Journal of Personality and Social Psychology, 48,* 1127–1140.

Schank, R. C., & Abelson, R. P. (1977). *Scripts, plans, goals, and understanding.* Hillsdale, NJ: Lawrence Erlbaum.

Seibold, D. R., Cantrill, J. G., & Meyers, R. A. (1985). Communication and interpersonal influence. In M. L. Knapp & G. R. Miller (Eds.), *Handbook of interpersonal communication* (pp. 551–611). Beverly Hills, CA: Sage.

Swann, W. B., Pelham, B. W., & Roberts, D. C. (1987). Causal chunking: Memory and inference in ongoing interaction. *Journal of Personality and Social Psychology, 53,* 858–865.

Tenney, B. (1988). *A taxonomy of spouses' compliance-gaining messages.* Unpublished master's thesis, University of Wisconsin-Madison, Madison.

von Cranach, M., Machler, E., & Steiner, V. (1985). The organisation of goal-directed action: A research report. In G. P. Ginsburg, M. Brenner, & M. von Cranach (Eds.), *Discovery strategies in the psychology of action* (pp. 19–61). London: Academic Press.

Vroom, V. H., & Yetton, P. W. (1973). *Leadership and decision making.* Pittsburg: University of Pittsburg Press.

Wiseman. R. L., & Schenck-Hamlin, W. J. (1981). A multidimensional scaling validation of an inductively derived set of compliance-gaining strategies. *Communication Monographs, 48,* 251–270.

Wheeless, L. R., Barraclough, R., & Stewart, R. (1983). Compliance-gaining and power in persuasion. In R. N. Bostrom (Ed.), *Communication yearbook, vol. 7* (105–145). Beverly Hills, CA: Sage.

Cognitive Processes Underlying the Retrieval of Compliance-Gaining Strategies: An Implicit Rules Model

Janet R. Meyer
University of Wyoming

A cognitive approach to the study of communication assumes that behavior is influenced by the manner in which a situation is represented in working memory. This chapter exemplifies that approach in that its primary aim is to outline a model of the cognitive processes that underlie the retrieval of compliance-gaining strategies. The model attempts to account for the manner in which situations containing a compliance-gaining goal are represented in working memory, and the processes by which these representations shape the retrieval of strategies.

The notion of a schema is essential to the first point. Schemata are cognitive structures that organize information about situations, goals, and the kinds of communication behavior that can be used to achieve goals in particular types of situations.

Regarding the second point, the most basic and central claim of the model to be developed in this chapter is that rules for the production of communication behavior are stored as implicit rules. That is, rules are not stored in explicit, symbolic form, but are stored instead as multi-pathway associations between two types of schemata.

Situation schemata contain information about the communicative goal at hand as well as a configuration of relevant situational features. The other type of schematic representation, strategy schemata, organizes knowledge about a communication strategy that has proven successful under similar circumstances in the past. A single situation schema can send activation simultaneously to one or more associated strategy schemata.

The association between the two types of schemata is equivalent to a rule that specifies "Under these circumstances, use this strategy." Such rules are implicit, however; they have not been translated into verbal form, and, in fact, would be difficult for the individual to verbalize in their entirety (Reber & Allen, 1978; Reber, 1976; Reber et al., 1980; McClelland, Rumelhart, & Hinton, 1986; Rumelhart & McClelland, 1986).

The first section of this chapter outlines the general processing assumptions underlying the model. The second section describes the nature of strategy schemata as well as the form and content of situation schemata. The next section describes the cognitive mechanisms that allow a situation schema to influence the retrieval of a compliance-gaining strategy in a specific situation. The final section considers the role of active and passive processes in the acquisition of implicit rules.

GENERAL PROCESSING ASSUMPTIONS

The perspective developed in this chapter adopts many of the general processing assumptions of "distributed" models of memory (McClelland & Rumelhart, 1985; McClelland, Rumelhart & Hinton, 1986). The most basic units in memory are taken to be primitive elements that send excitatory and inhibitory impulses to each other. These elements represent basic components of perceptual experience, such as lines and colors, and of semantic meaning, such as the distinction between good and bad or between animate and inanimate. A simple concept is represented by a large number of highly interconnected primitive elements distributed throughout memory. Higher-level concepts can be abstracted from configurations of relatively lower-level concepts. Both situation and strategy schemata are viewed as higher-level concepts in this sense. The representation of the concept in working memory is equivalent to a particular pattern of activation across the primitives that comprise it.

Unlike theories that assume that rules for the production of behavior are acquired actively as the result of testing and rejecting hypotheses and have an explicit, symbolic representation in long-term memory (even though they may not be consciously retrievable) (Anderson, 1987; Dulaney, Carlson, & Dewey, 1984, 1985; Lewis & Anderson, 1985), the present model assumes that knowledge equivalent to an "if-then" rule is stored in the connections formed between one distributed representation and another (Rumelhart & McClelland, 1986). To the extent that rules *emerge* from the associative connections linking a situation schema and a strategy schema, it may be said that individuals store implicit rules.

The abstract knowledge that an individual possesses about a familiar concept or event is organized in long-term memory by a schema. Schemata are abstracted when similar configurations of primitive elements are activated on repeated occasions. Individuals possess a large number of schemata that connect the features of, and hence organize abstract knowledge about, typical situations containing a compliance-gaining goal. Additionally, schemata can integrate the various components of higher-level plans to employ particular communication strategies.

An activated schema consists of a coalition of highly interconnected features that provide excitatory feedback to each other. Once a schema is activated, mutually reinforcing feedback among features within the schema serves to maintain in working memory a representation of the relatively higher-level entity that the schema represents (Feldman & Ballard, 1982). The features that participate in one schema may also participate in a large number of other schemata. One schema can be "associatively" related to another through multiple paths connecting the primitive elements in one to the primitive elements in the other. Thus a situation schema, once activated, can activate a strategy schema by spreading excitation to it.

Assumptions about the manner in which schemata are abstracted are derived from McClelland and Rumelhart's (1985) distributed model of prototype abstraction. According to these authors, an initial episodic experience of a concept (such as a dog) is represented as a pattern of excitation over a large number of primitive units. Subsequent experiences of the same concept involve similar patterns of excitation over many of the same units. Multiple experiences of a concept are stored in the same set of connections as a composite memory trace. After repeated experiences of different patterns of the concept in different contexts, some of the connections between units in the composite become strengthened as the result of frequency of activation, while others decay. As a consequence, a prototypical representation of the concept is abstracted.

In the early experiences of a new concept, the representation of the concept and the contexts in which it occurs are inseparable. It is only after repeated experiences that a prototype or schema emerges. If a particular subset of prototypical features is repeatedly encountered in a particular context, however, those features will remain associated with that context. In this manner, such a model is able to store both a prototype and a specific exemplar of a prototype (such as a pattern representing a specific dog, Rover), or it can store contextual variations of a prototype as distinct patterns involving many of the same connections (McClelland & Rumelhart, 1985).

Although McClelland and Rumelhart's (1985) model allows exemplars of a concept that are repeated to be stored as an abstract pattern, it does not allow the memory traces of specific episodes to be retained for long. The present model assumes that episodic representations of compliance-gaining situations, although subject to decay, are also permanently stored. As will be argued in the final section of this chapter, being reminded of these specific memories plays an important role in the acquisition of situation schemata and of more highly differentiated rules.

THE STRUCTURE OF IMPLICIT RULES

Cognitive Representations of Strategies

A compliance-gaining strategy is defined as a cognitive representation that integrates three components: one, a sequence of one or more speech acts, such as request, promise, request-promise, explanation-request, and so forth; two, a strategic component that is expressed or implied by the propositional content of the message, such as appealing to the altruistic instincts of the listener, implying a reward, and reminding the listener of a debt owed; and, three, a relational message, such as politeness, dominance, aggressiveness, and so forth. After an individual has employed a particular configuration of these components on repeated occasions, he or she will acquire both a cognitive script and a strategy schema. The script specifies an abstract sequence of actions for producing that particular strategy while the higher-level schematic representation of the strategy can be viewed as an overall plan for the strategy. (The distinction here is analogous to that between a script that specifies the sequence of allophones required to pronounce a word and a representation of the lexical item as a whole.) It is the overall representation of a strategy as a whole that is initially activated by a situation schema.

Cognitive Representations of Situations

A speaker's perception of a situation at the time he or she is activating a compliance-gaining goal is organized by a schema that contains two types of information: a representation of a particular type of compliance-gaining goal and communication-relevant situational knowledge.

Past research on the underlying dimensions of compliance-gaining situations implies that the knowledge contained in a situation schema might be conceived of as a set of values along some number of perceptual dimensions (Cody & McLaughlin, 1980; Cody, Woelfel, & Jordan, 1983; Dillard & Burgoon, 1985; Hertzog & Bradac, 1984). Thus, it might be postulated that acquisition of a situation schema is synonymous with the development of a cognitive structure that contains a representation of the goal and a representation of each value.

The assumption that a representation of a concept can be described as a set of values assigned to a number of dimensions is consistent with the definition of a "prototype" that has been accepted in most past research. In those works, a prototype has been treated as a knowledge structure that contains the modal values (assuming categorical dimensions) or the mean values (assuming continuous dimensions) on each of some number of independent perceptual dimensions (Medin, Altom, & Murphy, 1984; Posner & Keele, 1968; Reed, 1972). The assumptions made here concerning the way in which those features are stored depart from past research in two ways, however. First, the critical features contained in a schema for a particular type of compliance-gaining situation are often related to each other and to the type of action requested in meaningful ways (Medin, Wattenmaker, & Hampson, 1987), and hence are highly interconnected by paths that represent causal and other kinds of relationships among the features. For instance, the perceptions that the hearer is a stranger (low intimacy), that the hearer will object to doing the action (high resistance), and that the speaker's right to ask is questionable (low rights), might be connected by a number of pathways that store the knowledge that the perception of low rights follows from the fact that the hearer is a stranger and that the hearer will object to carrying out the action.

The second departure from past research is that the exact configuration of primitives that constitutes a speaker's representation of any situational feature is dependent upon the situation schema in which the feature participates. This assumption is consistent with research and theory that suggest that the meaning of any concept is context-dependent (Anderson & Ortony, 1975; Asch, 1946; Barclay et al., 1974; Tulving & Thomson, 1973). The logic here is that a speaker's representation of a feature such as high rights contains as part of its conceptual meaning some of the reasons underlying the perceived right to make the request. These reasons could stem from a variety of factors such as a position of authority over the hearer, the perception that the hearer is in some way indebted to the speaker, the fact that the hearer is a close friend, the fact that the requested action is a small one, or the fact that the action is to the personal benefit of the hearer. Whether any or all of these perceptions constitute part of the meaning of high rights will depend upon the features contained in the schema.

In summary, a speaker's representation of a compliance-gaining situation is organized by a schema that contains an abstract representation of a compliance-gaining goal, a configuration of communication-relevant situational features, and knowledge about the relationships among the features. Situational features can become part of a schema simply because they have been processed simultaneously with a particular type of goal on multiple occasions; that is, they have covaried. There is evidence to suggest, however, that a schema will be more likely to form, if thoughts about the nature of the relationships among features are also processed by the individual (Craik & Lockhart, 1972). This aspect of schema development is thought to result in more and stronger connections among the primitive elements.

The specificity of a situation schema will depend upon the two major components of that schema, the goal and the configuration of situational features. Goal specificity will vary depending upon the extensiveness and variety of an individual's experience with any general type of goal. An individual who seldom pursues a particular type of compliance-gaining goal might possess only a single situation schema that contains a relatively general representation of the requested action. In contrast, an individual who has entertained such a goal in a number of different contexts could abstract several situation schemata, each of which contains a more highly differentiated representation of the action requested.

The number of situational features contained in the situation schema will vary across rules and across individuals. When a speaker retrieves an implicit rule that contains a relatively higher differentiated situational component, it should be easier to create messages that address all critical features of an immediate situation than when the situational information contained in the rule is more general. Such differences are likely to combine with a speaker's representation of the characteristics of a specific hearer to contribute to the individual differences in adaptive ability tapped by measures of cognitive complexity, cognitive abstractness (for example, see O'Keefe & Delia, 1982), and self-monitoring (Snyder, 1979).

For any given type of compliance-gaining goal, an individual potentially could abstract a number of different situation schemata where each contains a different configuration of situational features. Furthermore, an individual could possess a large number of situation schemata that contain the same configurations of situational features but different types of compliance-gaining goals. Because the processing assumptions specify that the primitive elements that participate in one schema also participate in many others, and they specify that a general schema as well as more highly differentiated variations of it are stored in the same sets of connections as a composite memory trace, the model allows individuals to store in memory a very large number of relatively specific situation schemata.

The Content of Situation Schemata

Past research on the perceptual dimensions of compliance-gaining situations is suggestive of the kind of communication-relevant knowledge that might be contained within the situational component of an implicit rule. A multidimensional scaling study conducted by Cody and McLaughlin (1980) indicates that situation schema might contain information pertinent to the amount of *resistance* expected, the *intimacy* of the relationship between the speaker and hearer, whether the hearer is *dominant* or *submissive* with respect to the speaker, the degree of *personal benefits* to the speaker, whether *relational consequences* are short-term or long-term, and/or the extent to which the speaker believes he or she has a *right* to ask. Using a similar methodology, Hertzog and Bradac (1984) found four dimensions that appeared to underlie subjects' perceptions of compliance-gaining situations. These included the resistance to persuasion and dominance dimensions reported by Cody and McLaughlin, as well as a *values/rules* dimension (which distinguished situations in which the target was asked to violate some role or role-related rule from situations where the target was asked to respect and adopt some value held by the speaker), and a *gender-relevance* dimension (which distinguished situations in which the speaker and hearer were of the opposite sex from situations in which the relationship between the sex of the speaker and the sex of the hearer was irrelevant).

In addition to these factors, the knowledge contained in a schema for a particular type of compliance-gaining situation could include knowledge that bears directly upon the strategic component of some strategies, such as knowledge pertinent to a debt, reward or reciprocal favor; knowledge related to preconditions for the performance of and understanding of speech acts, such as knowledge about whether the hearer has the ability to do the action (Labov & Fanshel, 1977); knowledge about general personality characteristics of the hearer or about the hearer's perspective (Burleson, 1983; 1984); and situation-specific knowledge that becomes critical only in the context of a particular request type, such as in the case of borrowing, whether or not the speaker trusts the hearer (Tracy et al., 1984).

All of the situational factors listed above may be relevant to the compliance-gaining attempt not only in terms of goal accomplishment, but also because they provide the speaker with information pertinent to relational goals such as making a good impression, conveying a positive view of the hearer, and addressing the negative face needs of the hearer (cf., Dillard, p. 46 in this volume). Such goals may be activated simultaneously with a compliance-gaining goal. If one or more relational goals has frequently occurred together with the compliance-gaining goal and features of a specific situation schema, then the relational goals can come to form part of the situation schema. In this case, the strategy activated by the situation schema would likely be the one that had proven most successful in the individual's past experience in addressing both the instrumental goal and relational goals.

COGNITIVE PROCESSES UNDERLYING STRATEGY RETRIEVAL

The Relationship Between Situation Schemata and Strategy Schemata

Once a situation schema has become activated, activation will spread from it to one or more strategy schemata. Given the tenets of a distributed model, at least two explanations can be posited regarding the manner in which goals and situational features interact to influence the retrieval of a strategy. These explanations are of fundamental importance here since they relate to the question of what constitutes an implicit rule. One explanation holds that each component of a situation schema is independently associated to particular strategies. An alternative explanation would posit that strategies are associated to the schema as a whole.

According to the first explanation, each goal and situational feature active in working memory would contribute to strategy selection independent of the other goals and situational features that are simultaneously activated. That is, the amount of activation sent to a strategy by a given situational feature would be the same regardless of the overall configuration of situational features. The strategy most likely to be selected, or in other words, the most highly activated strategy, would be the one receiving the most activation from all sources of activation.

Although the above explanation probably has some merit, it seems inadequate given the assumptions about situation representation described in the preceding section. To begin with, such an explanation implies that a strategy could be selected as the result of activation converging upon it from situational features that had not previously occurred together in the individual's experience. That is, each feature may have occurred in quite different contexts in the past. If the success of a particular strategy, given a particular feature, often depends upon the presence or absence of other features, the activation process described above would not provide a very reliable means for retrieving the most appropriate strategy for a particular circumstance.

Second, the meaning of individual situational features is often dependent on the overall configuration of features. In this view, any association formed from a feature and a strategy would be an association from a context-sensitive representation of the feature and the strategy. The strategies activated by a given feature should depend upon the particular representation of the feature that is currently activated. If it is assumed that the meaning of a feature is dependent on the schema it participates in, then the strategies activated by a given feature would depend on the specific schema activated.

Third, if situation schemata contain not only features but also knowledge about the relationships among the features, then a strategy would become associated not only to the features but also to the knowledge about the relationships among features. For these reasons, the present theory posits that the relationships between situation schemata and strategy schemata are best viewed as associations of the situation schema as a whole and the strategy schema as a whole. Hence, the central claim of the model is that *after finding, from multiple situations that contain the same goal and similar configurations of situational features, that a particular strategy consistently produces a successful outcome, an individual will form an implicit rule that takes the form of an association of a schematic representation of the goal and configuration of situational features and a schematic representation of the strategy. In new situations containing a goal and a configuration of features that match the schema, the individual will retrieve the situation schema and, as the result of activation spreading from it, the associated strategy schema.*

The ease of retrieving a situation schema will be a positive function of the strength of the connections among the components of the schema. The strength of these links will increase with frequency of activation as will the strength of the links that connect the pragmatic, strategic, and relational components within a higher-level schematic representation of a compliance-gaining strategy. Because a situation schema that is more frequently activated will require less stimulation from the knowledge active in working memory in order to be retrieved, it will be more accessible for organizing an individual's perception of a situation. Similarly, a strategy schema that is more frequently activated will be more accessible in that it will require a smaller amount of activation from a situation schema to be retrieved, and hence it will be retrieved more quickly than a less accessible one.

The strength of a particular strategy is independent of the strength of the various situation schemata that might activate it. Thus, a large number of situation schemata could be associatively connected to a single strategy that is highly accessible across numerous contexts, such as a direct request. Similarly, a highly accessible situation schema could be associated either to a single highly accessible strategy or to a number of different strategies. This suggests that individual differences in the selection of compliance-gaining strategies may be attributable to variations in the accessibility of either alternative situation schemata or particular strategies or both.

Retrieving a Strategy in a Specific Request Situation

The retrieval of a compliance-gaining strategy in a specific situation may be described as a three-stage process. At the first stage, activation spreads from the speaker's representation of the situation in working memory, which causes activation of an appropriate situation schema. A schema may be retrieved in this manner when information that is active in working memory matches only a subset of the information contained in the schema (Anderson, 1983; McClelland & Rumelhart, 1985). Once retrieved, the schema organizes the speaker's perception of the situation and causes the speaker to attend to information in the immediate situation that matches information contained in the schema. Such a schema may also serve as the basis for "filling in" information not contained in the immediate situation.

At the second stage, excitation from the activated situation schema is sent to strategies associated with it. Relatively more activation goes to strategies that are strongly associated to the situation schema. The strength of the association from a situation schema to a strategy schema, that is, the rule, increases as a function of three factors: the frequency of activation of the link (which strengthens existing connections) (Anderson, 1983; Rumelhart & McClelland, 1986); the recency of activation of the link (due to memory decay) (Anderson, 1983); and the amount of reflection upon the relationship of the features to the strategy (which would increase the number of pathways from the situation schema to the strategy) (Craik & Lockhart, 1972).

At the third stage of the retrieval process, one of the strategies receiving activation from the situation schema is selected. If competing strategies are activated by a schema, the most highly activated strategy will be the one that is initially retrieved. The level of activation of a given strategy is a positive function of the strength of the strategy schema (independent of its association to any particular situation schema) and of the amount of activation converging upon it from the currently activated situation schema. A strategy that is strong due to frequency of use will require less activation from a situation schema and hence may often be retrieved first.

Although the most highly activated strategy will be retrieved initially, a speaker may not use the first strategy that comes to mind. Automatic adoption of the initially retrieved strategy may occur under heavy capacity load or under time pressure, but if the speaker does have time to evaluate outcomes, this extra knowledge could help a strategy outcome take one of two forms. For example, by activating a strategy schema in a particular situation, a speaker could be reminded of an earlier episode in which the same strategy was utilized, and consequently could retrieve the outcome in that episode. Thus, tenants involved in a housing dispute might recall that the last time they threatened a landlord, the outcome was failure.

Alternatively, a speaker might retrieve a representation of an outcome acquired from multiple situations in which the strategy currently being considered was utilized in similar contexts. This possibility is suggested by the general processing assumptions of distributed models. According to these assumptions, if an individual repeatedly found that when a particular strategy was employed within a certain configuration of situational features, a specific outcome resulted, he or she would acquire abstract knowledge that could be utilized to predict the outcome of the strategy in the current situation. This knowledge would take the form of an association between the strategy and the outcome. Once the former representation was activated, the outcome could be retrieved. The cognitive representation of an outcome retrieved in this manner potentially could include information about a specific compliance-resisting strategy, a speech act (agreement, refusal, complaint), a generalized relational response (acceptance, rejection, disconfirmation), and/or a simple representation of positive or negative affect. The information stored in the representation of an outcome should be that information that was most frequently attended to across all occurrences of that outcome.

Retrieving Overly General Schemata

For any compliance-gaining situation, an individual will be able to retrieve *some* situation schema that can be employed to organize and maintain an overall representation of the situation in working memory. In addition to that knowledge organized by the situation schema, however, working memory will always contain situational knowledge that is not contained in the schema. This situational knowledge may contain features that are critical to the selection of an effective strategy. To the extent that the retrieved schema does not accurately represent the configuration of features present in the particular situation, it is overly general.

One of two things could occur if an overly general situation schema is employed. First, an individual might employ the strategy most strongly associated with that schema, despite the fact that it fails to address all communication-relevant features of the immediate situation. This would be particularly likely under time pressure or if there were additional demands on processing capacity such as an on-going conversation.

Alternatively, the individual might attempt to integrate the initial strategy with other strategies that had been activated by situational features that were active in working memory but not contained in the schema. In such cases, the schematic and the nonschematic features contribute independently to strategy selection. The most highly activated strategy will be the one receiving the most activation from all sources. Because the nonschematic features typically might occur in very different situational contexts from the immediate one, a strategy activated as such may often be less than optimal for the immediate situation.

When a speaker's representation of a situation is organized by a schema, each situational feature that is active in working memory will tend to send more of its activation to other activated features (and less activation to associates outside the schema) than when the situation is not organized by a schema. This mutually reinforcing feedback within a schema will allow a speaker to represent a given goal and communication-relevant features with fewer demands on processing capacity than would be required to represent the same information in the absence of a schema. In such instances, speakers generally will be quicker and more fluent at producing effective compliance-gaining messages.

THE ACQUISITION OF IMPLICIT RULES

The acquisition of implicit rules, as well as the development of any more highly differentiated components of an existing rule, comes about as the result of a reminding process or as a combination of active and reminding processes. Active processes are characterized by attempts to articulate some of the situational features of the rule. Reminding occurs when the memory of a specific compliance-gaining episode is activated because of the similarity between the configuration of goals and situational features in the past episode and the present one.

An implicit rule can be acquired solely as the result of reminding-based processes in the following way: Imagine that an individual encountered a new type of compliance-gaining situation containing a set of features that had not previously co-occurred and that successfully utilized a new strategy in that situation. The situation, the strategy, and the link between them would be stored in an episodic memory trace. If a similar episode were encountered later, activation from the features of the immediate situation would cause the individual to be reminded of the previous one. The likelihood of being reminded of an earlier episode will be positively related to the number of features in the immediate situation that match those in the situation stored in memory, and will be negatively related to the amount of time that has passed since the earlier episode. Once reminding has occurred, the strategy employed in the previous episode will be retrieved and instantiated in the immediate situation.

At this point, the episodic memories of the two situations are stored as a composite memory trace, as are the episodic memories of the twice-instantiated, higher-level strategy plan. The individual will thus possess the beginning of a schema for the situation, a schema for the strategy, and a weak association connecting them, in which the features common to both schemata are strongest. Should the same type of situation occur a third time, the individual would retrieve the situation schema, employ it to organize the immediate situation, and retrieve the associated strategy schema. At this point, the selection of a strategy is guided by an implicit rule.

Suppose that in a later situation, however, the strategy contained in the implicit rule failed. Failure might be attributed to the presence of a critical feature, such as high resistance, that was not contained in the situation schema and hence was not addressed. The acquisition of a rule containing a more highly differentiated situational component could occur either as the result of reminding-based processes or as an outcome of more active processes.

In the former case, if a subsequent situation contained both the situational features of the rule that failed and the critical feature that was not addressed, the speaker could be reminded of the earlier episode, recall that the strategy failed, and try a new strategy. At that point, the speaker would possess the beginning of a more highly differentiated situation schema that contained the features of the old schema plus the new critical feature.

Assume that the new strategy produced the desired outcome. In a later, similar situation, the speaker could retrieve the more finely discriminated situation schema, retrieve the strategy that succeeded, and use it in the immediate situation. With frequency of use, the strength of the associative links between the more highly differentiated schema and the successful strategy would become even stronger and the connections to the failed strategy would weaken with disuse.

Rule acquisition and/or differentiation could also occur through relatively more active processes. By reflecting upon a failed compliance-gaining attempt, a speaker might realize that a critical situational feature was not appropriately addressed and thus might formulate a hypothetical rule that linked the feature to a more optimal strategy. Initially, a rule of this sort would be stored in episodic memory along with any unarticulated situational information that was active in working memory at the time the rule was formulated (Ross, 1984; Tulving & Thomson, 1973). If such a rule were utilized repeatedly with the same situational features, the various episodes would be stored as a composite in memory. Consequently, a situation schema, including both an explicit verbal component (describing some aspect of the situation) and an unarticulated contextual component, would be abstracted and would become connected to the strategy schema. At that point, the individual would possess an implicit rule.

The retrieval assumptions outlined above imply that the likelihood of retrieving such an implicit rule would be greater if the situational features of an immediate situation matched the unarticulated component of the rule than if they did not, since those features would provide additional retrieval cues. It would be correct to assume that the unarticulated component of the implicit rule had an impact upon the selection of a strategy in the same manner as the articulated component.

In this sense, even when speakers consciously reflect upon the relevance of particular situational features to the success or failure of a strategy, and then develop their own conscious rules for strategy selection, tacit situational knowledge will also influence the selection of a strategy. The influence of this tacit knowledge will be primarily outside conscious awareness (Reber & Allen, 1978). This is true for two reasons: First, the dependability of an explicitly formulated rule is often contingent upon the presence of other situational features that were not articulated; and second, the number of situational features that actually exert an influence upon the retrieval of a communication strategy is probably very large. It is unlikely that an individual would be able to articulate all of them.

REFERENCES

Anderson, J. R. (1983). *The architecture of cognition.* Cambridge, MA: Harvard University Press.

Anderson, J. R. (1987). Skill acquisition: Compilation of weak-method problem solutions. *Psychological Review, 94,* 192–210.

Anderson, R. C., & Ortony, A. (1975). On putting apples into bottles—A problem of polysemy. *Cognitive Psychology, 7,* 167–180.

Asch, S. I. (1946). Forming impressions of personality. *Journal of Abnormal and Social Psychology, 41,* 258–290.

Barclay, J. R., Bransford, J. D., Franks, J. J., McCarrell, N. S., & Nitsch, K. (1974). Comprehension and semantic flexibility. *Journal of Verbal Learning and Verbal Behavior, 13,* 471–481.

Burleson, B. R. (1984). Age, social-cognitive development, and the use of comforting strategies. *Communication Monographs, 51,* 140–153.

Burleson, B. R. (1983). Social cognition, empathic motivation and adults' comforting strategies. *Human Communication Research, 10,* 295–304.

Cody, M. J., Canary, D. J., & Smith, S. W. (in press). Compliance-gaining goals and episodes. In J. Daly & J. Wiemann (Eds.), *Communicating*

strategically. Hillsdale, NJ: Lawrence Erlbaum.

Cody, M. J., & McLaughlin, M. L. (1980). Perceptions of compliance-gaining situations: A dimensional analysis. *Communication Monographs, 47,* 132–148.

Cody, M. J., Woelfel, M. L., & Jordan, W. J. (1983). Dimensions of compliance-gaining situations. *Human Communication Research, 9,* 99–113.

Craik, F. I. M., & Lockhart, R. S. (1972). Levels of processing: A framework for memory research. *Journal of Verbal Learning and Verbal Behavior, 11,* 671–684.

Dillard, J. P., & Burgoon, M. (1985). Situational influences on the selection of compliance-gaining messages: Two tests of the predictive utility of the Cody-McLaughlin typology. *Communication Monographs, 52,* 289–304.

Dulaney, D. E., Carlson, R. A., & Dewey, G. I. (1984). A case of syntactical learning and judgment: How conscious and how abstract? *Journal of Experimental Psychology: General, 113,* 541–555.

Dulaney, D. E., Carlson, R. A., & Dewey, G. I. (1985). On consciousness in syntactic learning and judgment: A reply to Reber, Allen and Regan. *Journal of Experimental Psychology: General, 114,* 25–32.

Feldman, J. A., & Ballard, D. H. (1982). Connectionist models and their properties. *Cognitive Science, 6,* 205–254.

Hertzog, R. L., & Bradac, J. J. (1984). Perceptions of compliance-gaining situations: An extended analysis. *Communication Research, 11,* 363–391.

Labov, W., & Fanshel, D. (1977). *Therapeutic discourse: Psychotherapy as conversation.* NY: Academic Press.

Lewis, M. W., & Anderson, J. R. (1985). Discrimination of operator schemata in problem-solving: Learning from examples. *Cognitive Psychology, 17,* 26–65.

McClelland, J. L., & Rumelhart, D. E. (1985). Distributed memory and the representation of general and specific information. *Journal of Experimental Psychology: General, 114,* 159–188.

McClelland, J. L., Rumelhart, D. E., & Hinton, G. E. (1986). The appeal of parallel distributed processing. In D. E. Rumelhart, J. L. McClelland, and the PDP Research Group. *Parallel distributed processing: Explorations in the microstructure of cognition: Vol. 1. Foundations* (pp. 3–44). Cambridge, MA: MIT Press.

Medin, D. L., Altom, M. W., & Murphy, T. D. (1984). Given versus induced category representations: Use of prototype and exemplar information in classification. *Journal of Experimental Psychology: Learning, Memory and Cognition, 10,* 333–352.

Medin, D. L., Wattenmaker, W. D., & Hampson, S. E. (1987). Family resemblance, conceptual cohesiveness

and category construction. *Cognitive Psychology, 19,* 242–279.

O'Keefe, B. J., & Delia, J. G. (1982). Impression formation and message production. In M. E. Roloff & C. R. Berger (Eds.), *Social cognition and communication.* Beverly Hills, CA: Sage.

Posner, J. J., & Keele, S. W. (1968). On the genesis of abstract ideas. *Journal of Experimental Psychology, 77,* 353–363.

Reber, A. S. (1976). Implicit learning of synthetic languages: The role of instructional set. *Journal of Experimental Psychology: Human Learning and Memory, 2,* 88–94.

Reber, A. S., & Allen, R. (1978). Analogy and abstraction strategies in synthetic grammar learning: A functional interpretation. *Cognition, 6,* 189–221.

Reber, A. S., Kassin, S. M., Lewis, S., & Cantor, G. (1980). On the relationship between implicit and explicit modes in the learning of a complex rule structure. *Journal of Experimental Psychology: Human Learning & Memory, 6,* 492–502.

Reed, S. K. (1972). Pattern recognition and categorization. *Cognitive Psychology, 3,* 382–407.

Ross, B. H. (1984). Remindings and their effects in learning a cognitive skill. *Cognitive Psychology, 16,* 371–416.

Rumelhart, D. E., & McClelland, J. L. (1986). On learning the past tenses of English verbs. In J. L. McClelland, D. E. Rumelhart, and the PDP Research Group. *Parallel distributed processing: Explorations in the microstructure of cognition: Vol. 2. Psychological and biological models* (pp. 216–271). Cambridge, MA: MIT Press.

Snyder, M. (1979). Self-monitoring processes. In L. Berkowitz (Ed.), *Advances in experimental social psychology* (Vol. 12). New York: Academic Press.

Tracy, K., Craig, R. T., Smith, M., & Spisak, F. (1984). The discourse of requests: Assessment of a compliance-gaining approach. *Human Communication Research, 10,* 513–538.

Tulving. E., & Thomson, D. M. (1973). Encoding specificity and retrieval processes in episodic memory. *Psychological Review, 80,* 352–373.

Politeness Behavior in Social Influence Situations

Tae-Seop Lim
University of Colorado

Most studies of social influence have focused on the way in which individuals select general message categories such as threat, liking, and moral appeal. Consequently, variations within these general categories, that is, the linguistic form of the expression, have been largely ignored. When generating an influence message, however, individuals must do more than just determine the generic approach. They must also attend to the myriad of details requisite to the completion of an utterance. In other words, individuals must determine "how to say" as well as "what to say."

One important aspect of "how to say" is politeness (Craig, Tracy, & Spisak, 1986; Lim, 1988; Shimanoff, 1977; Tracy, in press; Tracy, Craig, Smith, & Spisak, 1984). If one assumes, as politeness theorists do, that all influence attempts constitute an intrusion on the target, then clearly the most polite course of action for the source is to refrain from seeking compliance altogether. There are obvious problems with that. One alternative would be to engage in social influence attempts that are forceful and explicit, but one runs the risk of antagonizing the target and reducing the likelihood of success. Politeness theory attempts to study the ground that lies between these two extremes. At issue is the manner in which speakers linguistically balance their own desires with the wishes and desires of the targets.

This chapter is composed of three major sections. In the first, I review and critique Brown and Levinson's (1978; 1987) politeness theory; in the second section, I present a new version of politeness theory; and finally, I apply the new theory to social influence situations.

BROWN AND LEVINSON'S POLITENESS THEORY

At the heart of Brown and Levinson's (1978; 1987) politeness theory is the concept of face. *Positive face* refers to an actor's desire to have the approval of others. *Negative face* is the desire to not be imposed upon by others. All social actors would like to have both types of face wants met, but because these are social desires, they can only be satisfied by other people. Thus, there exists a quid pro quo such that people behave in a certain manner to save the face of the others. The expectation is that others, although not necessarily the same others, will behave in kind. That is, people strive to preserve and promote others' face wants with the expectation that other actors will do the same for them. Although different cultures have different sets of criteria concerning what constitutes imposition and disapproval, the desire to avoid both is universal.

Difficulty arises from the fact that many communicative acts, especially instances of social influence, are face-threatening acts (FTAs). For example, a request to "Move out of the way" necessarily interferes with the hearer's negative face wants (desire for autonomy).

The degree to which face is threatened by a request is, in part, a function of three things: the social distance between the two actors, the relative power of the two actors, and the intrusiveness of the request. The *social distance* variable indexes the intimacy of the speaker and the hearer. *Power* encompasses not only relational power but also societally based distinctions such as status. *Intrusiveness* is roughly equivalent to request size, although what is considered small or large can only be judged within the context provided by a given culture. Brown and Levinson (1978) assume that either one type of face or the other is threatened by a request, but never both. The overall degree of face threat is determined by summing the threat value to that type of face with values representing distance and power.

The overall degree of face threat determines how polite a speaker will be. Brown and Levinson (1978) propose the existence of five general politeness strategies that vary along a continuum of "redressiveness." This refers to the extent to which the speaker attempts to mitigate the face threat to the hearer. When presented in order from

Table 5   **Brown and Levinson's Politeness Strategies**

ASSUME THAT THE SPEAKER DESIRES THAT THE HEARER CLOSE THE WINDOW.

Politeness	Strategy	Example
High	Don't do FTA	Do not make the request (no behavior)
	Go off record	Kind of breezy in here, don't you think?
	Negative politeness	If it wouldn't be too much trouble, would you mind shutting the window?
	Positive politeness	Hey friend, I think that we'd both be warmer if the window were closed.
Low	Bald on-record	Would you close the window?

most redressive to least redressive, the strategies are (1) do not do the FTA; (2) do it off-record, that is, inexplicitly, (3) use negative politeness, that is, mitigate the threat to the hearer's negative face; (4) use positive politeness, that is, mitigate the threat to the positive face; and (5) do it baldly on-record, that is, explicitly without redressing either face. Table 5 provides an illustration of each type of strategy.

Critique

There are several limitations to Brown and Levinson's (1978) politeness theory. First, it is confined to one kind of face threat at time. Consider the utterance "Can you do the work again, please?" Brown and Levinson would argue that this utterance threatens only the negative face of the hearer since it contradicts the hearer's desire not to be imposed on, but this request also clearly violates the hearer's desire to elude disapproval by implying that the work done is not satisfactory.

Second, this politeness theory is limited by utterances made to mitigate the effects of FTAs. This feature of the theory is unnecessarily restrictive for two reasons. One is that the absence of behavior often has implications for face wants, such as when someone does not show an expected expression. The second reason is that some behaviors appear to exist solely for the purpose of satisfying the face wants of another; they have no instrumental aspect at all. For example, greeting, parting, appreciating, apologizing, congratulating, as well as the various forms of phatic communication, are often performed without instrumental motivation.

A third limitation revolves around the definitions of positive and negative politeness. Although positive politeness is described as "simply representative of the normal linguistic behavior between intimates" (Brown & Levinson, 1978, p. 106), it is apparent that not all intimate linguistic behavior indicates approval. In-group identity markers such as "mate," "pal," and "buddy" typically impart approval, but their usual meaning can be inverted nonverbally or when they accompany certain types of utterances like "Step on my foot again, pal, and I'm gonna make sushi out of your face." In addition, intimate linguistic behavior is not the only way to convey approbation. The student who says "Professor Brown, I enjoyed your class very much" is unquestionably approving, but has communicated this approval without increasing intimacy.

The delineation of negative politeness is similarly troublesome. It seems true that most negative politeness strategies do perform "the function of minimizing the particular imposition that the FTA unavoidably affects" (Brown & Levinson, 1978, p. 134), but not all negative politeness strategies *prevent loss* of others' negative face; rather, some *promote* it. For example, when people greet or part with others of higher status, they often give deference using the "vous" (formal "you") form pronouns (Brown & Gilman, 1960), such as title plus last name, to show that they are aware of the power differential. There is no threat to face in such interactions and thus no concern for preventing loss of face, only for promoting it.

Brown and Levinson propose that when face threat is high, speakers will enact negative politeness, and when face threat is (relatively) low, there will be a preference for positive politeness. Other researchers have observed, however, that speakers often do not restrict themselves to a single strategy. Instead, complex combinations of positive and negative politeness occur in many conversations (Craig et al., 1986; Shimanoff, 1977). Moreover, some utterances are multifunctional. For example, the phrase "Would you mind doing a favor for me?" acknowledges the imposition, and in so doing shows the intention to preserve the hearer's negative face. The phrase also *simultaneously* promotes positive face by presuming a bond between the two actors that would predispose the hearer to agree.

Finally, empirical tests of the model reveal that a large portion of the variance in politeness can be explained by factors others than the three predictors specified by the theory, intrusiveness, social distance, and power (Baxter, 1984; Blum-Kukla, Danet, & Gherson, 1985). The theory would be enhanced if other factors were incorporated that increased its predictive power.

See Craig et al. (1986) or Lim (1988) for more complete analysis of the limitations of Brown and Levinson's politeness theory.

A NEW MODEL OF POLITENESS

The evidence discussed on the previous pages is not enough to conclude that Brown and Levinson's model is misleading, but it is sufficient to establish that it has several limitations to overcome. I therefore will present a revised version of Brown and Levinson's model. Of necessity, the presentation is an abbreviated one. The interested reader can find a more complete account in Lim (1988).

Positive face is defined as the desire for social approval, while *negative face* is defined as the desire for power. These conceptions represent a departure from the Brown and Levinson model in that both faces have active and passive aspects. The original, Brown and Levinson, treatment of negative face considered only that individuals wish to avoid being intruded upon by others. The more recent conceptualization incorporates this desire for autonomy, but sees it as only one portion of the desire for power continuum; people also want active control of their partner. Similarly, whereas Brown and Levinson's positive face was limited to the desire for approval, the newer treatment also includes the desire to avoid disapproval.

Either type of face can be threatened, and it is often the case that a single message will threaten both faces at the same time. Thus, by extension, it is also possible to redress or be polite to both faces simultaneously. Permitting the existence of positive and negative politeness also represents a significant departure from Brown and Levinson's work. It is expected that people will often use multiple forms of politeness within a single message or even a single phrase. Tables 6 and 7 list strategies that may be used to be positively and negatively polite.

Politeness is a function of two antecedents, considerateness and the obligation to save the face of the other. The concept of *considerateness* can be traced to Goffman's (1967) work that also provides a basis for face. It refers to the extent to which the speaker has concern for the face of the hearer. Incorporating considerateness into the politeness theory pays two important dividends. By assuming that variations in politeness are partially attributable to variations in considerateness,

Table 6   **Lim's Positive Politeness Strategies**

Politeness	Strategy	Example
High	Direct approval	It's really good.
	Absence of disapproval	(no behavior)
	Approval of acceptable aspects plus problems	It's really good except that it needs a few more arguments.
	Understatement of quality and quantity	It needs a little more work to be really good.
	Understatement of quantity	It needs a few more things added.
	Understatement of quality	It can be improved.
	Tentativeness plus negative evaluation	I'm not sure if it was done right.
	Request to improve	Could you please find more evidence to support it.
	Competence salvation	It's not the best work that you can do.
	Direct disapproval	It's weak.
Low	Attack on competence	I don't think that you can do it right.

the model invites the investigation of stable individual differences and transient emotional states (which may impact considerateness).

Obligation to save face is itself determined by the nature of the FTA and the actors' role requirements. FTAs vary in the extent to which they are intrusive, but intrusiveness judgments are made within the context of particular roles. For example, asking someone to type a 30-page paper may be highly threatening to negative face, unless that person is your secretary.

Table 7   **Lim's Negative Politeness Strategies**

Politeness	Strategy	Example
High	Deference/ self-abasement	Is there anything you want me to do?
	Absence of imposition	(no behavior)
	Off-record	Nobody can do it better than you.
	Hypothetical appreciation	I would greatly appreciate it if you did it.
	Subjunctive mood conventional indirectness	Could you do it?
	Please	Please
	Indicative mood conventional indirectness	Can you do it?
	Tentativeness	I know it's imposing a lot, but you gotta do it.
	On-record	I need you to do it.
	Obligation	You owe it to me to do it.
Low	Threat	If you don't do it, I will punish you.

POLITENESS IN SOCIAL INFLUENCE SITUATIONS

Politeness Behavior

As mentioned earlier, most speech acts, but especially acts of social influence, have the potential to threaten others' face. Lim's expanded politeness model claims that attempts at social influence may threaten the hearer's positive and negative face simultaneously. Because both types of face are threatened, most social influence messages will employ a mixture of the two types of politeness.

Proposition 1: Most social influence messages will manifest both positive and negative politeness.

There are several studies that are consistent with this proposition (Baxter, 1984; Craig et al., 1986). More recent evidence comes from Lim (1989). In that study, 400 persons were asked to perform four different face-threatening acts. Seventy-three percent of the participants in the study produced messages that showed both forms of politeness, 3 percent used only positive politeness, 22 percent used only negative politeness, and 3 percent did not use any form of politeness.

Intimacy and Politeness

As intimacy increases, so does the relational partner's obligation to satisfy positive face wants. When the relationship becomes so intimate that mutual acceptance is taken for granted, however, responsibility for the partner's positive face declines. In other words, the relationship between intimacy and the obligation to satisfy positive face is curvilinear. If accurate, then this reasoning should be reflected in the politeness of the social influence attempt.

Proposition 2: The functional form of the relationship between intimacy and positive politeness is best described by an inverted-U.

Although there is no evidence that bears directly on Proposition 2, there are several studies that speak to portions of the proposition. First, Lim (1989) and Baxter (1984) found that subjects used significantly more positive politeness with good friends than with acquaintances. The results of both studies are compatible with the claim that politeness increases as a function of intimacy at the lower end of the intimacy continuum. Second, Fitzpatrick and Winke (1979) found that in conflict situations, highly intimate pairs relied on very aggressive strategies (which are typically low in positive politeness). The finding supports the claim that politeness decreases as a function of intimacy at the upper end of the intimacy continuum.

It is reasonable to expect that negative politeness will behave somewhat differently. As two people grow closer, they become more and more interdependent and aware of the need for mutual assistance and interference (Roloff et al., 1988). Expectations of long-term, reciprocal attention to positive face allows the relational partners to impose upon one another with minimal redress to negative face in the short term.

Proposition 3: As relational intimacy increases, individuals will manifest a lower degree of negative politeness.

Several ethnographic studies of politeness support the above proposition. In their analysis of data drawn from several cultures, Brown and Levinson (1978) found that negative politeness declined as intimacy increased. In addition, two quantitative studies also show the same relationship between intimacy and politeness (Lim, 1989; Roloff et al., 1988).

Power and Politeness

Superiors have higher needs not to be disapproved of and not to be imposed on by their status inferiors. Thus, as the relational power of the hearer increases, the speaker is under increasing obligation to satisfy the hearer's face wants. When individuals want to be considerate, therefore, they will show increased politeness in their influence messages.

Proposition 4: As the relational power of the hearer increases, speakers will manifest greater positive and negative politeness.

Several studies have reported that relational power was not a good predictor of politeness behavior. For example, Baxter (1984) reports only moderate-sized effects for relational power on politeness, and Lim (1989) found no significant effects at all. It can be argued, however, that neither study provided a strong test of Proposition 4. In both investigations, power was manipulated by informing subjects in the disparity condition that they were the leader of a group in which the hearer was a member, and informing the subjects in the power-equal condition they and the hearer were both equal members of a group. There are two potential problems with this manipulation. First, the actual power disparity may not have been great enough to demonstrate the predicted relationship. Second, since many people, but especially Westerners, believe that it is undesirable to openly display power differences, they may tend to limit verbal manifestations of power. Additional research is needed to refute or support Proposition 4.

Degree of Face Threat

Communicative acts vary in the degree to which they threaten the face of the hearer. It is axiomatic to the model of politeness outlined in this chapter that redress is attempted to the extent that the message is threatening.

> *Proposition 5:* As the degree of face threat inherent to a social influence attempt increases, speakers will manifest more positive and more negative politeness.

Lim (1988) found that the amount of face threat was a very strong predictor of politeness behavior. The greater the face threat, the more positive and negative politeness speakers incorporated into their messages.

Marked Politeness Behavior

When speakers make unusual or "marked" linguistic choices, they signal to the hearer that they want to renegotiate their relationship with the hearer (Scotton, 1983). Speakers may wish to permanently alter the relationship, or to simply alter the relationship within the context of a particular interaction. This latter type of change is accomplished by emphasizing some existing feature of the relationship, such as reminding the hearer of a status difference.

Solidarity Moves

A solidarity move is indicative of an attempt to increase the closeness between a speaker and a hearer. It shows that the speaker likes and is interested in the hearer by emphasizing in-group membership, indicating shared wants and shared knowledge, or claiming obligations to help each other (Brown & Levinson, 1978). Thus, solidarity moves address positive face wants.

Solidarity moves indicate that the speaker believes that the hearer has an obligation to help achieve the speaker's goal, and that the speaker does not have to be concerned about the hearer's negative face because of the closeness of their relationship. In other words, solidarity moves also suggest that the speaker should be exempted from the rule of politeness.

Power Displays

This form of marked behavior attempts to increase the relational power of the speaker. Although power differences are, in many ways, less observable in everyday interaction than intimacy differences (Brown & Gilman, 1960), sometimes individuals attempting to exert social influence may feel that to make the power disparity more prominent would be helpful. Power displays function as a warning that the speaker has the ability to invoke the hearer's obligation to comply and that the speaker does not have to be concerned with the hearer's face wants.

Distancing Moves

A distancing move is the antithesis of a solidarity move; it emphasizes the lack of intimacy between the two parties. Such a move emphasizes that the speaker wants to focus on the obligations that exist between strangers.

Determinants of Marked Politeness

It is difficult to predict what kind of marked politeness behavior individuals will employ in a given situation unless we understand their emotional states or their specific goals. Solidarity moves are expected to be used when individuals are in a positive, cooperative mood and the intended act of social influence is judged to be better achieved in a closer relationship. Power displays and distancing moves are expected to be more frequent when the speaker is in an antagonistic mood or when the speaker is willing to sacrifice the relationship to the influence goal.

CONCLUSION

This chapter provides a brief overview of politeness phenomena. Lim's (1988) politeness model seems to be able to make several contributions to the study of social influence. First, it provides a theoretical framework that can explicate the influences of various situational and individual difference variables on the production of influence messages. Second, it moves toward an account of a micro level decision process in which people determine the specific linguistic forms of their influence messages. Third, it attempts to extend our understanding of why people produce marked social influence messages. Although this effort is preliminary, it is important in that it pushes forth in a direction that is new to the study of compliance-gaining.

REFERENCES

Baxter, L. (1984). An investigation into compliance-gaining as politeness. *Human Communication Research, 10,* 427–456.

Blum-Kukla, S., Danet, B., & Gherson, R. (1985). The language of requesting in Israeli society. In J. P. Forgas (Ed.), *Language and social situations* (pp. 113–139). New York: Springer-Verlag.

Brown, R., & Gilman, A. (1960). The pronouns of power and solidarity. In T. A. Sebeok (Ed.), *Style in language* (pp. 253–276). Cambridge, MA: MIT Press.

Brown, P., & Levinson, S. (1978). Universals in language usage: Politeness phenomena. In E. Goody (Ed.), *Questions and politeness: Strategies in social interaction* (pp. 56-289). Cambridge, England: Cambridge University Press.

Brown, P., & Levinson, S. (1987). *Politeness.* Cambridge, England: Cambridge University Press.

Craig, R. T., Tracy, K., & Spisak, F. (1986). The discourse of requests: Assessment of a politeness approach. *Human Communication Research, 12,* 437–468.

Fitzpatrick, M. A., & Winke, J. (1979). You always hurt the one you love: Strategies and tactics in interpersonal conflict. *Communication Quarterly, 27,* 3–11.

Goffman, E. (1967). *Interaction ritual: Essays in face-to-face behavior.* Garden City, NY: Doubleday Anchor.

Lim, T. S. (1988, November). *A new model of politeness in discourse.* Paper presented at the annual meeting of the Speech Communication Association, New Orleans, LA.

Lim, T. S. (1989, May). *Positive and negative politeness in performing face-threatening acts.* Paper presented at the annual meeting of the International Communication Association, San Francisco.

Roloff, M. E., Janiszewski, C. A., McGrath, M. A., Burns, C. S., & Manrai, L. A. (1988). Acquiring resources from intimates: When obligation substitutes for persuasion. *Human Communication Research, 14,* 364–396.

Scotton, C. M. (1983). The negotiation of identities in conversation: A theory of markedness and code choice. *International Journal of Sociology of Language, 44,* 115–136.

Shimanoff, S. B. (1977). Investigating politeness. In E. O. Keenan & T. L. Bennet, (Eds.), *Discourse across time and space* (pp. 213–241). Los Angeles: University of Southern California.

Tracy, K. (in press). The many faces of facework. In H. Giles & P. Robinson (Eds.), *The handbook of language and social psychology.* Chichester, UK: John Wiley.

Tracy, K., Craig, R. T., Smith, M., & Spisak, F. (1984). The discourse of requests: Assessment of a compliance-gaining approach. *Human Communication Research, 10,* 513–538.

The Logic of Regulative Communication: Understanding the Rationality of Message Designs

Barbara J. O'Keefe
University of Illinois, Urbana-Champaign

I n many communication situations, behavior is uniform; that is, virtually every speaker produces the same sort of message. In such situations, messages are relatively homogenous in content and organization, and all messages appear equally well designed to meet the objectives of the communicator. This is the case, for example, in apartment descriptions. Linde and Labov (1975) observed that apartment descriptions appear to be produced to a uniformly applied formula, which leads people to reason in very similar ways about what information to communicate and how to communicate it.

Regulative communication situations, however, seem to call out substantial individual variation in message design. A *regulative* situation is one in which one person is faced with the need to control or correct the the behavior of another (for a general discussion of this type of situation and message diversity within it, see Seibold, Cantrill, & Meyers, 1985). As Seibold et al. point out, there are a number of ways that one might think about the regulative situation and the message variations that might occur in it. O'Keefe and McCornack extended this point:

> One might, for instance, interpret the regulative situation as essentially being a conflict situation, since it intrinsically involves a conflict between the two parties; and so one could conceive of regulative messages as ways of pursuing and resolving conflict. One might interpret such a situation as a compliance-gaining situation, since one important and natural thing the regulator might try to do is gain some kind of commitment or assent from the message target; and so one could conceive of regulative messages as ways of gaining compliance. One might interpret such a situation as calling for a complaint-and-remedy sequence, since the occasion for regulation is generally some fault or lapse on the part of the message target. And so on. In fact, one reason why regulative situations evoke such diversity in message production is precisely that any of these alternative ways of defining the situation and organizing communication could be employed by a message producer, just as these alternative perspectives are available to the analyst (1987, p. 68).

In an effort to explain why and how individuals can come to have such differing ways of approaching communication situations, I have argued that understanding the observed range of functional variation in regulative messages requires a two-dimensional analysis: Message producers set themselves different kinds of goals, and message producers reason differently in constructing messages to serve whatever goals they select (O'Keefe, 1988a).

This chapter provides an overview and discussion of research associated with this "rational goals" approach to functional message analysis. The first section outlines this approach to the analysis of message designs. The second section discusses applications of this model in the study of regulative communication.

OVERVIEW

Functional Message Analysis

Obviously, one can approach the analysis of discourse systems with any of a number of very different research interests. One might suppose that the discourse a person produces reflects, in many detailed ways, that person's personal history and psychological idiosyncrasies; the object of a discourse analysis based on this supposition might be an archaeology of that individual. One might suppose that the discourse produced by a community reflects a common system of lexical practices; the object of an analysis based on this supposition might be a dictionary. Likewise, an analysis of a discourse system might produce a phonology or a rhetoric, depending on what kinds of suppositions the researcher makes and the kinds of regularities the researcher is seeking to identify.

The perennial concern of the rhetorician, and the recent concern of many communication theorists, has been to describe discourse systems *functionally*, to characterize the fit between messages and the jobs they are meant to do. Use of functional analysis follows naturally from the concerns that have traditionally motivated rhetorical and communication theories. To understand the role of discourse in society, one must understand the relationship between what is said and what effects are brought about; to elucidate the rationale for speech, one must understand what might be achieved through speaking. Hence, functional analysis is grounded in the assumption that message designs are systematically related to speaker intentions and communicative effects. It presumes that messages are adapted to fit the circumstances of their production and that their content and structure reflect the process of adaptation.

There are a number of different ways to go about analyzing adaptation in message content and structure. The most common approach to functional analysis involves the compilation of lists of message types associated with the pursuit of a particular function or goal. This approach is familiar to communication researchers through research on *communication strategies*: compliance-gaining strategies, compliance-resisting strategies, relationship disengagement strategies, identity management strategies, comforting strategies, regulative communication strategies, and so on.

This compilation begins with identification and systematization of functionally significant variations in messages. The object is to isolate a set of message types that represent the "natural kinds" of messages that are produced in a given kind of situation. This taxonomic approach to message analysis is employed by researchers who are interested in constructing message typologies (for example, Marwell & Schmitt, 1967; Wiseman & Schenck-Hamlin, 1981) and by those developing message analysis systems in which message types are defined and ordered in terms of some abstract dimension like listener-adaptation (for instance, "constructivist" coding systems; see Clark & Delia, 1976; Delia, Kline, & Burleson, 1979).

Rational Goal Analysis

In a series of recent papers I have argued for an alternative to the standard "strategy repertoire" model of message adaptation—"rational goal analysis" (O'Keefe, 1985, 1987, 1988a, 1988b, 1988c; O'Keefe & Shepherd, 1987). Rational goal analysis provides an account or description of message designs in terms of the goals being pursued by the message producer and the principles of discourse organization that mediate between goals and messages. Rational goal analysis recognizes that message types exist, but explains them as relevant alternatives to say in a given situation. The thrust of a rational goal analysis is the elucidation of *principles of coherence* rather than the enumeration of alternative message types. It is a form of what Jacobs (1985) has described as the "strategic inference model" of discourse production and comprehension. The most prevalent contemporary approach to rational goal analysis explains discourse coherence in terms of speech act theory. A number of theorists have developed theories of message organization based on the speech acts theory; because it is a theory of the rational adaptation of utterances to goals and contexts, most views of communication based on the speech acts theory would qualify as "rational goal analyses" of messages. Examples of such analyses can be found in the work of Levinson (Brown & Levinson, 1978; Levinson, 1979) and Goffman (1969). An especially well-developed version of such a view can be found in the work of Jacobs and Jackson (Jacobs, 1985; Jacobs & Jackson, 1983a, 1983b, 1989).

The Logic of Message Design

While I have argued that a rational goals model offers many advantages as an approach to functional message analysis, I have also questioned the assumption, common to most rational models, that there is a universal sense of relevance or rationality that organizes all communication processes (O'Keefe, 1988a, 1988c, 1989). Rational goal analyses generally account for variation in messages in terms of variation in goals, but assume that individuals with the same goals will produce similar messages. My work suggests that even individuals with similar goals can differ systematically in what kinds of things they think are relevant to communicative situations. Consequently, a two-dimensional analysis is required (minimally) to understand functional variation in messages: People differ in their motivations or goals, and people differ in their beliefs about the communication they employ in reasoning about message designs.

Observation of variations in messages across a number of different genres suggests that individuals may employ any of three different sets of beliefs about message design (*message design logics*) in producing and understanding messages (O'Keefe, 1985, 1988a). Each of these three message design logics can be understood as a constellation of related beliefs and operations: a communication-constituting concept, a conception of the functional possibilities of communication, unit formation procedures, and principles of coherence. The three message design logics identified in my original formulation are called expressive, conventional, and rhetorical.

An *expressive* message design logic reflects the view that communication is a process of expressing and receiving encoded thoughts and feelings. Characteristically, those using an expressive logic fail to distinguish between thought and expression; in producing messages, they "dump" their current mental state, and assume that others produce messages the same way. Expressive communicators do not generally alter expression systematically in the service of achieving effects, nor do they ordinarily find anything other than "literal and direct" meaning in incoming messages.

A *conventional* message design logic is based on the view that communication is a game played cooperatively, according to social conventions and procedures. Within conventional logic, thought and expression are related in a less isomorphic way by subordinating expression to achievement of effects. Language is treated as a means of expressing propositions, but these propositions are specified by the social effect one wants to achieve. That is, utterance content is specified in the sense that uttering a given set of propositions under certain conditions counts as performing an action that is associated in sociocultural practice with the effect the message producer wants to achieve; for example, uttering a certain kind of proposition under the right conditions counts as performing a request, and performing a request is a way to get certain wants satisfied simply by exploiting conventional obligations among individuals. Conventional communicators treat communicative contexts (the roles, rights, and relations that situations contain) as having fixed parameters (that is, they take social structure—roles and norms—to be manifest to all while being relatively inflexible) and design messages by performing what they take to be the contextually appropriate actions.

A *rhetorical* message design logic reflects a view of communication as the creation and negotiation of social selves and situations. The rhetorical view subsumes knowledge of conventional means to achieve goals within the view that social structure is flexible and created through communication. Rather than seeing selves and situations as fixed by convention, and rather than seeing meaning as fixed in form and context, self, situation, and meaning are bound together in dramaturgical enactment and social negotiation. For the rhetorical communicator, social reality is created by what and how something is said or written, and thus messages are designed to portray a scene that is consistent with one's wants; the discourse of others is closely interpreted to determine the nature of the drama and the perspective they are enacting. (Examples of each of the design logics will be provided later.)

The three design logics form a natural developmental progression; that is, there is a logically necessary order to the acquisition of expressive, conventional, and rhetorical premises about communication. Since a rhetorical message design system exploits conventional knowledge so as not to derive action directly from representations of context, but to bring contexts into being, mastery of the conventional system is prerequisite to rhetorical functioning. Since a conventional message design system exploits the ability to express propositions so as not to generate messages directly but to generate expressions that count as actions in given contexts, mastery of the expressive system is prerequisite to conventional functioning. Hence, the first logic that must be acquired is expressive; without it systematic relations between verbal expressions and propositions cannot be understood. The second message design logic to be acquired is conventional, since without it the ability to use propositions to bring about effects by relying on structures of intersubjective meaning cannot be developed; acquiring this premise does not involve discarding the expressive premise, but rather subsuming it within a more abstract and organized conception of communication. Similarly, the rhetorical message design logic is the last of these to be acquired; when it is acquired the conventional system is not discarded, but rather subsumed within a system that creates the possibility of invoking conventional meaning rather than following conventional patterns.

O'Keefe and Delia (1988) summarized research on the development of oral and written communication skills that supports this analysis. They argued that a message design logic hypothesis provides an account of age- and experience-related changes in message production skills that is superior to classical accounts, such as the hypothesis that development in role-taking skill causes developments in communication skill.

The three message design logics are ordered not only developmentally, but also in terms of their functional utility—their intrinsic capability for generating effective messages, especially in difficult communication situations (discussed below). Each move up the hierarchy of message design systems opens up additional possibilities for the use of language. Attaining a conventional level of functioning makes expression an option or a goal that one might choose, rather than the guiding principle behind the message production system. Attaining a rhetorical level of functioning makes affirmation of pre-existing roles and routines a choice, rather than a necessary foundation from which all meaning derives.

In short, movement up this hierarchy permits an individual to focus on goals and to adapt language more and more finely to their service. An expressive message design logic is, as many theorists have noted (e.g., Britton, Burgess, Martin, McLeod, & Rosen, 1975; Gusdorf, 1965), not well adapted from the standpoint of generating a means to an end. That is why expression is so often conceived of as the opposite of instrumental functioning. A conventional message design logic offers only those opportunities for action that are congruent with existing situation parameters, but a rhetorical message design logic permits reshaping situations to serve communicative aims. The developmental ordering of the three message design logics does not result from some accident of history or general development in mental capacities, but rather from the extension of control over verbal communication through the development of increasingly functional and integrated communication concepts.

THE LOGIC OF REGULATIVE COMMUNICATION

Individual Differences in Regulative Message Design

Although the message design logic model is distinctive in that it offers a general model of functional design that is relevant to any interpersonal task, most initial applications have been directed at explicating variation in regulative communication. According to the model, there is a set of message variables that are controlled by message design logic; these features should vary together across message genres. Consequently, the messages produced by expressive, conventional, and rhetorical communicators should display features that are diagnostic of the logic employed in their production.

One implication of this property is that the model can be applied in a fairly straightforward manner to develop message classification systems for virtually any suitable interpersonal task. The prototype system was designed to classify regulative messages on the basis of the design principle they revealed. Subjects were asked to respond to the Group Leader problem, a task in which the message producer must deal with a procrastinating group member. In the scenario for this hypothetical situation, subjects are told that a group member, Ron, has repeatedly failed to make group meetings and produce his work. The subject is assigned the role of group leader and is asked to deal with a circumstance in which the due date is imminent but Ron has not finished his work.

The Group Leader scenario has a couple of features that lead it to elicit different messages from individuals whose design logics differ. First, Ron is represented as having repeatedly failed to conform to the group's decisions and procedures; this leads subjects to have a negative impression of Ron and a number of salient beliefs about his past conduct that are not particularly relevant for dealing with the present situation. Second, the group is portrayed as having a particular organization and set of commitments that might or might not be subject to renegotiation but which are relevant to dealing with Ron's failure to perform; the ways in which the group's arrangements might be altered to secure a good outcome are fairly easy to see and plainly advantageous. In short, the presence of salient but irrelevant and negatively valenced beliefs about Ron's past behavior and the desirability of reorganizing the situation make this scenario especially useful for detecting differences in design logic.

An expressive message design principle, applied to the set of beliefs and feelings evoked by the Group Leader scenario, leads people to produce a distinctive type of message. They tend to contain few elements; the elements they do contain are strongly and affectively toned. The elements of an expressive message might all be thoughts that were evoked by a particular action taken by Ron, they might be items of information that the message producer happened to encounter all at one time, or they might be items from a chain of associations. This produces the two most identifiable global properties of expressive messages—a lack of editing (so that socially unacceptable content or tenuously relevant content is included in the message) and a failure to engage the immediate task to be accomplished in the situation (so that messages may focus exclusively on past transgressions rather than present problems or they may perform some action that is emotionally satisfying but interferes with task accomplishment). Messages 1 through 3 display these properties.

1.   You stupid a—— f——. Why did you wait so long to tell us you were getting behind on your part? You f—— up all our grades. I'm getting you out of this group. Everybody feels the same way. I hope you have fun when you take the class next semester.

2. Ron, I can't believe you haven't finished your research. You have been inconsiderate to the group all along. Several members even suggested that you be taken out of the group but we decided to give you a chance. Now what are we supposed to do? It was your responsibility and you backed out. I'm afraid that I'm going to tell the T.A. that you haven't done your share. I will be so mad at you if we get a bad grade on this—I need an A in this course.

3. Ron, I am going to have to suggest to Professor Jones that you receive a D or E on your individual part of the presentation. Not only did you come late to the meetings but you completely skipped one of them, and now not finishing the part of the project you volunteered to do shows how immature and irresponsible you really are. Do you think you can bring me what you have done and I'll see if the rest of us can finish it?

Conventional messages reflect a view of message design as a matter of mentioning the feature or features of the context that, given the existing structure of rights and obligations in the situation, should serve as reasons for the message target to perform as required. The application of this sense of relevance to the Group Leader scenario produces a second type of message. In contrast to expressive messages, conventional messages contain some content that predicates a future goal-related action of the message target. Other elements in the message are mentions of contextual conditions that are either prerequisite to the performance of the desired action or backing for the leader's demand that the action be performed. Messages 4 through 6 exemplify this design logic.

4. Ron, you idiot, this speech is due next week and you are not getting anything done. Now, number one, you owe it to other people in the group who have spent a great deal of time and energy working on this to at least do your part. Number two, you have been slacking off altogether on this project. I hope you realize you will be getting an individual grade—and at this point I seriously doubt that it will be a high one. There is no excuse for this laziness, and I really don't appreciate it, so get going now, and have that material prepared by tomorrow.

5. I would ask Ron if he had serious family problems or was he just blowing us off. If he had serious problems, I would ask him to call the T.A. and tell him/her the situation with our group. If he was blowing us off, I would talk to my T.A. and explain the problem. If Ron had serious problems

I would encourage him to talk to someone. I would ask him to please consider what he is doing to our group. If he was blowing us off, I would insist he get his butt to the library and research.

6. Well, Ron, I'm sorry you don't have your part of the project done. We have given you several breaks thus far and I don't see how we can give you any more. The whole group is depending on you so I would suggest to you to get it done or at the most bring in what you have got done. If you don't get this done I'm going to have to give you an F for the project. If you can't hold up your responsibility with this group even under these adverse conditions (family problems) how are you going to make it in life.

Finally, a rhetorical design principle, applied to the Group Leader scenario, leads people to produce a third type of message. Rhetorical messages are derived from the view that situations are created in the process of communication. The materials contained in the scenario are treated not as givens, but as resources that can be called on in transforming the situation to facilitate goal attainment. The linguistic mechanisms through which these transformations are effected are motivational appeals, rhetorical labelling, accounting, explicit redescriptions of the context, and the like. In short, in the course of talking about one thing (what Ron should do), the rhetorical communicator elaborates the message in such a way as to reconstitute some important set of features of the situation (own identity, Ron's identity, Ron's motives, the group's procedures, and so on). Messages 7 through 9 exemplify this approach to message design.

7. First, Ron, we've all been counting on you to get this section that you volunteered for done. If you could have let us know earlier that you weren't going to have time to finish it, then we could all have started to work on it.

   Well, since it has to be done for our meeting tomorrow, I'll come to the library and help you finish up your research. Also, you should call to see if anyone else can help us get this finished. We were all counting on you. I wish you would have let us known earlier, because I need a good grade in this class.

8. Ron, I'm sorry you won't have everything ready by tonight. Can you give me some good reasons I can tell the group? I know you've been having problems all along and that's obvious to the rest of the group too. You need to be able to see how your personal problems have interfered in the group's

completion of the project. I'll be the first to sympathize with you but now we'll have to come up with some concrete solutions. You can't expect someone else to take over your research workload.

9. Well, Ron, it's due next week and we have to get it all to the typist. OK, if it's not done it's not. Tell you what. Why don't you jot down your main ideas so that we can include them in the introduction and conclusion. Also, tell me when you think your section should come in the whole project. Then get it to my apartment by 10:00 the next day because I have to get it to the typist by 2:00. Is this okay? I'll just explain to the group that you'll have it done but not by meeting time. We all want a good grade, so if you need the time to make your part better, go ahead. But if I can't get it to the typist in time, you'll have to type it. Alright, take it easy.

Message Design Logic, Situation Complexity, and Message Effectiveness

One key aspect of the message design logic model is its articulation of the relationship between message design logic and the communication situation in generating functional variation in messages. There are particular features of situations that elicit message variations due to differences in design logic. In some situations functional variations in messages are virtually nonexistent, and it appears that all messages are generated by the same expressive- or conventional-looking message design system. Many specific kinds of circumstances can make differences in design logic irrelevant, such as situations where there are few if any limitations on relevance (such as informal, unfocused conversation among close friends in which virtually anything a person happens to think of could be introduced as a topic or topical elaboration), situations that contain few if any interpersonal complications (in which no conflicts among goals exist or in which no obstacles to goal achievement are met), and situations in which there are few if any requirements to reorganize stored information in the service of goals (in which individuals can simply repeat or replay messages they have received and remembered).

In contrast to those kinds of communication situations, a situation in which goal achievement requires drawing a clear separation between subjective and intersubjective relevance, or in which it would be helpful to reorganize the communication context, will lead people who use different message design logics to generate different messages. This is because those employing conventional and rhetorical design logics distinguish between issues that are objectively relevant and those that are only subjectively relevant, whereas those relying on expressive logic do not. Those people who employ conventional design logic also operate within established situation parameters whereas those employing rhetorical logic make overt efforts to change the situation.

Following this analysis, one can see why the intrinsic structure of some communication situations, such as the group leader situation employed by O'Keefe (1988a), encourage functional message variation. The circumstances that make a situation regulative can provoke a good deal of negative thoughts about the message target that are not relevant to the attainment of intersubjectively defined situational goals. For example, the message target's present transgression may stimulate recall of past transgressions. Similarly, the inability or unwillingness of the message target to meet existing situation requirements combined with the intrinsically face-threatening character of attempts at regulation of conduct (Brown & Levinson, 1978), make redefining the communicative context desirable (see also Delia, O'Keefe, & Paulson, 1985; Murphy, 1988).

One additional implication of this analysis of the role of situation complexity in drawing out functional variation in messages is that messages generated by differing design logics should differ in effectiveness. The difference between an expressive and a conventional message design logic is, in large part, the difference between a system that simply reacts to circumstances and a system that responds to exigences with some appropriate remedy. The difference between a conventional and a rhetorical system is the difference between a system that is limited in its response by historically evolved structures and a system that draws on a wider range of resources by changing structures. Hence, differences in message design logic should lead to differences in the ability to accomplish whatever tasks are confronted in the situation. Messages generated by an expressive design logic should be judged as least effective and messages generated by a rhetorical design logic should be judged as most effective in meeting situational demands. In the case of regulative situations, these demands include attaining one's own wants and objectives, getting the message target to perform, and satisfying norms of civility and politeness that are relevant to all social situations (Brown & Levinson, 1978; Goffman, 1969). As the level of message design logic increases, therefore, messages should be perceived as more effective in managing the immediate practical task faced in the situation, in eliciting the desired performance from the message target, in satisfying the various parties involved in the situation, and in showing respect and consideration for the message target.

These expectations received initial support in an experiment conducted by O'Keefe and McCornack (1987). They found that as the level of message design logic increased, so did perceived effectiveness in regulation, perceived effectiveness in giving support to the message recipient, and the attractiveness of the message producer. A subsequent study produced more equivocal results (Bingham & Burleson, 1989). These findings are not easily interpretable as consistent or inconsistent with O'Keefe and McCornack, however; the earlier study used naturally produced messages while the later investigation employed experimenter-generated messages. This is, potentially, an important difference because we cannot be confident that experimenter-generated messages will capture the full range of variation in naturally occurring messages.

CONCLUSIONS

The objective of the theory of message design logic is to lay the groundwork for a model of message production by providing an analysis of the fit between message designs and the jobs they are meant to do. It should be emphasized, however, that while the analysis of message designs is a crucial foundation for models of message production, a message analysis is not the same thing as a model of message production. One assumption that has been endemic to the study of message production is that the description given to message structures will serve, in a fairly straightforward way, as a description of the underlying processes that produce the message. This assumption is quite apparent in most research on communication strategies. As noted earlier, the work typically begins with the identification of message types, which are generally referred to as strategies. Message production is quite explicitly described as a process of "selecting" among the strategies that people are presumed to have in their heads (for analyses and critiques of such research, see O'Keefe, 1987; Seibold, Cantrill, & Meyers, 1985). Because the term *strategy* implies that some sort of psychological process is going on, it invites researchers to assume that message types have (or ought to have) psychological reality *as types*.

But this "strategy selection" account of message production raises a number of issues that have never been satisfactorily addressed in the literature. The first issue concerns how individuals select message types. To explain message production, one would have to explain two fundamental things. First, one would have to explain how the individual chooses message types from the strategy repertoire. Second, one would have to explain how the individual generates an actual

message that instantiates the message type. Message types are difficult to evaluate in the abstract; what one can say or ought to say in
a given situation depends on particular features of that situation and
what exactly one might say about it. For example, if one is making
a request, the question of which is the better method to take, coun-
terarguing or emphasizing advantages to the other person, depends
on the actual kinds of objections the requestee might have and
whether one knows of any advantages that would accrue to the other.
To make any considered assessment of the utility of the available
message types, one would already need to have available for consideration all the relevant beliefs and ideas that the possible messages
might be built from and would have inferred how a message constructed from those materials would be received. That is, to pick a
message type one would need to have instantiated all the types in
messages that exemplified them.

What this suggests is that *either* individuals pick message types
first on some basis other than whether an actual successful message
can be constructed to fit the type *or* individuals constantly go through
a process of generating every possible message and then comparing
all the messages to find which is the best.

Although there is no clear evidence that either of these hypotheses
is incorrect, there is certainly no evidence to commend them. People
construct messages so rapidly and fluently that the idea that they
generate all possible messages and compare them is implausible. The
idea that people pick message types first and then figure out how to
use them is not quite as far-fetched, but it does make one wonder
how people might go about selecting message types prior to knowing
what they might do with the type. "Boy," our hypothetical strategy
selector might think, "I'm having a pretty lousy day. I think I'll go
with the threat. Now what can I threaten him with?"

A second difficulty with the standard strategy selection view involves the persistence of incompetent types of messages. Particularly
in the study of communication development one encounters recurring
types of messages that are plainly incompetent. For example, one
common sort of message small children produce in persuasive situations is the inexplicit request. In the study of adult regulative communication some people produce messages that are abusive and
incoherent and do not deal with the regulative task. It is difficult to
conceive of these message types as having been produced as the result
of some rational strategy for addressing the task. "Gee," the child
thinks, "I think I'll pick Inexplicit Request from my repertoire." "I've
got it!" the incompetent boss thinks, "Dumping a load of abuse on
this guy will be just the ticket for handling this tricky situation."

There is, of course, no hard evidence that such incompetent message types do not reflect an underlying strategy that was somehow selected. On the other hand, however, it is difficult to imagine how an individual would acquire a strategy for being defective and, moreover, choose to be defective.

A third issue raised by the strategy selection view involves the need to explain apparent inconsistencies in individuals' knowledge of communication. One common finding in the study of functional communication competence is that whereas individuals differ rather substantially in the kinds of messages they construct, there is substantial consensus among individuals regarding what is and is not a good message (see, for example, Burleson, Wilson, Waltman, Goering, Ely, & Whaley, 1986). This raises an interesting question for a strategy selection account: If people understand and appreciate nicer and more developmentally advanced strategies, then why don't they produce them? It would seem that in order to evaluate messages of different types, individuals would have to have information about what the message is designed to do, how it does that, and what its likely effects would be. In short, they should know the "strategy." But people who know the strategies really ought to be able to produce sophisticated messages themselves.

These three puzzles all arise from a peculiar feature of the strategy selection model—the reification of message types. If we reject this reification, however, and instead assume that individuals generate messages as messages and that every message is produced as an individual's immediate and only solution to the communication problems being confronted, then dilemmas of choice can be sidestepped. If incompetent messages are just message types and are not selected "strategies," then there is no need to account for their persistence in the population or for the rationale behind their use. And if individuals do not produce or understand messages as "types," then the fact that they appreciate messages they cannot produce is no mystery.

From the standpoint of explaining message production, rational models generally and the message design logic model in particular offer a significant alternative to a strategy selection account. The three message design logics function as three principles guiding an individual's sense of relevance. As individuals have different kinds of communicable ideas relevant to different situations, the messages they produce differ in systematic ways.

Moreover, the message any individual produces in a situation is precisely the package of communicable content that the individual sees as relevant in the situation; the individual is guided by his or her message design principle, and does not face any significant choice in producing the message. If the message is dysfunctional or incoherent it is because the individual's communicable content is dysfunctional or incoherent, and neither the goals nor the message design process caused that individual to alter his or her thoughts prior to expression. Individuals produce messages as messages, and if they fail to produce a particular type of message it is because they fail to perceive the relevance of a particular kind of content. Individuals appreciate messages as messages and not as types, however, and assess them by their effects; therefore, the fact that individuals can appreciate messages they do not themselves produce is no problem for the kind of rational model of message design that O'Keefe has proposed.

A rational model recognizes that message types occur, but explains message types as relevant alternatives to say in a given situation. Message designs are the product of the interaction between an individual's sense of relevance and the demands of the communicative event. We observe different message types because the requirements of events differ, and because individuals construct different concepts of communication, which endow them with different conceptions of relevance.

In short, any strategy selection model faces a number of theoretical obstacles, such as difficulty in accounting for strategy choice, difficulty in explaining the production of incompetent messages, and difficulty in explaining the disparity in knowledge of message effectiveness and ability to produce messages. A rational model, which asserts that message production is guided by systematic principles determining what content is relevant to a given situation, provides a foundation for explaining message production that avoids these difficulties.

REFERENCES

Bingham, S. G., & Burleson, B. R. (1989). Multiple effects of messages with multiple goals: Some perceived outcomes of responses to sexual harassment. *Human Communication Research, 16,* 184–216.

Britton, J., Burgess, T., Martin, N., McLeod, A., & Rosen, H. (1975). *The development of writing abilities* (pp. 11–18). London: Macmillan.

Brown, P., & Levinson, S. (1978). Universals in language usage: Politeness phenomena. In E. Goody (Ed.), *Questions and politeness* (pp. 56–323). Cambridge, England: Cambridge University Press.

Burleson, B. R., Wilson, S. R., Waltman, M. S., Goering, E. M., Ely, T. K., & Whaley, B. B. (1986). Item desirability effects in compliance-gaining research: Seven studies documenting artifacts in the strategy selection procedure. *Human Communication Research, 14,* 429–486.

Clark, R. A., & Delia, J. G. (1976). The development of functional persua-

The Logic of Regulative Communication 103

sive skills in childhood and early adolescence. *Child Development, 47,* 1008–1014.

Delia, J. G., Kline, S. L., & Burleson, B. R. (1979). The development of persuasive communication strategies in kindergartners through twelfth-graders. *Communication Monographs, 46,* 241–256.

Delia, J. G., O'Keefe, B. J, & Paulson, L. (1985, November). *Construct differentiation, situational complexity, and the analysis of individual differences in alternative modes of communicative action.* Paper presented at the annual meeting of the Speech Communication Association, Denver.

Goffman, E. (1969). *Strategic interaction.* Philadelphia: University of Pennsylvania Press.

Gusdorf, G. (1965). *Speaking.* Evanston, IL: Northwestern University Press.

Jacobs, S. (1985). Language. In M. L. Knapp & G. R. Miller (Eds.), *Handbook of interpersonal communication.* Beverly Hills, CA: Sage.

Jacobs, S., & Jackson, S. (1983a). Speech acts structure in conversation: Rational aspects of pragmatic coherence. In R. Craig & K. Tracy (Eds.), *Conversational coherence: Form, structure, and strategy* (pp. 47–66). Beverly Hills, CA: Sage.

Jacobs, S., & Jackson, S. (1983b). Strategy and structure in conversational influence attempts. *Communication Monographs, 50,* 285–304.

Jacobs, S., & Jackson, S. (1989). Building a model of conversational argument. In B. Dervin, L. Grossberg, B. O'Keefe, & E. Wartella (Eds.), *Rethinking communication, Vol. II: Paradigm exemplars* (pp. 153–171). Beverly Hills, CA: Sage.

Levinson, S. (1979). Some pre-observations on the modelling of dialogue. *Discourse Processes, 4,* 93–110.

Linde, C., & Labov, W. (1975). Spatial networks as a site for the study of language and thought. *Language, 51,* 924–939.

Marwell, G., & Schmitt, D. R. (1967). Dimensions of compliance-gaining behavior: An empirical analysis. *Sociometry, 30,* 350–364.

Murphy, M. A. (1988). *The effects of construct differentiation and equal-peer vs. legitimate authority relationships on message design in compliance-gaining situations.* Unpublished doctoral dissertation, University of Illinois, Urbana-Champaign.

O'Keefe, B. J. (1985, November). *The functional integration of communication concepts: Evidence for individual differences in reasoning about communication.* Paper presented at the annual meeting of the Speech Communication Association, Denver.

O'Keefe, B. J. (1987, November). *Models of functional communication competence: A rational alternative to strategy repertoires.* Paper presented at the annual meeting of the Speech Communication Association, Boston.

O'Keefe, B. J. (1988a). The logic of message design: Individual differences in reasoning about communication. *Communication Monographs, 55,* 80–103.

O'Keefe, B. J. (1988b, March). *Message design logic and the management of multiple goals.* Paper presented to the 9th Annual Conference on Discourse Analysis, Temple University, Philadelphia.

O'Keefe, B. J. (1988c, November). *Message design logic and the management of multiple goals: Consequences of diversity in conceptions of rationality.*

Paper presented at the annual meeting of the Speech Communication Association, New Orleans.

O'Keefe, B. J. (1989). *Theory and practice in the constitution of communication processes.* Paper presented at the 10th Annual Conference on Discourse Processes at Temple University, Philadelphia.

O'Keefe, B. J., & Delia, J. G. (1988). Communicative tasks and communicative practices: The development of audience-centered message production. In B. Rafoth & D. Rubin (Eds.), *The social construction of written communication* (pp. 70–98). Norwood, NJ: Ablex.

O'Keefe, B. J., & McCornack, S. A. (1987). Message design logic and message goal structure: Effects on perceptions of message quality in regulative communication situations. *Human Communication Research, 14,* pp. 68–92.

O'Keefe, B. J., & Shepherd, G. J. (1987). The pursuit of multiple objectives in face-to-face persuasive interactions: Effects of construct differentiation on message organization. *Communication Monographs, 54,* 396–419.

Seibold, D. R., Cantrill, J. G., & Meyers, R. A. (1985). Communication and interpersonal influence. In M. L. Knapp & G. R. Miller (Eds.), *Handbook of interpersonal communication.* Beverly Hills, CA: Sage.

Wiseman, R. L., & Schenck-Hamlin, W. (1981). A multidimensional scaling validation of an inductively-derived set of compliance-gaining strategies. *Communication Monographs, 48,* 251–270.

Contexts

Communicating Sexual Desire: Message Tactics for Having and Avoiding Intercourse

Timothy Edgar
University of Maryland, College Park

Mary Anne Fitzpatrick
University of Wisconsin, Madison

I ntimacy is a slippery concept. For some theorists, an intimate relationship is defined through overt behaviors such as self-disclosure, declarations of liking and loving, and hugging and caressing (Lewis, 1978). Others prefer to define intimacy by strong, positive emotions like trust (Wheeless, 1976). Another view holds that commitment is the essential ingredient (Kingsbury & Minda, 1988). A fourth camp rejects the affective connotations of the term "intimacy" and focuses instead on behavioral interdependence (Kelley et al., 1983).

A particular persuasive context that captures elements of all these perspectives is the sexual encounter. A sexual episode presents individuals with an extraordinary situation that is arguably more vulnerable and volatile than almost any other interaction context. This is especially true for couples in the early stages of a sexual relationship. Ambiguity is high and mutual expectations and patterns of behavior have not been learned. During sexual arousal, individuals experience heightened emotional states and undergo unique physiological changes. Undoubtedly, this affects the persuasive choices people make. A course of action that would be appropriate in another context may be discarded in favor of messages that simultaneously aim to gain satisfaction while protecting vulnerability. Inappropriate choices may lead to conflict, embarrassment, and frustration.

Research literature exists that addresses the issue of interpersonal influence in sexual interactions, but with few exceptions (see Edgar & Fitzpatrick, 1988) communication scholars virtually have ignored the topic. Similarly, researchers from other fields (primarily psychology) who have focused their investigations on sexual message strategies have, in turn, ignored the body of literature compiled by communication researchers. The work on sexual bargaining is devoid of any reference to the methodological, pragmatic, and theoretical ideas offered by communication scholars. To borrow Donn Byrne's classic metaphor, researchers in these areas have spent their time building castles in their own sandboxes without even glancing in the direction of the other kids in the playground.

This state of affairs is unfortunate. Never before has there been such a tremendous societal need to increase understanding about sexual compliance. We live in an age where the potential consequences of sexual behavior have moved in a dangerous direction. In times past, individuals confronted the risk of pregnancy and the emotional scars of unwanted or dissatisfying intercourse, but now sexually involved couples also face the specter of AIDS. Because the disease is transmitted most commonly through sexual contact, individuals must give more careful consideration to the types of sexual behaviors in which they participate and the partners with whom they interact. Skillful compliance-gaining and resistance potentially can save one's life (Edgar & Fitzpatrick, 1988; Edgar, Hammond, & Freimuth, 1989).

It is our primary goal to demonstrate that two independent lines of investigation in the compliance-gaining area could benefit from mutual attention. The literature on sexual bargaining and the literature on interpersonal persuasion have much to say to one another. We hope to open the dialogue.

MEANS OF INFLUENCE

Communication researchers have been particularly strong in the development and refinement of typologies of influence strategies (see, for example, Cody, McLaughlin, & Jordan, 1980; Schenck-Hamlin, Wiseman, & Georgacarakos, 1982; Witteman & Fitzpatrick, 1986).

Sexual compliance investigators also have developed schemes for describing persuasive tactics. In this section we will delineate the methods used in constructing those taxonomies, explain how message types can be categorized as either direct, indirect, or sequenced, and offer a critique and some suggestions.

Taxonomy Development

In the sexual compliance literature, three primary studies have focused on the construction and implementation of influence taxonomies. The authors of these studies have taken a variety of approaches in developing their typologies and utilizing them to draw conclusions about persuasive behavior. Jesser (1978) conducted the earliest of the investigations. His approach was to develop a checklist of seduction strategies by drawing from the extant literature on sexual interaction and from suggestions from college students in a free-response pilot study. The student sample provided information regarding an encounter that they actually had participated in. Twenty items, most of which described nonverbal behavior, emerged from the procedure.

Instead of a checklist, McCormick (1979) used an essay technique in which participants were asked to write out the means they would use in a hypothetical seduction. According to the scenario, the respondents had known their imaginary partner for less than three weeks and had "necked" but intercourse had yet to occur. They were to describe in as much detail as they desired how they would influence the date to have sex. Judges then coded the essays with a system made up of ten strategy types that evolved from a pilot study that had used the same scenario.

A more recent study by Perper and Weis (1987) relied on a slightly different method. Like McCormick, their subjects (all female) responded to an open-ended question about sexual compliance strategies, and the essays were content analyzed. Instead of coding the answers with a pre-formulated typology, however, Perper and Weis searched for consistent themes within the data set. An idea or tactic was labeled as a theme if at least two respondents explicitly described the same phenomenon. Thirty-six different themes emerged.

Types of Messages

The results of the three studies indicate that sexual influence messages can be subsumed under three general headings: direct, indirect, and sequenced.

Direct Messages

Generally, sex researchers use "direct" to mean any sexual compliance message in which the persuasive force of the message depends on the target's awareness of how the source is attempting to gain compliance (McCormick, 1979). That is, the intent of the message is clear; there is no ambiguity about what the persuader desires.

Jesser (1978) included only one direct strategy on his checklist. This message type was described by the words "ask directly." As expected, Jesser found that a majority of his male subjects reported using this approach as a common means of sexual influence. Only "touching" was checked more often. He was surprised, however, to find that over half of the females also indicated that they had made direct requests to have sex. Those females who used direct strategies were less conventional, more assertive, more likely to be involved with men who employed similar tactics, and tended to perceive their male partners as capable of handling a direct request.

Perper and Weis (1987) also identified just one direct message strategy. The only theme in their analysis that referred to overt intent was "Ask." In contrast to the Jesser study, a much smaller number of females indicated that a direct approach was the preferred means of influence. Approximately 20% of the women claimed that they would request explicitly that their male partners have sex with them. The difference in the results is interesting in light of the fact that Jesser's subjects reported on actual past behavior while respondents in the Perper and Weis study based their answers on a hypothetical scenario. It may indicate a lack of equivalence between the two methods (cf., Dillard, 1988).

Of the three studies, only McCormick (1979) explicitly acknowledged that direct strategies can take on different forms and structures. Six of McCormick's ten message categories describe direct verbal strategies (McCormick, 1987). Table 8 provides the category labels and definitions for the six strategies. McCormick found little difference between males and females in the usage of direct messages.

Indirect Messages

The type of compliance-gaining strategy given the greatest attention in the sexual compliance literature is the indirect message. In general, an indirect tactic is one in which there is room for doubt about the persuader's intent. In the parlance of current politics, these messages are designed to have plausible deniability.

Most commonly, "indirect" equates with "nonverbal," but some researchers have identified indirect messages that are at least in part

Table 8   **Definitions for McCormick's Direct Verbal Strategy**
Types

Strategy	Definition
Reward	Giving gifts, providing services, and flattering the date in exchange for compliance
Coercion	Punishing or threatening to punish non-compliance by withdrawing resources or services or by sharing negative feelings
Logic	Using rational, but not moral, arguments to convince the date to have sex
Information	Tell the date that sex is desired in a straightforward or direct manner
Moralizing	Telling the date that it is the agent's legitimate or socially sanctioned right to have sexual intercourse
Relationship Conceptualizing	Influencing a date by talking about the relationship and indicating concern for the date's feelings

verbal. For instance, McCormick discusses *manipulation*. She defines this behavior as hinting through means of subtly changing one's appearance, the setting, or the conversational topic. In a similar vein, Jesser makes reference to indirect sex talk, teasing, giving compliments, and using code words as choices on his checklist. Perper and Weis discovered in their subjects' essays examples such as engaging in sexy romantic talk, laughing, offering a drink, and inviting a potential sex partner back to one's residence. They argue that hinting is an option that many females choose. If women desire to have sex with a man, they can drop subtle hints and then let him "take it from there." This strategy may appeal especially to women who feel uncomfortable with deviations from traditional sex roles. Hinting allows them to gain compliance while maintaining the "rules of the game" on a surface level.

McCormick also classifies *deception* as an indirect strategy. She characterizes this behavior as persuasion that relies on false information. Christopher (1988) believes that males use deception as a secondary tactic when their initial attempt at compliance is met with resistance. He describes how a man might try to bargain for sex by offering to build the relationship even though he has no intention of doing so.

As noted above, the most common sort of indirect message identified in the sexual compliance literature is nonverbal behavior. McCormick, who uses the term *body language* in her typology, states unequivocally that nonverbal strategies are by far the most important for gaining sexual compliance. Although most researchers agree that both sexes rely heavily on nonverbal messages, opinions diverge over which sex utilizes nonverbal communication most frequently as a sexual compliance technique. McCormick states that women are more likely than men to express interest nonverbally, but Byers and Lewis (1988) found that almost all of their male subjects reported using nonverbal strategies to initiate a sexual encounter. It is clear that these conflicting results deserve further attention.

There appear to be two major reasons for why individuals rely so heavily on nonverbal strategies for sexual influence. First, subtlety is consistent with the belief that sex should be spontaneous and retain an air of mystery. To discuss the act blatantly can make it seem cold, clinical, and mechanical (Byrne, 1983). People like to maintain the illusion that they have been "swept off their feet." Males especially believe that talking openly about sex reduces the chances of successfully gaining compliance (Gross & Bellew-Smith, 1983). Second, nonverbal strategies allow the individual to reduce vulnerability (LaPlante, McCormick, & Brannigan, 1980). When one uses a direct verbal statement, there are limited options for denying intent if the attempt at compliance is not well received; but if one chooses to persuade through nonverbal actions, the individual can easily stop or draw back if the desired response does not occur (Perper & Weis, 1987). In a situation as emotionally charged as sexual interaction, the chance to save face is always welcome.

Sequenced Messages

The third general type of influence strategy in the sexual bargaining literature is what we call a sequenced approach. The primary characteristic of this strategy is the enactment of multiple behaviors to achieve one's goal of seduction. McCormick described this phenomenon from an *active* perspective. That is, she centered the focus of analysis on the persuader alone. In her original study, the final category in her typology was labeled *seduction*. McCormick defined it as a step-by-step plan that includes body language, manipulation, and other techniques. Thus, seduction refers to a combination of verbal and nonverbal messages. Both males and females reported that seduction was the course of action most commonly used to persuade a partner to have sex.

Perper and Weis also discussed message sequences, but unlike McCormick they emphasized the *interactive* nature of sexual compliance. That is, they identified patterns of persuasive behavior in which *both* partners are mutual participants in the act of seduction. They argued that much of what happens in a sexual encounter is "a temporally organized, interactive sequence of events rather than a mere list of strategies" (p. 468). For example, the females in their sample told how they would express an interest to their male partners through a variety of signals and then let the men take the lead in expressing a desire for intercourse. Compliance-gaining, thus, becomes a ritual act in which both partners eventually become aware of the other's persuasive intent and the probable outcome. A continued effort to persuade is not really necessary, but the "strategic" behavior does fulfill a playful and stimulating function as the sequence is carried out.

Critique and Recommendations

To achieve understanding of the influence process in any interaction context, researchers must develop taxonomies of messages that rigorously describe and allow for consistent measurement of the phenomena in question. The taxonomies generated by sexual interaction scholars are useful to a point, but some methodological shortcomings present problems in application and in the construction of sound theory. The works by Jesser and by Perper and Weis provide such little information about the nature of direct verbal messages that the categories are rendered almost meaningless. To describe the behavior without acknowledging the variety of ways in which verbal strategies can be structured slights the complexity of the process of persuasion.

McCormick's categorization of direct messages does address the issue in a much more sophisticated manner. She recognizes that the variability of the persuasive force of different messages rests not simply in the explicitness of the message but also in the adornment of the basic theme. Validity for McCormick's categories comes from a comparison between her descriptions of message types and those found in the communication literature. Her definitions of *reward, coercion, logic, information,* and *moralizing* closely match Wiseman and Schenck-Hamlin's (1981) conceptualization of *promise, threat, explanation, direct request,* and *guilt*. Her sixth direct verbal strategy—*relationship conceptualizing*—has a very similar meaning to Witteman and Fitzpatrick's (1986) *us* message.

One problem with existing sexual influence taxonomies is the tendency to mix unrelated items together. This inappropriate fusion can be seen both in terms of message modes and units of analysis. On the first point, recognizing the significance of nonverbal messages in seduction is necessary, but combining verbal and nonverbal channels in the same taxonomy causes confusion and diminishes the researcher's ability to make worthwhile theoretical statements about either mode. The same problem exists for units of analysis. Our comprehension of sexual influence is clouded when taxonomies combine strategies made up of single message types with those made up of multiple messages.

To make real knowledge gains, researchers in the area of sexual bargaining and compliance-gaining need to make firm theoretical decisions on both issues. Furthermore, we suggest that they look to more rigorous methodologies, such as multidimensional scaling (see e.g., Falbo, 1977), for empirically assisted taxonomy development. Also, increased emphasis on behavioral data would ground the work more firmly in real life interaction. Unfortunately, the highly intimate nature of sexual behavior may preclude the possibility of designing naturalistic behavioral studies. Researchers may triangulate on the phenomenon by combining multiple methods such as role play and recall, but work remains to be done that demonstrates the equivalence of those methods.

RESISTANCE MESSAGES

Thus far, we have discussed the methods of influencing others and the attempts to get them to comply with our requests. One should be careful, however, to avoid advocating a magic-bullet view of interpersonal persuasion. That is, we cannot assume that a potential persuader can fire the right message and in one shot hit the target and ensure compliance. The study of both communication and sexual bargaining necessitates a consideration of the responses that individuals make to persuasive efforts. Accordingly, we must address the issue of resistance to compliance attempts.

Resistance

If the target of compliance wishes to refute the desires of the source, what communicative options does she or he have? Several communication scholars have addressed the issue by identifying a variety of resistance strategies from which one may choose. For instance, in a recent study of influence behavior among friends, Manusov (1989) found examples of twenty-eight different resistance tactics. Factor analysis resulted in categorizing the strategies under four general headings: *direct, challenging, avoidance,* and *distributive.*

There is, however, a conceptual roadblock to a clear understanding of resistance messages. This is true for the sexual scenario as well as for other interpersonal contexts. Making an obvious distinction between influence and resistance is not an easy task, and some messages should not be singularly defined. That is, specific actions that occur in the course of an entire interaction episode may be viewed simultaneously as attempts to refuse and to gain compliance. The same message that indicates that one does not desire to go along with the wishes of the other person can also communicate a preference for the course of the other's behavior. Consider this example of a sexual interaction that occurs between a male and a female. They are kissing one another but the level of their physical involvement has gone no further. At one point the man begins to unbutton the woman's blouse and verbally indicates to her that he wants them to have intercourse. To his advance she replies, "No, stop it." He continues to undress her, however, and replies, "Don't worry. Everything will be OK." The male's initial advances may be viewed strictly as an effort to gain compliance, but subsequent behaviors in the sequence of events are multilayered in their intent. The female's response is an attempt to resist his wishes as well as an endeavor to get him to comply with what she wants, that is, discontinue unbuttoning her blouse. His retort has the same structural characteristics. Telling her that everything will be all right acknowledges her attempt to counter-persuade but indicates that he prefers not to abide by her wishes. His message also is a second bid to achieve his original goal. Thus, they both have attempted to resist and to gain compliance with single messages.

Despite this conceptual dilemma, several sexual influence researchers have attempted to identify strategies for resistance to intercourse. McCormick (1979), for instance, argued that the same set of messages (with the exception of seduction) that she classified as tactics for requesting sex are also utilized to refuse sexual advances. In addition, she found that both males and females are more likely to rely on direct rather than indirect techniques when resisting. The use of indirect resistance messages, especially nonverbal ones, by women frequently results in misunderstanding. Because nonverbal action is often more ambiguous, a male may misread or even choose to misinterpret the female's message. Abbey and Melby (1986) found that males generally tend to view nonverbal cues in a more sexual manner than females. Byers (1988) and Christopher (1988) both argue that too many females are not direct enough in communicating their intent and may need to express their desires more definitively.

One study that examined three different ways in which a female can say "No" to a male's sexual advances is reported in Byers and Wilson (1985). A mixed-sex group of subjects was shown videotapes portraying a man and woman engaging in romantic physical activity. In all situations the female on tape had agreed to a lower level of sexual intimacy, but had not consented to the higher level desired by the male. The woman's strategy for refusal varied on the tapes. In one instance the actress simply said "No" without explanation, in another her "No" coincided with an excuse that she was expecting company, and the final condition involved a "No" response with an explanation that they did not know each other well enough to engage in the behavior. After watching the tapes, male subjects were asked to role-play how they would respond if they were the male on tape. Females role-played on the basis of how they would expect the typical man to act in the scenario. Across conditions, most of the men indicated that they would stop their advances, but many said they would do so reluctantly. For example, 35% of the males reported that they would comply but desired further information from the female about her reticent attitude. Men with liberal views were more willing to comply than males with conservative values.

Another type of direct resistance message, the *mixed message*, communicates resistance and compliance on different levels (cf., Fung, Kipnis, & Rosnow's [1987] synthetic strategies). Most typically, the literal meaning of the message denotes a refusal, but the true intent of the message is an agreement to comply with a sexual advance. In heterosexual relationships, the common belief is that the female is the one most likely to behave in this manner.

The one study that has explored this phenomenon in the greatest depth was conducted by two female researchers at Texas A & M University (Muehlenhard & Hollabaugh, 1988). They claim that many individuals hold the notion that a large number of females communicate *token resistance* to their male partners. That is, some women say no to sexual advances when they actually mean yes (see also Buss, 1987, on acting coy). Pilot data from their own work supplied evidence that many men believe that this is a commonplace female strategy. The purpose of their subsequent research was to determine to what extent the practice exists in reality. They asked a sample of 610 college females if they had ever behaved in the following manner:

> You were with a guy who wanted to engage in sexual intercourse and you wanted to also, but for some reason you indicated that you didn't want to, although *you had every intention to and were willing to engage in sexual intercourse.* In other words, you indicated "no" and you meant "yes." (p. 874)

Almost 40 percent of the subjects claimed to have engaged in token resistance with a man. Muehlenhard and Hollabaugh classified the women's reasons for doing so into three categories. Some *practical* reasons revolved around fears of appearing promiscuous and of sexually transmitted diseases. Reasons classified as *inhibition-related* showed concern for emotional, religious, and moral issues. Game playing, anger with partner, and desire to be in control were considered *manipulative*. One reason for the use of token resistance may be that it allows a female to feel and behave on the surface in a manner consistent with what she believes she is "supposed" to do, yet on another level she can express her true feelings.

In relating token resistance to other variables, Muehlenhard and Hollabaugh found that those females who engage in this behavior hold beliefs compatible with traditional sex roles. For instance, token resistors were more likely to "believe that token resistance is a common behavior among women, that male-female relationships are adversarial, that it is acceptable for men to use physical force in male-female relationships, and that women enjoy it when men use force in sexual relationships" (p. 877).

Perper and Weis (1987), who describe a similar pattern of behavior as *incomplete rejection*, warn that mixed messages can result in acute miscommunication and potential problems for both parties. They fear that messages by females that perpetuate stereotypes may encourage men to do likewise and "enact the role of an ardent male who does not take no for an answer" (p. 467). Muehlenhard and Hollabaugh agree that token resistance is a contributing factor in discouraging honest communication in the compliance process. Restrictive gender roles are maintained and both females and males lose out.

SEXUAL INTERACTION

We have argued that message production in sexual influence situations is a function of a complex interaction process. Declaring the behavior to be complex without specifying the cognitive mechanisms that direct message choice, comprehension, and perceptions of effectiveness would leave this area of research theoretically barren. To explain why people utilize specific message types, sexual compliance researchers have referred most frequently to the literature on script theory and sexual norms (especially as they apply to heterosexual couples) to account for the manner in which persuasive messages are produced.

Although some individuals report that they had not considered a sexual strategy until moments before the start of intercourse

(Strassberg & Mahoney, 1988), many sex researchers believe that attempts at sexual compliance and resistance are carefully planned (McCormick & Jesser, 1983). The planning, however, does not begin from scratch but follows a standard script (Gagnon & Simon, 1973). The script, which is often learned from one's own peer group (McCormick, Brannigan, & LaPlante, 1984), allows the individual to "define the situation, name the actors, and plot the behavior" (Gagnon & Simon, 1973, p. 19). According to McCormick (1987), sexual scripts give the individual information grounded in stereotypes about how participants in the "play" are expected to act and the likely sequence of events. Changes in one's sexual compliance behavior are often difficult due to tightly defined scripts (Grauerholz & Serpe, 1985). McCormick (1987) agrees that the scripts for sexual interactions are frequently strong and involve expectations about the order as well the occurrence of exchanges. She points out, however, that despite the strength of the script, it is essential that some ambiguity remain so that the individual may fill in the gaps as needed. McCormick argues that competency with sexual communication may be the result of learning how to gear a generic script to a specific partner and situation.

Within our society the content of sexual scripts is governed largely by sex role stereotypes. The standard script for heterosexual behavior says that males are expected to be the initiator and to get as far as possible. The female's role is to set the limits on sexual interaction while simultaneously preserving a good reputation (Peplau, Rubin, & Hill, 1977). Generally, individuals are familiar with the basic content of sexual scripts by the time they reach adolescence (McCormick, 1987).

Although we might like to believe that people do not continue to follow traditional scripts, much evidence suggests that many still do. For instance, Grauerholz and Serpe (1985) found that females reported feeling more comfortable in resisting sexual intercourse and less at ease in initiating sex. In a study by LaPlante et al. (1980), both male and female subjects indicated that in their own experiences males most frequently played the role of initiator and females most commonly used persuasive strategies to avoid intercourse with an aroused date.

Still, a few studies suggest that females especially are allowing themselves some flexibility within the confines of the standard sexual script. Both Jesser (1978) and Perper and Weis (1987) found that large percentages of women in their samples indicated that they used persuasive strategies to initiate sexual encounters with men, but the specific nature of these strategies seems to be influenced by male-female sex roles. Perper and Weis believe that females are more willing to utilize initiation strategies when they feel that they also are skilled in the use of rejective strategies.

CONCLUSION

Oscar Wilde once remarked that intellectuals are the only group of people who have found something other than sex worthy of consuming their attention. Presumably, sex represents *the* vital and engrossing portion of the human experience for everyone else.

Sexual influence researchers represent an unusual combination of Wilde's two groups. By making intimate negotiations the focus of intellectual inquiry, these intellectuals have managed to return their attention to that most fundamental of activities—sex. They have recognized that the elemental concerns manifested in the interaction that surrounds the act of intercourse have far-reaching societal and theoretical implications. The time has come for communication scholars to contribute to these issues.

As we argued earlier in this chapter, the work on sexual influence contains methodological and theoretical weaknesses. The research, however, does provide a solid base for further investigations. The potential exists for the establishment of an exciting and significant new sub-area of compliance-gaining. Nowhere is this more true than in the work grounded in script theory. While learning about the ways in which individuals cognitively represent action sequences, we might also shed much-needed light on the communicative barriers to practicing safe sex (Edgar, Freimuth, & Hammond, 1988). Further investigations of sexual bargaining scripts will allow us to probe the degree to which expectations about the employment of safe sexual practices have penetrated the expectation sets of individuals in sexual encounters. Furthermore, we will be able to see the placement of such expectations in the sequence of interpersonal behavior, and we will be able to evaluate the perceived likelihood that safe sex will be practiced by the individual possessing a given type of script.

REFERENCES

Abbey, A., & Melby, C. (1986). The effects of nonverbal cues on gender differences in perceptions of sexual intent. *Sex Roles, 15,* 283–298.

Buss, D. N. (1988). The evolution of human intrasexual competition: Tactics of mate attraction. *Journal of Personality and Social Psychology, 54,* 616–628.

Byers, E. S. (1988). Effects of arousal on men's and women's behavior in sexual disagreement situations. *Journal of Sex Research, 25,* 235–254.

Byers, E. S., & Lewis, K. (1988). Dating couples' disagreements over the desired level of sexual intimacy. *Journal of Sex Research, 24,* 15-29.

Byers, E. S., & Wilson, P. (1985). Accuracy of women's expectations regarding men's responses to refusals of sexual advances in dating situations. *International Journal of Women's Studies, 8,* 376–387.

Byrne, D. (1983). Sex without contraception. In D. Byrne & W. A. Fisher (Eds.), *Adolescents, sex and contraception* (pp. 3–31). Hillsdale, NJ: Lawrence Erlbaum.

Christopher, F. S. (1988). An initial investigation into a continuum of marital pressure. *Journal of Sex Research, 25,* 255–266.

Cody, M. J., McLaughlin, M. L., & Jordan, W. J. (1980). A multidimensional scaling of three sets of compliance-gaining strategies. *Communication Quarterly, 28,* 34–46.

Dillard, J. P. (1988). Compliance-gaining message selection: What is our dependent variable? *Communication Monographs, 55,* 162–183.

Edgar, T., & Fitzpatrick, M. A. (1988). Compliance-gaining in relational interaction: When your life depends on it. *The Southern Speech Communication Journal, 53,* 385–405.

Edgar, T., Freimuth, V. S., & Hammond, S. L. (1988). Communicating the AIDS risk to college students: The problem of motivating change. *Health Education Research: Theory and Practice, 3,* 59–65.

Edgar, T., Hammond, S. L., & Freimuth, V. S. (1989). The role of the mass media and interpersonal communication in promoting AIDS-related behavioral change. *AIDS and Public Policy Journal, 4,* 3–9.

Falbo, T. A. (1977). A multidimensional scaling of power strategies. *Journal of Personality and Social Psychology, 35,* 537–547.

Fung, S. S. K., Kipnis, D., & Rosnow, R. L. (1987). Synthetic benevolence and malevolence as strategies of relational compliance-gaining. *Journal of Social and Personal Relationships, 4,* 129–141.

Gagnon, J. H., & Simon, W. A. (1973). *Sexual conduct: The social sources of human sexuality.* Chicago: Aldine.

Grauerholz, E., & Serpe, R. T. (1985). Initiation and response: The dynamics of sexual interaction. *Sex Roles, 12,* 1041–1059.

Gross, A. E., & Bellew-Smith, M. (1983). A social psychological approach to reducing pregnancy risk in adolescence. In D. Byrne & W. A. Fisher (Eds.), *Adolescents, sex and contraception* (263–272). Hillsdale, NJ: Lawrence Erlbaum.

Jesser, C. J. (1978). Male responses to direct verbal initiatives of females. *Journal of Sex Research, 14,* 118–128.

Kelley, H., Berscheid, E., Christensen, A., Harvey, J. H., Huston, T. L., Levinger, G., McClintock, E., Peplau, L. A., & Peterson, D. R. (1983). *Close relationships.* New York: W. H. Freeman.

Kingsbury, N. N., & Minda, R. B. (1988). An analysis of three expected relationship states: Commitment, maintenance, and termination. *Journal of Social and Personal Relationships, 5,* 405–422.

LaPlante, M., McCormick, N., & Brannigan, G. (1980). Living the sexual script: College students' views of influence in sexual encounters. *Journal of Sex Research, 16,* 338–355.

Lewis, R. A. (1978). Emotional intimacy among men. *Journal of Social Issues, 34,* 108–121.

Manusov, V. (1989, May). *How can you resist me?: Compliance resistance among friends.* Paper presented at International Communication Association, San Francisco.

McCormick, N. B. (1979). Come-ons and put-offs: Unmarried students' strategies for having and avoiding sexual intercourse. *Psychology of Women Quarterly, 4,* 194–211.

McCormick, N. B. (1987). Sexual scripts: Social and therapeutic implications. *Sexual and Marital Therapy, 2,* 3–27.

McCormick, N. B., Brannigan, G. G., & LaPlante, M. N. (1984). Social desirability in the bedroom: Role of approval motivation in sexual relationships. *Sex Roles, 11,* 303–314.

McCormick, N. B., & Jesser, C. J. (1983). The courtship game: Power in the sexual encounter. In E. R. Rice & N. B. McCormick (Eds.), *Changing boundaries: Gender roles and sexual behavior* (pp. 64–86). Palo Alto, CA: Mayfield Publishing Co.

Muehlenhard, C. L., & Hollabaugh, L. C. (1988). Do women sometimes say no when they mean yes? The prevalence and correlates of women's token resistance to sex. *Journal of*

Personality and Social Psychology, 54, 872–879.

Peplau, L., Rubin, Z., & Hill, C. T. (1977). Sexual intimacy in dating couples. *Journal of Social Issues, 33,* 86–109.

Perper, T., & Weis, D. L. (1987). Proceptive and rejective strategies of U.S. and Canadian women. *The Journal of Sex Research, 23,* 455–480.

Schenck-Hamlin, W. J., Wiseman, R. L., & Georgacarakos, G. N. (1982). A model of properties of compliance-gaining strategies. *Communication Quarterly, 30,* 92–100.

Strassberg, D. L., & Mahoney, J. M. (1988). Correlates of the contraceptive behavior of adolescents/young adults. *Journal of Sex Research, 25,* 531–536.

Wheeless, L. R. (1976). Self-disclosure and interpersonal solidarity: Measurement, validation, and relationships. *Human Communication Research, 3,* 47–61.

Wiseman, R. L., & Schenck-Hamlin, W. (1981). A multidimensional scaling validation of an inductively derived set of compliance-gaining strategies. *Communication Monographs, 48,* 251–270.

Witteman, H., & Fitzpatrick, M. A. (1986). Compliance-gaining in marital interaction: Power bases, processes, and outcomes. *Communication Monographs, 53,* 130–143.

An Organizational Perspective on Interpersonal Influence

Kathleen J. Krone and John T. Ludlum
The Ohio State University

W hile not always made explicit, the practice of influence is integral to understanding organizations. The earliest theories of organization focused attention on downward influence and authority (e.g., Taylor, 1911). Human relations approaches fostered interest in peer and upward influence (e.g., Likert, 1961), while systems logic required that we reconceptualize influence as a multilayer process that occurs at several levels of abstraction simultaneously (e.g., Kast & Rosenzweig, 1972). Ultimately, whether we understand organizations as machines, organisms, or cultures (Morgan, 1986), the process of influence remains central.

The purpose of this chapter is to bring into sharper focus one part of the influence process in organizations—the production and selection of compliance-gaining messages. Due to space limitations and the need for a coherent focus, our chapter is limited in two notable ways. First, we avoid discussion of many of the personal and situational variables that undoubtedly affect compliance-gaining activity. Instead, we emphasize factors that are uniquely important to compliance-gaining in an organization context.

Second, we do not attempt to give equal time to all aspects of the influence process. For the most part, we address questions such as "What sort of organizational features are associated with different sorts of influence tactics?" Our decision to emphasize message content reflects the state of the literature, since the vast majority of existing research addresses issues of tactic content. We also extend consideration to the frequency of influence activity. Since only a very small base of research directly addresses this issue, we have used work on frequency of communication in general as a springboard to derive hypotheses about influence in particular. This move required the assumption, perhaps justifiable, that as amount of communication increases so does amount of compliance-gaining. We do not mean to imply a strong relationship such that influence always occupies a fixed-size piece of the communication pie, but rather that as frequency of communication increases, frequency of influence behavior will never decrease and, in fact, will usually increase.

AN ORGANIZATIONAL PERSPECTIVE ON INTERPERSONAL INFLUENCE

In the field of communication, most compliance-gaining investigations have been conducted as studies of interpersonal behavior. Implicitly at least, the interpersonal perspective takes the dyad as the backdrop within which influence messages are created. An organizational perspective on interpersonal influence insists on a broader view, one that requires situating the dyad within a larger social aggregate. To look beyond the dyad reveals some important differences between the interpersonal and the organizational perspectives.

Influence in organizational settings often takes place for reasons that are different from those that explain why influence takes place in interpersonal settings. Kipnis, Schmidt, and Wilkinson (1980) provide a list of influence goals from their organizational investigation: initiating (organizational) change, assigning work, improving performance (of the target), gaining assistance with one's own job, and obtaining personal benefits (such as raises and better working hours). Even a cursory examination of these goals reveals that they reflect concern for issues that are not dyad specific.

Influence in organizations may take place by different means than in interpersonal settings. For example, while tactics like coalition-building and appeals to higher authority (Kipnis et al., 1980) are not inconceivable in interpersonal transactions, their absence in interpersonal message taxonomy studies suggests that they occur in that context infrequently, if at all (e.g., Cody, McLaughlin, & Jordan, 1980; Wiseman & Schenck-Hamlin, 1981). Conversely, tactics such as us-oriented messages—"Do it because it would be good for our marriage" (Witteman & Fitzpatrick, 1985)—would be nonsensical in organizational contexts. Thus, the configuration of influence tactics that are both available and appropriate differ in interpersonal and organizational settings.

In order to lend some theoretical coherence to this chapter we have attempted to compact some of these observations into three principles that jointly shape the production of influence messages in organizational contexts.

Principle 1: Compliance-gaining is shaped, in part, by the agent's perceptions of the *effectiveness* of different messages.

Principle 2: Compliance-gaining is shaped, in part, by the agent's perceptions of the *organizational appropriateness* of different messages.

Principle 3: Compliance-gaining is shaped, in part, by the relative *availability* of different influence tactics.

DIRECTION OF THE INFLUENCE ATTEMPT

One distinguishing feature of organizations is the arrangement of individuals according to the degree of formal authority they hold in the hierarchy. Intuitively, this arrangement might be expected to exert some impact on compliance-gaining. In general, however, individuals indicate that they prefer the use of rational tactics, regardless of the direction of the influence attempt. With respect to downward influence, while some student subjects report a willingness to use coercive (e.g., Goodstadt & Hjelle, 1973; Goodstadt & Kipnis, 1970; Instone, Major, & Bunker, 1983) and reward (Riccillo & Trenholm, 1983) tactics, actual managers generally report a preference for the use of rational tactics with their subordinates (Kipnis & Cosentino, 1969; Kipnis, Schmidt & Wilkinson, 1980; Kipnis & Lane, 1962). Research on upward influence suggests that student subjects (e.g., Offerman & Kearney, 1988; Offerman & Schrier, 1985) and organizational employees (e.g., Cheng, 1983; Mowday, 1978; Schilit & Locke, 1982; Krone, 1985) respond similarly. Both tend to emphasize rational, withdrawal, and information-based tactics. In horizontal influence attempts, members of actual job evaluation committees also report using rationality tactics most frequently (Benson & Hornsby, 1988).

Preference for tactics other than rationality tends to show more variability as a function of direction. Specifically, managers say that they are more likely to employ assertiveness tactics, such as direct, unadorned requests, with subordinates than with co-workers, and they are more likely to use the same tactics with co-workers than with superiors. Managers also report that they are more likely to employ sanctions with subordinates than with co-workers or superiors, and they are less likely to use exchange to influence superiors than to influence subordinates or co-workers (Erez, Rim, & Keider, 1986; Kipnis et al., 1980).

When faced with target resistance, agents generally report selecting stronger follow-up tactics, but these choices also seem to vary somewhat with direction. Although managers responded to resistance with increases in persistence and personal negative actions regardless of direction, they also reported increases in the use of coalition-building with superiors and co-workers, and increases in administrative punishments for subordinates (Kipnis et al., 1980).

Some studies, discussed below, also suggest variables that may interact with direction to impact the influence process. These include relative power, the goals motivating the influence attempt, and the type or quality of relationship between the agent and the target.

Direction and Relative Power

Although many studies seem to assume that supervisors have more power than subordinates and that co-workers are power equals, formal status differences are not necessarily equivalent to power differences. Hierarchical position usually defines status, while control of needed resources defines power (e.g., Bradley, 1978).

Available research shows that decreased power among subordinates is accompanied by an increased tendency to employ some forms of ingratiation (Michener, Plazewski, & Vaske, 1979) and "politeness" (Baxter, 1984). Decreased power among supervisors (e.g., the ability of subordinates to remove a leader via a vote of confidence) does not appear to be related to the use of threat or punishment (Michener & Burt, 1975). Mainiero (1986) reports that those with low dependency jobs (defined as a measure of relative power) relied on "alternatives" (i.e., finding other methods or individuals who can provide what is needed) more often and on "acquiescence" (accepting power imbalance and acting in a helpless, dependent manner) less often, than those with high dependency jobs.

If any generalization can be drawn from this set of studies, it is that low power agents rely on soft tactics in order to influence others. While intuitively appealing, this generalization is based solely on laboratory studies conducted with students in hypothetical situations.

As is true in most areas of organizational science, a broader data base built on real organizational participants is needed.

Direction and Agent Goals

Compliance-gaining agents in organizations attempt to persuade supervisors, subordinates, and co-workers for a variety of reasons. Available research consistently reports that agents' goals, that is, reasons for attempting influence, vary with direction and also affect their compliance-gaining choices. These reasons almost certainly cause them to use or avoid certain tactics. For example, agents who would ordinarily oppose the use of threat might threaten another if they perceived their objective as in the target's best interest (cf., Fung, Kipnis, & Rosnow, 1987). Similarly, the simultaneous presence of "interpersonal" and "identity" goals (Clark & Delia, 1979) might cause agents to avoid tactics that could threaten either a relationship or their own self-image (e.g., Clark, 1979).

With respect to influence goals and direction, managers tend to turn to their superiors for personal benefits (Kipnis et al., 1980; Erez et al., 1986), and are more likely to ask subordinates to improve their job performance or to do their jobs (Kipnis et al., 1980; Erez et al., 1986). Some research shows that managers tend to ask co-workers for assistance (Kipnis et al., 1980), while other research suggests that managers seek assistance on job-related issues from their supervisors (Erez et al., 1986). Mowday's (1978) work indicates that elementary school principals were most likely to choose targets within the "chain of command" when their goal was to influence budgetary versus personnel decisions.

Regardless of direction, compliance-gaining agents appear to select stronger tactics when pursuing organizational goals. Subordinates concerned with "personal benefits" (e.g., promotion) reported that they were more likely to employ ingratiation tactics with their supervisors than subjects who were asked to pursue an "organizational goal" (e.g., convincing a supervisor to hire new personnel in order to help meet company objectives); and that subordinates in the "organizational goal" condition reported that they were more likely to employ "rational persuasion," "upward appeal," and "blocking," than subjects in the "personal benefits" condition (Ansari & Kapoor, 1987). Harper and Hirokawa (1988) found that agents selected different tactics depending on whether their goal was to influence subordinates' "obligatory work-related actions" (e.g., coming to work on time) or their "non-obligatory work-related actions" (e.g., providing more ideas to management). In particular, managers reported using more punishment-based tactics (e.g., threat, negative esteem) under the obligatory condition and more rationale-based tactics (direct request, explanation) under the non-obligatory condition.

A series of studies that used goals to predict the likelihood of strategy use found that assigning work was associated with the use of assertiveness, that managers who intended to sell ideas were likely to employ rationality, and that managers attempting to obtain personal benefits were likely to employ ingratiation and exchange tactics (Erez et al., 1986; Kipnis et al., 1980; Schmidt & Kipnis, 1984). Overall, agents select stronger, more explicit tactics when pursuing organizationally endorsed goals and relatively weaker ones when pursuing other types of goals.

Direction and Relationship Quality

Research concerned with direction treats all hierarchical or non-hierarchical relationships in a similar fashion. Studies of interpersonal compliance-gaining suggest, however, that relationship quality molds message making in a variety of ways. Intimacy is negatively related to verbal aggressiveness (Dillard & Burgoon, 1985), as well as politeness and the degree to which the request is elaborated (Roloff, Janiszewski, McGrath, Burns, & Manrai, 1988).

Investigations of relationship quality in organizational compliance-gaining are few. Still, they suggest that perceptions of weak interpersonal bonds with a target (i.e., lower trust, respect, and liking), contribute to the use of multiple strategy mixes, including increased selection of deceptive strategies (Perreault & Miles, 1978), and that students who were role-playing supervisors in a high-trust condition perceived that persuasion would be more successful with their subordinates and coercion would be less successful than those students in medium- and low-trust conditions (Riccillo & Trenholm, 1983). In general, when relationships are characterized by liking, closeness, and respect, compliance-gaining agents tend to select softer, rational tactics. Studies of relationship quality and compliance-gaining in organizations would benefit from additional theoretical anchoring and greater sensitivity to a range of relationship types found in organizations. One promising approach is suggested by vertical dyad linkage theory (Graen, 1976) and the related body of research on leader-member exchange (see Dienesch & Liden, 1986 for a review and critique). The results of one study that utilized this framework revealed that subordinates who perceived higher quality exchanges with their supervisors selected more open persuasion tactics and fewer manipulation tactics in their upward influence attempts than did subordinates who perceived lower quality exchanges (Krone, 1987).

Organizations also make possible types of relationships that are less evident in other communication contexts and that might affect compliance-gaining in unique ways. For instance, mentor and peer relationships have been identified as crucial to the development of adults' careers in organizations (Kram, 1985; Kram & Isabella, 1985). While both relationships are influential in shaping individuals' career choices, peer relationships typically occur across status equals and often last longer than mentor relationships. Three distinct types of peer relationships have been identified—information peer, collegial peer, and special peer—that vary in qualities such as level of trust and self-disclosure (Kram & Isabella, 1985).

FORMAL STRUCTURE

Formal structures regulate interaction among individuals and groups (Hall, 1977; Perrow, 1979). Some theorists distinguish between formal structural "properties" of organizations and structuring "processes." *Structural properties* refer to concrete attributes of organizations that can be objectively determined, such as size, while *structuring processes* describe policies and/or formally sanctioned activities that might more directly constrain or facilitate other organizational processes (Dalton et al., 1980). Research on how structural properties and structuring processes affect compliance-gaining is sparse. Consequently, there are two aims for the following sections: to summarize what little literature that does exist, and to explore tentative linkages between formal organizational structure and compliance-gaining.

Structural Properties

Organizational/Subunit Size

Research examining the effects of organizational size on the overall quantity and quality of communication has yielded inconsistent results (Jablin, 1987), probably due to the effects of intervening variables. Specifically in terms of influence, Schilit (1987) reports that middle-level managers from small organizations (less than 100 employees) tend to be more active in their attempts to influence risky, strategic decisions than are middle-level managers from large organizations (greater than 3,000 employees). Another study indicates that managers in organizations of 6,000 or more employees appear to use rational tactics with their supervisors more often than do managers in organizations of less than 599 employees (Erez & Rim, 1982). Vast differences in organizational size may be necessary to detect differences in the overall frequency of compliance-gaining and the use of specific compliance-gaining tactics.

As work group or subunit size increases, so does the use of rules, plans, and policies to coordinate work (Van de Ven, Delbecq, & Koenig, 1976); and thus, compliance-gaining may become more impersonal as well. As subunit size increases, supervisors report using more assertions, sanctions, and appeals to higher levels of authority in their attempts to influence their subordinates' behavior. Increases in work group size do not appear to affect the influence tactics supervisors use with their co-workers (Kipnis et al., 1980). The results are more mixed with respect to supervisors' upward tactic choices with the next level of management. Some research suggests that managers of larger work units (sixteen or more subordinates) use significantly more personal, negative, and clandestine tactics with their supervisors than do managers of smaller units (Erez & Rim, 1982), while other research reports no differences in upward tactic choices for managers of small and large work groups (Kipnis et al., 1980). Beyond these two studies, little exists to suggest additional ways in which work group size alone might affect compliance-gaining choices.

Span of Control

Span of control indexes the number of subordinates reporting directly to a supervisor (Fayol, 1949). A field study reported by Kipnis and Cosentino (1969) indicates that span is positively associated with the use of official warnings to correct subordinates' performances. In laboratory research, students with a large span (eight individuals) threatened to fire a problem employee in an organizational simulation sooner than did students with a small span (three individuals) (Goodstadt & Kipnis, 1970). In the same study, subjects with a smaller span of control gave praise, promised raises, and gave raises more often to their satisfactory workers than did students with a larger span of control. Combined with the results of another work (Kipnis et al., 1980), these studies indicate that span of control is positively associated with the use of more impersonal, coercive tactics to correct performance problems.

It seems likely that span effects are mediated by the increases in relational quality that are possible, and perhaps even structurally encouraged, in small-span supervisory relationships. Empirically, however, the question of the direct versus indirect effects of span of control on compliance-gaining remains open. Another issue that is completely unresearched concerns the impact of supervisory span of control on *subordinate* influence behavior. If the relationship quality hypothesis advanced above is correct, span should affect compliance-gaining in both directions.

Hierarchical Level

Since frequency of message sending and receiving (Bacharach & Aiken, 1977; Hannaway, 1985) and participation in decision making (Blankenship & Miles, 1968; Jago & Vroom, 1977) tend to increase with hierarchical level, we might expect more frequent compliance-gaining communication at higher organizational levels as well. Although we could locate no research that directly examined compliance-gaining frequency across levels, two studies suggest that the use of specific influence tactics varies with organizational level. Kipnis et al. (1980) found that, regardless of the direction of the attempt, one's level in the organization was directly associated with one's use of rationality and assertiveness tactics, but the relatively greater use of sanction by higher level employees was limited to attempts to influence those below them in the hierarchy. Similarly, Krone (1985) found that subordinates at higher levels reported using more open persuasion in their attempts to influence their supervisors' strategic and work decisions than did subordinates at lower organizational levels. Erez and Rim (1982) report that nonmanagers report using more negative and clandestine tactics toward their supervisors than do managers or assistant managers.

Structuring Processes

Complexity

As organizations become more structurally differentiated, they become more complex. *Vertical complexity* refers to the number of different hierarchical levels relative to an organization's size. *Horizontal complexity* refers to the number of departments into which an organization is divided (Zey-Ferrell, 1979). Depending on how it is operationalized, horizontal complexity appears more consistently related to organizational communication than does vertical complexity (e.g., Jablin, 1987). In particular, as the number of occupational specialties increases (one way in which horizontal complexity has been operationalized), so too does attendance at organization-wide committee meetings and volume of unscheduled communication across other work units (Hage, Aiken, & Marrett, 1971).

As scheduled and unscheduled communication across work units increases, compliance-gaining across units should also increase. Assuming that it does, increased horizontal complexity may have interesting implications for compliance-gaining activity. For instance, to the extent that increased horizontal complexity is associated with the emergence of various occupational communities, their members may have been socialized to share unique values, norms, and perspectives concerning work and other matters (VanMaanen & Barley, 1984). Related research suggests that horizontal diversity may be associated with opinion diversity and lack of consensus on potentially important organizational issues (Welsh & Slusher, 1986). Differences in occupational orientation also suggest differences in attitudes toward the use of various compliance-gaining tactics, knowledge about a range of compliance-gaining tactics, skill in the use of various tactics, and/or willingness to use certain tactics. When faced with increased audience diversity, to what extent do members of interdepartmental work units incorporate greater variety in the types of arguments used or reasons given for compliance? Conversely, to what extent do compliance-gaining agents in heterogeneous groups avoid tailoring reasons and arguments to the needs of a diverse audience? It seems possible that agents opt instead for increasing ambiguity in their messages, permitting targets to provide their own reasons for complying.

The extent to which horizontal complexity affects compliance-gaining activity may also depend on the degree of interdependence among the subunits. When diverse units are required to work cooperatively to accomplish tasks, the frequency of compliance-gaining in the form of political activity tends to increase (Pfeffer, 1981). Thus, increasing specialization across highly interdependent work units may affect compliance-gaining activity and message choice to a greater extent than it would among more autonomous units. Interestingly, Welsh and Slusher (1986) observed that political activity such as coalition formation and attempts to influence decision criteria was most frequent between college departments that were moderately interdependent. Less political activity took place between departments that were either high or low in interdependence. Possible relationships between horizontal complexity, subunit interdependence, and compliance-gaining activity seem to warrant further empirical attention.

Formalization

An organization is formalized to the extent that work-related behaviors and job requirements are made explicit through rules, policies, and regulations. Some theorists add the additional stricture that these performance requirements must be seriously enforced (Hage, 1965).

The degree to which employees report detailed job descriptions for their positions is significantly associated with a reduction in (1) the overall frequency of unscheduled communication, (2) unscheduled communication with individuals at the same level in different work units and (3) unscheduled communication with individuals at lower levels in different departments (Hage, et al., 1971). Highly specific job descriptions, policies, and procedures may act as a substitute for downward and interdepartmental communication (e.g., McPhee, 1985) and, by extension, compliance-gaining.

The types of compliance-gaining tactics selected under more or less formalized conditions remains a matter of some speculation. Since high formalization includes high enforcement of organizational expectations, it seems likely that when individuals do attempt compliance, albeit infrequently, they increasingly select tactics that include appeals to honor the formal organizational rules and chain of command. In the absence of explicitly defined organizational policies and procedures, rule-conforming appeals are less available to compliance-gaining agents than are information-based, relationship-based or politically based tactics. Indeed, the results of one study reveal that under orderly and unambiguous conditions, subordinates reported using rational influence tactics most frequently, while under chaotic and ambiguous conditions, they reported using political tactics such as ingratiation, threat, and blocking most frequently (Cheng, 1983).

Centralization

Centralization refers to the distribution of decision making authority throughout an organization (Dalton, Todor, Spendolini, Fielding, & Porter, 1980). Generally, as decentralization increases, so does the frequency of organizational communication. Decentralization is positively correlated with the frequency of attending organization-wide committee meetings, the frequency of attending department meetings, and the frequency of unscheduled interaction with people in different departments on the same status level and at higher levels (Hage, Aiken, & Marrett, 1971). Other research reports a significant, positive association between decentralization and communication especially for subordinates' upward, downward, lateral, and total communication and the upward, lateral, and total communication of department heads (Bacharach & Aiken, 1977). Decentralization and participation in decision making also shape relationships among organizational members. There is some evidence that members of a high participation work group report greater trust in their supervisor and a greater desire to interact than members of a low participation work group (Harrison, 1985). Furthermore, the extent to which organizations are decentralized can also affect the prevalence of differents types of compliance-gaining goals. For instance, decentralization formally sanctions subordinates' attempts to influence certain types of decisions, while centralization does not.

In an attempt to examine more carefully how centralization might affect the use of specific types of influence, Krone (1985) studied subordinates' self-reports of upward influence attempts across five different organizations. Her results reveal a negative relationship between work-unit centralization and the use of explicit persuasive tactics.

While available research suggests that centralization of authority affects the frequency of certain types of upward influence, we found no research that examined downward or lateral compliance-gaining choices under varying centralization conditions. Under centralized conditions, we would expect downward influence to include increases in the use of formal authority and information-based strategies that reflect the centralization of knowledge that accompanies centralization of authority. Compliance-gaining among status equals might also vary under centralized versus decentralized conditions. Under both conditions, agents may attempt to influence each others' interpretations of significant organizational events; however, under decentralized conditions status equal agents may also attempt to shape each others' opinions with respect to important decision matters.

TASK CHARACTERISTICS

At least two dimensions of a task may be relevant to compliance-gaining in organizations. The first, *task routineness*, refers to variety (i.e, number of exceptional cases encountered in the work) and analyzability (i.e., logical versus speculative information search upon encountering exceptions) (Perrow, 1970). The second, *task interdependence*, refers to the extent to which a task requires coordination among group members (Thompson, 1967). Generally, as routineness decreases or interdependence increases, so does the amount of horizontal communication, including the number of group meetings (Van de Ven, Delbecq, & Koenig, 1976).

Apparently, task routineness does affect managers' choice of influence tactics (Schmidt & Kipnis, 1984). Specifically, managers of nonroutine units reported greater variety in their upward influence attempts than did managers of routine work units. Managers who directed nonroutine units frequently used reason, assertiveness, and higher authority with their supervisors, although typically, assertiveness and higher authority are less often used in upward influence attempts. Managers of nonroutine units may have increased power in the organization that permits the use of stronger upward influence tactics (Kipnis et al., 1980; Perrow, 1970).

How task interdependence in groups affects compliance-gaining choices remains a speculative matter. As noted earlier, job dependence tends to be associated with an increase in the extent to which agents select acquiescence and a decrease in the extent to which they select alternatives (Mainiero, 1986). High task interdependence, however, compels work group members to rely on each other to accomplish group goals. Thus, high task interdependence may be associated with a more even distribution of talent and resources among members, greater orientation to a group, and the accomplishment of its goals. Relatedly, Tjosvold (1985; 1988) reports that subjects in a high power, cooperative condition provided more assistance and instruction to their group members than did subjects in low power, competitive, or individualistic conditions.

COMPLIANCE-GAINING ACROSS ORGANIZATIONAL BOUNDARIES

Interorganizational Compliance-Gaining

Wilkinson and Kipnis's (1978) work on interorganizational compliance gaining examined the use of weak versus strong tactics. Results indicated a preference for strong tactics when the agent company faced resistance from the target company, when the target company was less powerful than the agent company, and when the agent company was in a reactive mode and responding to some activity initiated by the target company (Wilkinson & Kipnis, 1978). The first two findings appear similar to those conditions under which individual agents report selecting more forceful tactics.

One untried but potentially fruitful approach to study of interorganizational influence would be to focus on boundary-spanning activity. Adams (1983) proposed a conceptual model of organizational boundary systems that illustrates the centrality of influence activity for those whose work involves linking their organization to another. Boundary role people (BRPs) are often called upon to influence their counterparts in other organizations as well as their constituents in the focal organization. Similarly, they are positioned so as to receive influence attempts from external BRPs and their own constituents. Many organizational positions require boundary-spanning activity, including receptionists, sales representatives, purchasing agents, and lobbyists (Adams, 1980). It would be interesting to examine how compliance-gaining activity between BRPs from different organizations compares to compliance-gaining activity with members of their constituent group. Because some BRPs must be able to represent their constituents' interests to the external group and must also argue the interests of the external group to their consituents (Adams, 1980), they may have a relatively varied repertoire of arguments resulting from their need to adopt the perspective of more than one audience.

Organization-Client Compliance-Gaining

The principle of availability specifies that the influence process is fashioned by the presence or absence of different premises. The research on organization-client interaction illuminates this principle. Influence attempts seem to be affected by either party's "rights" in a given situation and the extent to which clients have been socialized to bureaucratic behavior. A study of compliance-gaining interviews between tax enforcement officers and delinquent tax payers reveals that tax collectors argue critically, describe sanctions, and assure cooperation, while clients provide accounts, excuses, and explanations for nonpayment (Gilchrist, 1982). Other research confirms that when clients are in a weaker position with respect to an organization they use more altruistic appeals, and when they are in a stronger position they use more normative appeals (Katz & Danet, 1966). Thus, some persuasive appeals tend to be chosen over others because they are made available by the relative power of the interactants.

Other research speaks to the way in which clients' socialization to bureaucracy affects message production. Katz and Danet (1966) report that more "modern" individuals, that is those who were more socialized to bureaucratic behavior, rely more on normative appeals and less on altruistic appeals relative to more "traditional" individuals. A later study looked at client occupational status as a predictor of the extent to which individuals made use of role-related information in their persuasive appeals to Israeli customs officials. High status agents were more likely to mention only those roles that were officially relevant to their specific problem (Danet & Gurevitch, 1972). These findings underscore the fact that availability is not an objective feature of the agent-target relationship, but that it depends on the manner in which the interaction is conceived (cf., Meyer, this volume).

CONCLUSIONS AND
RECOMMENDATIONS

Our primary goal was to bring into sharper focus established and possible relationships between contextual features of organizations and compliance-gaining. In doing so, we braved a descent into occasionally "confusing particularity" (Poole, 1985, p.80), but have emerged with a number of insights. Most importantly, we know that specific contextual features of organizations systematically affect compliance-gaining choices. Our review also revealed a number of under-researched areas including compliance-gaining choices among status equals in organizations, compliance-gaining in organizational groups, the effects of structuring processes on compliance-gaining, and compliance-gaining choices across organizational boundaries.

Research on compliance-gaining in organizational contexts reveals vulnerabilities similar to those of compliance-gaining research in general. Methodologically, all the research procedures provided subjects with the opportunity to cognitively monitor their compliance-gaining decisions and, thus, may be subject to errors in recall or "social desirability" effects (Burleson & Wilson, 1988), as well as tendencies to ignore the more "mindless" aspects of much compliance (e.g., Langer, 1978). In addition, organizational compliance-gaining research is more representative of subjects' perceptions and preferences for compliance-gaining tactics than it is of actual compliance-gaining behavior.

In a more specific vein, although it is established that individuals generally indicate a preference for rational forms of influence, less is known about the structure, content, and effectiveness of rational arguments. Moreover, with a few exceptions (Perreault & Miles, 1978; Kipnis & Schmidt, 1988), existing research reveals little about when and how compliance-gaining agents supplement their use of rational strategies with other types of tactics. While it may be the case that agents use rational tactics most often, perhaps it is the infrequent use of more subtle or political tactics that actually helps them accomplish their goals. Existing compliance-gaining measures seem to reduce all organizational politics to a question of how frequently three or four tactics get used (coalition formation, upward appeal, blocking and ingratiation-impression management) and reveal little about the specific communication behaviors involved in these processes. Because individuals report using these tactics less often than rational ones, or restrict their use to specific situations, we may be left with an overly rational depiction of organizational compliance gaining.

In addition, because work groups and organizations often impose goals on their members, organizations are ideally suited as contexts in which to explore the pursuit of multiple and sometimes conflicting goals via compliance-gaining choices and interaction. At a minimum, each organizational member acts to establish, maintain, and occasionally relinquish a variety of relationships at work, to manage multiple role identities (e.g., formal roles and occupational roles), and to accomplish work-related tasks. In varying degrees, these goals might be reflected in compliance-gaining choices. Within organizational contexts, individual goals are embedded in, and may conflict with or be constrained by, work group and organizational goals. Moreover, individuals may choose group or organizational goals to support the pursuit of individual goals.

Finally, our knowledge of organizational compliance gaining stands to be meaningfully informed by moving beyond checklist methods of data collection to examinations of influence attempts as they occur within natural discussions among workers (see Boster, this volume). In particular, interaction analyses can reveal how the content of widely reported tactics such as rational argument is accepted, rejected or questioned in a compliance-gaining attempt; how previously unmeasured strategies such as humor or ambiguity function in compliance-gaining interaction; and how relative power expressed through conversational dominance relates to compliance-gaining choices and outcomes.

REFERENCES

Adams, J. S. (1980). Interorganizational processes and organization boundary activities. In L. L. Cummings & B. Staw (Eds.), *Research in organizational behavior,* (Vol. 2, pp. 321–355). Greenwich, CT: JAI Press.

Adams, J. S. (1983). The structure and dynamics of behavior in organizational boundary roles. In M. D. Dunnette (Ed.), *Handbook of industrial and organizational psychology* (pp. 1175–1199). New York: John Wiley & Sons.

Ansari, M. A., & Kapoor, A. (1987). Organizational context and upward influence tactics. *Organizational Behavior and Human Decision Processes, 40,* 39–49.

Bacharach, S. B., & Aiken, M. (1977). Communication in administrative bureaucracies. *Academy of Management Journal, 20,* 356–377.

Baxter, L. A. (1984). An investigation of compliance-gaining as politeness. *Human Communication Research, 10,* 427–456.

Benson, P. G., & Hornsby, J. S. (1988). The politics of pay: The use of influence tactics in job evaluation committees. *Group & Organizational Studies, 13,* 208–224.

Blankenship, H. V., & Miles, R. E. (1968). Organizational structure and managerial decision behavior. *Administrative Science Quarterly, 13,* 106–120.

Bradley, P. H. (1978). Power, status and upward communication in small decision-making groups. *Communication Monographs, 45,* 33–43.

Burleson, B. R., & Wilson, S. R. (1988). On the continued undesirability of item desirability: A response to Boster, Hunter and Seibold. *Human Communication Research, 15,* 178–191.

Cheng, J. L. C. (1983). Organizational context and upward influence: An experimental study of the use of power tactics. *Group & Organizational Studies, 8,* 337–355.

Clark, R. A. (1979). The impact of self-interest and desire for liking in the selection of communication strategies. *Quarterly Journal of Speech, 65,* 187–206.

Clark, R. A., & Delia, J. G. (1979). Topoi and rhetorical competence. *Quarterly Journal of Speech, 65,* 187–206.

Cody, M. J., McLaughlin, M. L., & Jordan, W. J. (1980). A multidimensional scaling of three sets of compliance-gaining strategies. *Communication Quarterly, 28,* 34–46.

Dalton, D. R., Todor, W. D., Spendolini, M. J., Fielding, G. J., & Porter, L. W. (1980). Organizational structure and performance: A critical review. *Academy of Management Review, 5,* 49–64.

Danet, B., & Gurevitch, M. (1972). Presentation of self in appeals to bureaucracy: An empirical study of role specificity. *American Journal of Sociology, 77,* 1165–1189.

Dienesch, R. M., & Liden, R. C. (1986). Leader-member exchange model of leadership: A critique and further development. *Academy of Management Review, 11,* 618–634.

Dillard, J. P. & Burgoon, M. (1985). Situational influences on compliance-gaining message selection: Two tests of the predictive utility of the Cody-McLaughlin typology. *Communication Monographs, 52,* 289–304.

Erez, M., & Rim, Y. (1982). The relationships between goals, influence tactics, and personal and organizational variables. *Human Relations, 35,* 871–878.

Erez, M., Rim, Y., & Keider, I. (1986). The two sides of the tactics of influence: Agent vs. target. *Journal of Occupational Psychology, 59,* 25–39.

Fayol, H. (1949). *General and industrial management* (C. Storrs, Trans.). London: Pitman.

Fung, S. S. K., Kipnis, D., & Rosnow, R. L. (1987). Synthetic benevolence and malevolence as strategies of relational compliance-gaining. *Journal of Social and Personal Relationships, 4,* 129–141.

Gilchrist, J. A. (1982). The compliance interview: Negotiating across organizational boundaries. In M. Burgoon (Ed.), *Communication yearbook, vol. 6* (pp. 653–673). Beverly Hills, CA: Sage.

Goodstadt, B. E., & Hjelle, L. A. (1973). Power to the powerless: Locus of control and the use of power. *Journal of Personality and Social Psychology, 27,* 190–196.

Goodstadt, B. E., & Kipnis, D. (1970). Situational influences on the use of power. *Journal of Applied Psychology, 54,* 201–207.

Graen, G. (1976). Role-making processes within complex organizations. In M. D. Dunnette (Ed.), *Handbook of industrial and organizational psychology* (pp. 1455–1525). Chicago: Rand McNally.

Hage, J. (1965). An axiomatic theory of organizations. *Administrative Science Quarterly, 10,* 289–320.

Hage, J., Aiken, M., & Marrett, C. B. (1971). Organizational structure and communications. *American Sociological Review, 36,* 860–871.

Hall, R. H. (1977). *Organizations: Structure and process.* Englewood Cliffs, NJ: Prentice-Hall.

Hannaway, J. (1985). Managerial behavior, uncertainty and hierarchy: A prelude to synthesis. *Human Relations, 38,* 1085–1100.

Harper, N. L., & Hirokawa, R. Y. (1988). A comparison of persuasive strategies used by female and male managers I: An examination of downward influence. *Communication Quarterly, 36,* 157–168.

Harrison, T. M. (1985). Communication and participative decision making: An exploratory study. *Personnel Psychology, 38,* 93–116.

Instone, D., Major, B., & Bunker, B. B. (1983). Gender, self confidence, and social influence strategies: An organizational simulation. *Journal of Personality and Social Psychology, 44,* 322–333.

Jablin, F. M. (1987). Formal organizational structure. In F. M. Jablin, L. L. Putnam, K. H. Roberts, & L. W. Porter, *Handbook of organizational communication* (pp. 387-419). Newbury Park, CA: Sage.

Jago, A. G., & Vroom, V. H. (1977). Hierarchical level and leadership style. *Organizational Behavior and Human Performance, 18,* 131–145.

Kast, F. E., & Rosenzweig, J. E. (1972). General systems theory: Applications for organization and management. *Academy of Management Journal, 15,* 447–465.

Katz, E., & Danet, B. (1966). Petitions and persuasive appeals: A study of official-client relations. *American Sociological Review, 31,* 811–822.

Kipnis, D., & Cosentino, J. (1969). Use of leadership powers in industry. *Journal of Applied Psychology, 53,* 460–466.

Kipnis, D., & Lane, W. (1962). Self-confidence and leadership. *Journal of Applied Psychology, 46,* 291–295.

Kipnis, D., & Schmidt, S. M. (1988). Upward-influence styles: Relationship with performance evaluations, salary and stress. *Administrative Science Quarterly, 33,* 528–542.

Kipnis, D., & Schmidt, S. M. (1982). *Profiles of organizational influence strategies: Influencing your subordinates.* San Diego: University Associates.

Kipnis, D., Schmidt, S. M., & Wilkinson, I. (1980). Intraorganizational influence tactics: Explorations in getting one's way. *Journal of Applied Psychology, 65,* 440–452.

Kram, K. E. (1985). *Mentoring at work: Developmental relationships in organizational life.* Glenview, IL: Scott-Foresman.

Kram, K. E., & Isabella, L. A. (1985). Mentoring alternatives: The role of peer relationships in career development. *Academy of Management Journal, 28,* 110–132.

Krone, K. J. (1985). Subordinate influence in organizations: The differential use of upward influence in decision making contexts. Unpublished doctoral dissertation, University of Texas at Austin.

Krone, K. J. (1987). The effects of leader-member exchange on subordinates' upward influence attempts. Paper presented at the annual conference of the International Communication Association, Montreal.

Langer, E. (1978). Rethinking the role of thought in social interaction. In J. H. Harvey, W. J. Ickes, & R. F. Kidd (Eds.), *New directions in attribution* research, (Vol. 2, pp. 35–58). Hillsdale, NJ: Lawrence Erlbaum.

Likert, R. (1961). *New patterns of management.* New York: McGraw-Hill.

Mainiero, L. A. (1986). Coping with powerlessness: The relationship of gender and job dependency to empowerment-strategy usage. *Administrative Science Quarterly, 31,* 633–653.

McPhee, R. D. (1985). Formal structure and organizational communication. In R. D. McPhee & P. K. Tompkins (Eds.), *Organizational communication: Traditional themes and new directions* (pp. 149–177). Beverly Hills, CA: Sage.

Michener, H. A., & Burt, M. R. (1975). Use of social influence under various conditions of legitimacy. *Journal of Personality and Social Psychology, 32,* 398–407.

Michener, H. A., Plazewski, J. G., & Vaske, J. J. (1979). Ingratiation tactics channeled by target values and threat capability. *Journal of Personality, 47,* 36–56.

Morgan, G. (1986). *Images of organization.* Beverly Hills, CA: Sage.

Mowday, R. T. (1978). The exercise of upward influence in organizations. *Administrative Science Quarterly, 23,* 137–156.

Offerman, L. R., & Kearney, C. T. (1988). Supervisor sex and subordinate influence strategies. *Personality and Social Psychology Bulletin, 14,* 360–367.

Offerman, L. R., & Schrier, P. E. (1985) Social influence strategies: The impact of sex, role, and attitudes toward power. *Personality and Social Psychology Bulletin,, 11,* 286–300.

Perreault, W. D., & Miles, R. H. (1978). Influence strategy mixes in complex organizations. *Behavioral Science, 23,* 86–98.

Perrow, C. (1970). *Organizational analysis: A sociological view.* Belmont, CA: Wadsworth.

Perrow, C. (1979). *Complex organizations* (2nd ed.). Glenview, IL: Scott-Foresman.

Pfeffer, J. (1981). *Power in organizations.* Marshfield, MA: Pitman Publishing Inc.

Poole, M. S. (1985). Communication and organizational climates: Review, critique, and a new perspective. In R. D. McPhee & P. K. Tompkins (Eds.), *Organizational communication: Traditional themes and new directions* (pp. 79–108). Beverly Hills, CA: Sage.

Riccillo, S. C. & Trenholm, S. (1983). Predicting manager's choice of influence mode: The effects of interpersonal trust and worker attributions on managerial tactics in a simulated organizational setting. *Western Journal of Speech Communication, 47,* 323–339.

Roloff, M., Janiszewski, C. A., McGrath, M. A., Burns, C. A., & Manrai, L. A. (1988). Acquiring resources from intimates: When obligation substitutes for persuasion. *Human Communication Research, 14,* 364–396.

Schilit, W. K. (1987). Upward influence activity in strategic decision making: An examination of organizational differences. *Group & Organizational Studies, 12,* 343–368.

Schilit, W. K., & Locke, E. A. (1982). A study of upward influence in organizations. *Administrative Science Quarterly, 27,* 304–316.

Schmidt, S. M., & Kipnis, D. (1984). Managers' pursuit of individual and organizational goals. *Human Relations, 37,* 781–794.

142   *Contexts*

Taylor, F. W. (1911). *Principles of scientific management.* New York: Harper & Row.

Thompson, J. D. (1967). *Organizations in action.* New York: McGraw-Hill.

Tjosvold, D., (1985). Power and social context in superior-subordinate interaction. *Organizational Behavior and Human Decision Processes, 35,* 281–293.

Tjosvold, D. (1988). Cooperative and competitive dynamics within and between organizational units. *Human Relations, 41,* 425–436.

Van de Ven, A. H., Delbecq, A. L., & Koenig, R. (1976). Determination of coordination modes within organizations. *American Sociological Review, 41,* 322–338.

VanMaanen, J., & Barley, S. R. (1984). Organizational communities: Culture and control in organizations. In B. M. Staw & L. L. Cummings (Eds.), *Research in organizational behavior,* (Vol. 6, pp. 209–264). Greenwich, CT: JAI Press.

Welsh, M. A., & Slusher, E. A. (1986). Organizational design as a context for political activity. *Administrative Science Quarterly, 31,* 389–402.

Wilkinson, I., & Kipnis, D. (1978). Interfirm use of power. *Journal of Applied Psychology, 63,* 315–320.

Wiseman, R. L., & Schenck-Hamlin, W. J. (1981). A multidimensional scaling validation of an inductively-derived set of compliance-gaining strategies. *Communication Monographs, 48,* 251–270.

Witteman, H., & Fitzpatrick, M. A. (1986). Compliance-gaining in marital interaction: Power bases, processes, and outcomes. *Communication Monographs, 53,* 130–143.

Zey-Ferrell, M. (1979). *Dimensions of organizations: Environment, context, structure, process, and performance.* Santa Monica, CA: Goodyear.

Developing Strategic Communication

Beth Haslett
University of Delaware

As children acquire language, they simultaneously acquire a standard of appropriate communication. They learn what, when, where, and how to communicate with others. They learn that knowledge permits them to make strategic decisions about communication. Strategic communication occurs when actors utilize their knowledge of what is appropriate in order to maximize the likelihood of achieving some goal.

Not all communication is strategic. Some communication is very routine. Some is so severely constrained, that is, ritualized, that few communicative choices may be available, especially to children. When influencing others, however, it is assumed that there are choices that one can make among alternative messages, and that whatever strategy is chosen, it is the one in the speaker's mind that can maximize the likelihood of achievement. This is not a simple task, because communication has both a referential and a social function. That is, any message expresses a content as well as reflects the social relationship(s) among the interactants (Watzlawick, Beavin & Jackson, 1967; Olson & Hilyard, 1981).

In what follows, we will examine the communicative skills and sociocognitive knowledge that support the development of strategic communication. In particular, we will discuss both the conceptual and performance abilities needed for strategic communication, and we will trace their development in family and peer interactions. Since family and peer interactions provide the most important learning environments for young children (Bruner, 1975a; Haslett, 1984), we will emphasize those contexts. Finally, since conflict settings offer very useful opportunities to look at children's strategic communication, we will consider them as well.

DEVELOPING STRATEGIC COMMUNICATION

Communicating strategically requires certain levels of conceptual knowledge and performance skills. Conceptual knowledge includes an awareness of the importance of communication in establishing relationships with others and in exerting influence, of differences between the self and others, of message clarity and accuracy, of social settings and their behavioral and communicative requirements, and of message adaptation to others. On the performance dimension, children need to develop the language skills needed to perform different communicative acts, and to have opportunities for learning and polishing those skills.

This knowledge and skill emerges gradually over time. Early in life, infants recognize the survival value of communication, and this recognition provides the motivation to acquire communicative knowledge and skills. During the first year, infants distinguish between the self and others, and demonstrate intentionality. Intentional behavior presupposes a recognition of the animacy of the self and others, and the independence of others' actions. By the end of their first year, infants recognize that they can influence the actions of others through their own intentional behavior; this understanding provides the basic awareness necessary for strategic communication.

As the child matures during its preschool years, this awareness becomes much more refined. Children discriminate among the different behaviors required for different roles; they use different behaviors with friends than they do with family members. Children also become increasingly skilled at communicating accurately and they learn scripted behaviors for different situations, such as going to the pool or attending Sunday school. Finally, children learn to adapt their messages to the unique personal characteristics of others.

For the most part, knowledge and skill at influencing others is learned through family and peer interaction. The social relationships unique to each setting enable the child to acquire skill and knowledge in different social realms. In the family context, adult-child interaction provides infants and young children with their first emotional bonds as well as authority relationship. Peers, in contrast, offer opportunities for competition and collaboration with equals. Most striking is that while adults attempt to accomodate to children and to figure out their wants, peers ordinarily will not make an attempt to accomodate, perhaps because they are cognitively ill-equipped to do so, and later have no desire to do so. In following sections, we look at each underlying aspect of the child's developing communicative strategies, and how they are facilitated in both family and peer settings.

Instrumental and Relational Functions of Communication

During their first year of life, infants become aware of the survival value of communication. Through cries, vocalizations, and gestures, they learn to establish relationships with others and to signal their own needs (Bruner, 1975b). Indeed, two important gestures—pointing and reaching—are viewed as prototypes for verbal commands and requests (Bates, 1979).

Trevarthen's work (1977, 1979a, 1979b) suggests that infants' understanding of communication proceeds in stages. During *primary intersubjectivity*, from birth to 15 months, infants increasingly control their own involvement with others, through cycles of interaction and withdrawal (e.g., averting eye gaze, turning away from the adult, and so forth). After nine months, infants "clearly conceive of others [as] having interests, purposes and helpful powers" (1982, p. 100). *Secondary intersubjectivity* develops during the following year, in which strong growth is followed by a period of consolidation (that is, a period of little growth or a state of stability), and then subsequent cycles of growth and stability follow. By the end of the second year, children demonstrate a strong motivation for interpersonal communication and a social sensitivity to others.

Intentionality

Bates (1979) argues that intentionality emerges at nine months. At this time, infants send a signal, repeat the signal, and then alter the signal in order to achieve their goal. This altered signal is believed to reflect the infant's intentionality. At approximately the same time, mothers infer intentionality on the infant's part, and begin to hold the infant accountable for what he or she does (Dore, 1983). Shotter (1984) makes this point even more strongly when he argues that children's selfhood emerges through being held accountable for their actions, and that such accountability begins in the earliest interactions between infants and adults.

When language begins—at the two-word stage, at approximately eighteen months—a young child's intentionality in communication becomes much more precise. Chalkley (1982) notes that the preverbal child can accomplish a number of communicative acts: making requests, expressing emotional states, referring, expressing an opinion without demanding action, and making offers. She suggests that three other functions—intending to greet someone, setting the stage for an exchange, and shaping an exchange—appear to develop later in the preverbal stage.

With the onset of two word utterances, however, communicative acts become more powerful and complex. As Chalkley notes:

> With the advent of two-word speech, the child can now use language to *inform* the other person about something new. . . the ability to perform the function of informing may capture some of the power of language—a power that allows the speaker to share a set of experiences with the listener. This affords them the opportunity to interact within the context of shared knowledge. . . .
>
> The child's interest in information is also reflected in the set of *comment-upon* functions. . . one encounters a proliferation of functions that merely comment upon certain aspects of the situation or properties of an object. (1982, p.99)

She also suggests that another important communicative act, that of prohibition (trying to prevent the actions of another), emerges with language and is the first function that "clearly hinges upon some understanding of social rules" (Chalkley, 1982, p. 99).

Differentiating the Self and Others

Another important development during the first year is that of differentiating between the self and others. An awareness of the independence of the self and others appears to emerge at the same time as intentionality. It seems reasonable to assume that separation of self from others may be a precursor of intentionality. If the self were not separate from others, there would be no need to express intentionality because the child would control the other automatically and intent would always be understood.

Self versus Others

During the first year of life, the infant begins to develop a separate sense of self. The year-old child recognizes the animacy and independence of action of others, as well as the fact that people exert mutual influence on one another (Wolf, 1981). Trevarthen (1979a, 1979b) points out that children develop complex exchanges of involvement and withdrawal with caretakers during the first fifteen months. Clearly, these exchanges reflect the child's awareness of being involved with another and, in part, the child's growing ability to control this involvement.

From this primitive separation of self from others comes increasing differentiation among others, in the form of person perception and role taking. At about eighteen months of age, as the child begins to experience interactions with other family members and subsequently with peers, increasingly fine discriminations about others and their behavior becomes possible.

Person Perception

As a function of time and exposure to an increasingly diverse set of experiences, children become aware of differences among others in terms of their relationships with others, others' goals and needs, and the roles that others play. These differences, of course, are viewed from different perspectives as the child matures. For example, the criteria for being a friend at three years are quite different from being considered a friend at fifteen (Gottman & Parker, 1986; Mueller & Cooper, 1986).

At three, children adapt their messages to others in terms of simplicity, politeness, and topic (Chalkley, 1982). Damon (1981) points out that children learn about authority and love relationships from their adult caretakers, and learn about friendship from their peers. Gender differences also emerge during early childhood, with children's play, interaction, and conversation becoming increasingly gender-differentiated (Brown & Levinson, 1987; Gottman, 1986; Haslett, 1984; Liss, 1983).

As children age, they develop "a systematic set of beliefs about the thoughts, feelings, intentions, motives, knowledge, and capacities of other people" (Gelman & Spelke, 1981, p. 171). With increasing age, children move from forming concrete characteristics of others to forming descriptions that reflect the feelings and thoughts of others (Chandler, 1977). From kindergarten to eighth grade, children's characterizations became more abstract, hierarchically organized, and moderated by situational or temporal factors (Scarlett, Press, & Crockett, 1971).

While person perception approaches focus on relatively enduring dispositions or traits, role-taking models emphasize children's ability to take the view of another. Higgins (1981) suggests that children proceed through a three-stage model:

1. situational role taking—in which children ask what they would do in that situation
2. there is an acknowledgment that people in the same situation may act differently
3. there is a comparison of one's behavior with that of another person

As they grow older, children display increasing sensitivity to differences between their own behavior and that of others in a wide variety of situations such as comforting (Burleson, 1984), prosocial behaviors, social reasoning (Forbes & Lubin, 1984), conflict (Haslett, 1983b), value analysis (Cosaro, 1985), and making requests (Becker, 1982).

The early verbal child is able to use language to inform and to comment on social norms. Chalkley (1982) suggests that, by three, children use language to request permission, invoke rules, offer judgments, make jokes, warn and tease others, and fantasize. Lastly, children are able to evaluate messages and clarify them. In brief, Chalkley argues that language enables children to inform others, to separate the content of a message from its function (as required for lying, joking, teasing, and a number of social functions), and to refer to abstract or nonpresent objects.

Finally, children's increasing awareness of differences among people is facilitated by different social models portrayed by the media. Current research suggests that children incorporate TV characters directly into their play, and pattern their behavior after social behavior viewed on television (Haslett & Alexander, 1988). Children's sensitivity to action and scene on television appears to require relatively sophisticated judgments concerning action sequences, motives for action, and awareness of contextual requirements (Pingree, 1983; Rice & Wartella, 1981).

Social Settings and Communicative Behavior

Just as children's social awareness of others increases, so too does their awareness of different social settings. They experience and observe behavior in a variety of social settings, such as school, church, home, and at play.

Understanding Social Contexts

Social relationships clearly influence a speaker's choices concerning message structure and content. These relationships may be modified by the social context, however, and in situations where the other participants are not known, contextual constraints may serve as the basic guideline for one's behavior. There is considerable evidence that young children rely heavily on contextual cues in interpreting utterances (Cook-Gumperz & Gumperz, 1976).

According to Cook-Gumperz and Gumperz (1976), children use contextual cues such as physical settings and formality, in conjunction with the interrelationships among cues, to help them identify the communicative activity in which they are participating. Adults and children appear to weight contextual cues differently (i.e., children weight all cues equally), and thus develop different understandings of what is happening (Gumperz & Herasimchuk, 1973). Older children underestimate the influence of specific situations and thus make the "fundamental attribution error" (Ross, 1981).

Scripts

Social knowledge about situations may also be found in scripts. Nelson's work (1981, 1986) is concerned with the development of scripted knowledge by young children. She defines scripts as concrete, well-defined action sequences, located in a given spatial and temporal context, and designed to achieve specific goals. The earliest examples of scripted activity are caretaking routines and play routines established between the adult-caretaker and infant (Bruner, 1975a, 1975b). Nelson (1981, 1986) found that preschoolers can verbalize and act out scripts. As these scripts become more practiced, children can begin to vary them. She argues that abstract categorical knowledge is built up from these scripts, and that similar scripts become combined. Although scripts represent routinized behaviors, variations can emerge over time, and thus some strategic communication is possible.

Message Clarity and Accuracy

The task of clear self-expression begins at birth. As children's knowledge and skills develop, their messages become more clear and more accurate—reflecting the increasing discriminations they are able to make. As we have seen, clear, intentional communication is in evidence by nine months of age, and some researchers suggest that signals can be detected even earlier (Izard, 1986; Stern, 1977).

The early verbal child can accomplish a number of communicative acts in an increasingly clear and complex fashion. The ability to evaluate and alter messages, for the purpose of making them more accurate and clear, develops late in the preschool years and is a particularly significant developmental milestone. Accuracy refers to the correctness of a message, while clarity refers to ease of understanding the message. This milestone represents the child's first acknowledgement of faulty messages, rather than faulty listeners, and can thus be viewed as an early attempt to self-repair a message.

Message Accuracy

Monitoring one's message accuracy begins to emerge at around age five, and can be viewed as part of the child's increasing metacognitive capacity (Flavell, 1981a, 1981b). The child may be corrected for mistakes in accuracy much earlier, at age three, for example, if the child confuses dogs with horses, but the child's ability to acknowledge that a message is not clear usually emerges later. As the child is able to comment upon a number of cognitive activities, communication also becomes an object or act that can be commented upon and corrected. The Robinsons' work on speaker-blame and listener-blame is of particular interest in regard to monitoring messages. They found that children generally tend to blame listeners at age five, but generally blame speakers at about seven years of age (Robinson & Robinson, 1977, 1978a, 1978b). Lloyd and Beveridge (1981) report that preschoolers could give adequate descriptions and modify messages when asked, although generally they had trouble recognizing deficient messages.

Adapting Messages Appropriately

Adapting messages that are sent to others involves an understanding of the differences between the self and others, especially in terms of goals and motives, and an appreciation of different social contexts and their communicative requirements. By age three, children adapt topics to younger children by simplifying their talk, and they use politeness strategies when talking to adults (Brown & Levinson, 1987). Situational adaptation is also evident through children's use of different scripts and routines in their social behavior.

Message adaptation also reflects the child's ability to metacommunicate. That is, children make comments that tell the listener how the message is to be interpreted. For example, comments like "I was only teasing" or "I didn't really mean it" function as metacommunicative remarks. These remarks emerge when children are about five years old, and they appear to depend upon children's awareness of message adequacy.

To summarize, in strategic communication, the child must choose among alternative strategies. In order to make these choices, children must acknowledge the independence of others, as well as their own choices. By the time they are three, *primitive strategies* appear. These reflect children's awareness of their own and others' motivations, their recognition of situational appropriateness, and their use of language to achieve personal goals. Politeness, for example, may be viewed as a primitive persuasive strategy that strengthens the likelihood of achieving goals. When they are four-and-a-half, children are utilizing *interpersonally oriented strategies*. These strategies are adapted to specific others and may incorporate coalitions with other children. At age six, a *reasoning strategy* begins to emerge. These strategies reflect a sequence of arguments or reasons designed to achieve one's goals. For example, a child begins to argue for something and is able to generate alternative reasons or a sequence of arguments that persuade others. These arguments or strategies are often quite sophisticated in their analyses of others and of situations.

As we have seen, an awareness of the instrumental and relational functions of communcation are essential to developing strategic capacity. In addition, sociocognitive knowledge about the self, about others, and about social settings plays an important role in encoding and decoding. In terms of exerting influence, speakers clearly modify their messages on these bases. If the child is to refine these developing influence skills, however, the knowledge base must be applied in real-life settings. It is to these developmental opportunities that we now turn.

I shall argue in the next section that the types of early communicative experiences children have play a critical role in determining what influence tactics they develop. Different developmental opportunities present the child with opportunities to develop different communicative skills (Wells, 1985). Language development itself seems similarly constrained by developmental opportunity (Bernstein, 1973; Dore, 1983).

INTERACTIONAL OPPORTUNITIES

Different contexts provide different opportunities for language development and for development of influence strategies. Language development is governed by cultural and subcultural differences as well as by family styles of interaction. As opportunities to develop influence strategies seem to be especially important in conflict resolution and persuasion, we shall focus on those two particular settings.

Developing Linguistic and Conversational Skills

The majority of language development occurs during the preschool years, with some complex grammatical constructions being acquired in middle childhood (Reich, 1986). As a child grows older, vocabulary and sentence complexity increases (Brown, 1975). As linguistic complexity increases, so does the child's capacity to express an increasingly diverse set of communicative functions (Haslett, 1983a).

At eighteen months, when most children use two word utterances, language emerges (preverbal stages and the use of single words are considered prelinguistic). With the emergence of language, children are more precise in conveying their thoughts, expressing needs, and referring to absent objects or past events. The earliest sentences usually consist of an action + object ("Hit John") or two terms ("Big wagon"). During their third year, children develop three term sentences (agent + action + object: "John hit the ball"). Also during their third year, children begin to use a variety of "wh" questions: negation, indirect utterances, and politeness conventions. All these developments indicate the child's growing flexibility in using a variety of linguistic structures (Reich, 1986).

Conversational skills also develop rapidly during one's preschool years (Haslett, 1984). Children use language to refer to their environment, express their views, question others, declare ownership, state demands, and so forth. Children are able to sustain topics of conversation, initiate interaction, respond to interruptions, and ask questions of both adults and peers. They are also able to adapt to communicative rules established in certain settings (such as don't interrupt your teacher, be quiet in church, and ask for something rather than grabbing it).

Many of these conversational skills, and to a lesser extent language itself, are influenced by family styles of interaction. Bernstein's work (1973) discusses the differences in communication across middle-class and lower-class families. Elaborated codes, involving the ability to take the perspective of others and using a variety of linguistic structures, are used by middle-class families. In contrast, lower-class families rely on restricted codes, which are less complex linguistically and rely on shared group values.

Culture also influences the linguistic and communicative skills a child develops. Ethnicity and gender are two important subcultural influences on language and communication (Schieffelin & Ochs, 1986; Goodwin, 1982). Different cultures emphasize different types of acquisition strategies and different types of linguistic and communicative skills (Schieffelin & Ochs, 1986). Generally, the culture and its social structure prescribe learning opportunities extended to young children. These developmental opportunities facilitate some skills while ignoring others (Wells, 1985).

Although there are a variety of cultural expectations and experiences, every social group develops ways of handling conflict and influencing others. It appears that argumentation and persuasion are two universal interactional challenges, although they are handled differently by different cultures. Conflict, according to many, provides one of the most significant developmental opportunities because it forces one to confront others' views.

PERSUASION, CONFLICT, AND STRATEGIC COMMUNICATION

Persuasion and Conflict Defined

Persuasive contexts are those in which one person exerts influence on another, but without explicit conflict. In contrast, conflict requires some expressed opposition between the communicators, and it requires that opposition is responded to rather than ignored or repaired immediately (Haslett, 1983a; Maynard, 1985; O'Keefe & Benoit, 1984). Both are instances of interpersonal influence.

Persuasion and conflict between adults and children and between peers are likely to be quite different. Social relationships between adult and child are shaped by status, age, authority, and skill differences. Among peers, persuasion and conflict take place between actors of roughly equal status, authority, and skill. Thus, the criteria for evaluating arguments and influence processes will be different, as well as the judgment of whether or not strategies are effective. Strategies, in general, must be evaluated against the relational, contextual, and task demands of the argument or influence attempt (i.e., what issues are at stake). With this in mind, we now turn to a more specific analysis of children's influence attempts and conflict resolution.

Persuasion

In a developmental context, the research of Delia and his colleagues, and that of Lubin and Forbes, represent the two most programmatic inquiries into persuasive strategies. Both attempt to look at the cognitive underpinnings of persuasive skills.

A series of studies assessed the relationships among persuasive strategies, construct complexity, and construct abstractness among children (Clark & Delia, 1976, 1977; Delia & Clark, 1977; O'Keefe & Delia, 1979). Elementary school children's perspective-taking ability was significantly related to construct complexity. Construct complexity generally predicted the number of different persuasive strategies used. Construct abstractness was significantly correlated with the complexity of persuasive strategies used among adults. Delia, Kline, and Burleson (1979) found that the level of persuasive strategy used increased significantly with age; the older the child, the greater the number of reasons identified for a target's rejection of a message. Cognitive complexity and construct abstractness correlated significantly with one another, and both significantly predicted the level of persuasive strategies and the potential bases for rejecting an appeal. O'Keefe and Delia (1982, 1986) found that older children, when persuading another, are more skilled at integrating multiple objectives and the other's goal than are younger children. Kindergartners and first graders used unelaborated requests, second through fifth graders used personal-need arguments, sixth through ninth graders used need arguments and some counter-arguments, and tenth through twelfth graders relied on counter-arguments in their persuasive attempts. Applegate (1982), analyzing naturalistic interaction, found that construct abstractness was significantly related to persuasive ability. As Kline's review (n.d.) of developing persuasive skills notes:

> it appears that as children grow older they. . . perceive persuasive situations in more complex ways, they develop more complex goal sets, they develop a more differentiated strategy repertoire, which they successfully use to create persuasive messages that are tailored to their message recipients' goals and desires. (p. 11)

Forbes and Lubin (1981) summarize the research trends in examining children's persuasive attempts. They conclude that children move from stereotypic conceptions of others to a focus on individual differences among them.

Their own research concerning the development of persuasive strategies among preschoolers sets up a three-tier model of strategic persuasion. The first, *mechanistic stereotype*, reflects the child's perception that everyone will react in the same way to a specific situation. In the second tier, *reaction subjectivism*, preschoolers acknowledge differences in how people react but view their own interpretation as the most valid.

Finally, in *constructive subjectivism*, children recognize that people have subjective perceptions and evaluations of others' behavior. Ritualistic persuasion, such as the use of entreaty, de-escalation of a request, and appeals to norms, are indicative of the first stage of social reasoning. In the second stage, children use appeals to history (past situations), testimonials, and positive affect. Stage-three reasoning involves clarification of the activity or intent. Forbes and Lubin found that stage-three reasoning always includes strategies from the prior two levels, and that level-two strategies encompass level-one strategies. This suggests that there is a hierarchical relationship among the three levels. Interviews with the children revealed a strong association between their reasoning and their use of persuasive strategies. They concluded that children move from "stereotypic, egocentrically formulated conceptions of others toward decentration and a consequent orientation to individual differences—both in the construction of and reaction to events in the social world" (Forbes & Lubin, 1984, p. 121).

Thus, in terms of influence attempts, we can see that children move from self-oriented, simple requests to strategies that match the message-to-listener characteristics. To do so requires, as O'Keefe and Benoit (1984) suggest, a mastery of turn-taking skills, language, conversational coherence, and repair. We can see this same developmental sophistication when we look at argumentation research.

Conflict

As previously noted, arguments involve some opposition that is taken up by the other interactant. Children's conflict strategies range from simple, repeated negation to complex sequences involving friends in the dispute (Haslett, 1983b).

By age three, children are using communicative tactics that reflect a sophisticated understanding of social relationships and their rights and obligations (Mitchell-Kernan & Kernan, 1977; Olson & Hilyard, 1981). Ervin-Tripp (1977) found that children altered their directives to account for age, dominance, and familiarity. Indirect requests are acquired and responded to at a very early age (such as "It's really hot in here, isn't it?" as a request to open the door) (Ervin-Tripp, 1977).

Olson and Hilyard (1981) analyzed young children's discourse in order to assess how they controlled others' actions. They suggest that any utterance has an assent value (truth value) and a compliance value (status-preserving). Their results indicated that young children do not separate truth conditions from social utility. "Claims of truth appear to be advanced if the gaining of assent may be instrumental in gaining compliance with some social goals. . . denials of truth will be offered if the social consequences of assent are perceived to be undesirable" (p. 324). They gave children narratives in which different requests were made to targets of varying status. They found that favors are more likely to be conventionally requested than rights, and that younger subjects tended to use direct commands to other peers but used conventionalized requests when addressing an adult. Adults tended to give responses that allowed others more options to respond. As Olson and Hilyard note:

> . . . in all of these cases, subjects aspired to the same goal, yet the utterance used to express that intention took a different form depending on the social relations beteen the participants. . . commands may be issued to lower status individuals, conventionalized requests must be issued to superiors, even if you are only asking for your rights. Second, presumed rights determine the form in which that illocutionary force will be expressed. Favors are largely expressed through conventionalized requests, although adults frequently add reasons. Rights may be expressed through conventionalized requests (to a high-status listener), commands (to a low status listener), occasionally through threats or through indirect speech acts, declaratives and questions. (1981, p. 329).

Maynard (1985, 1986) has systematically investigated children's development of argumentative skills. He notes, as do others, that this development reveals how children acquire a sense of social structure. His analysis reveals that children's argumentative strategies include negation, substitution, accounts, and presuppositional analysis (attacking a presumption about a person, activity, or event). The child's strategic choice has social consequences, especially for preserving face for oneself and one's opponent.

Haslett (1983b) also investigated preschoolers' arguments. Children's tactics change from reactive to active strategies as they become older. She suggests that as children develop more cognitive and communicative complexity, they can increasingly counter and anticipate others' reactions and thus adapt actively to them. By five years of age, children are able to engage in lengthy arguments, often involving multiparty confrontations and long sequences of reasoning and counter-proposals.

Other scholars have analyzed the underlying premises that seem to govern children's disputes. Brenneis and Lein (1977) found that arguing requires semantic continuity and redundancy between content and paralinguistic style. Eisenberg and Garvey (1981) found marked differences in children's adaptability in resolving disputes, i.e., their ability to give their opponents options for responses. Adaptability varied along four dimensions: the degree to which new information was added, conversational needs were met (e.g., recognizing that an explanation was called for), another's perspective was acknowledged, and fairness was recognized. Generally, the more adaptive the strategy, the more likely the dispute was to be resolved.

In summary, children's persuasive and conflict tactics show a fairly sophisticated mastery of a number of skills. These skills include sociocultural knowledge of norms, expectations, and individual differences. These skills reflect a pragmatic understanding of how to accomplish one's goals, even under adverse conditions, and an ability to select the optimal strategy for goal achievement.

Two important conclusions can be drawn from the general research in this area. First, social aspects of messages often take precedence over the content aspects of messages, even from early childhood. In fact, interpretations about what is meant are heavily biased toward the pragmatic, social dimension. Second, persuasive and conflict tactics appear to be selected on the basis of the specific issue involved (e.g., right or favor, truth or compliance, etc.), the social relationship between the participants (especially in terms of face requirements), and the outcomes or goals desired.

REFERENCES

Applegate, J. (1982). The impact of construct system development on communication and impression formation in persuasive contexts. *Communication Monographs, 49,* 277–289.

Bates, E. (1979). *The emergence of symbols.* New York: Academic Press.

Becker, J. (1982). Children's strategic use of requests to mark and manipulate social status. In S. Kuczaj (Ed.), *Language Development.* Hillsdale, NJ: Lawrence Erlbaum.

Bernstein, B. (1973). *Class, codes and control vol. 2.* London: Routledge Kegan Paul.

Brenneis, D., & Lein, L. (1977). You fruithead: A sociolinguistic approach to children's dispute settlement. In S. Ervin-Tripp & C. Mitchell-Kernan (Eds.), *Child's discourse* (pp. 49–65). New York: Academic Press.

Brown, P. & Levinson, S. (1987). *Politeness.* Cambridge, England: Cambridge University Press.

Brown, R. (1975). *A first language.* Cambridge, MA: Harvard University Press.

Bruner, J. (1975a). The ontogenesis of speech-acts. *Journal of Child Language, 2,* 1–19.

Bruner, J. (1975b). From communication to language—a psychological perspective. *Cognition, 3,* 255–287.

Burleson, B. (1984). Comforting communication. In H. Sypher & J. Applegate (Eds.), *Communication by adults and children.* Beverly Hills, CA: Sage.

Chalkley, M. (1982). The emergence of language as a social skill. In S. Kuczaj (Ed.), *Language and Development.* Hillsdale, NJ: Lawrence Erlbaum.

Chandler, M. (1977). Social cognition: A selective review of current research. In W. Overton (Ed.), *Knowledge and development.* New York: Plenum Press.

Clark, R., & Delia, J. (1976). The development of functional persuasive skills in childhood and early adolescence. *Child Development, 47,* 1008–1014.

Clark, R., & Delia, J. (1977). Cognitive complexity, social perspective-taking, and functional persuasive skills in second-to-ninth grade children. *Human Communication Research, 3,* 123–134.

Cook-Gumperz, J., & Gumperz, J. (1976). Context in children's speech. In J. Cook-Gumperz & J. Gumperz (Eds.), *Papers on language and context.* Berkeley: Language Behavior Research Laboratory.

Cosaro, W. (1985). *Friendship and peer culture in the early years.* Norwood, NJ: Ablex.

Damon, W. (1981). Exploring children's social cognition on two fronts. In J. Flavell & L. Ross (Eds.), *Social cognitive development.* Cambridge, England: Cambridge University Press.

Delia, J., & Clark, R. (1977). Cognitive complexity, social perception, and the development of listener-adapted communication in six-, eight-, ten-, and twelve-year-old boys. *Communication Monographs, 44,* 326–345.

Delia, J., Kline, S., & Burleson, B. (1979). The development of persuasive communication strategies in kindergartners through twelfth-graders. *Communication Monographs, 46,* 241–256.

Delia, J., & O'Keefe, B. (1979). Constructivism: The development of communication in children. In E. Wartella (Ed.), *Children communicating.* (pp. 157–186). Beverly Hills, CA: Sage.

Dore, J. (1983). Feeling, form and intention in the baby's transition to language. In R. Golinkoff (Ed.), *The transition from prelinguistic to linguistic communication.* Hillsdale, NJ: Lawrence Erlbaum.

Eisenberg, A., & Garvey, C. (1981). Children's use of verbal strategies in resolving conflicts. *Discourse Processes, 4,* 149–170.

Ervin-Tripp, S. (1977). Wait for me, roller-skate. In S. Ervin-Tripp & C. Mitchell-Kernan, *Child discourse.* (pp. 165–188). New York: Academic Press.

Flavell, J. (1981a). Cognitive monitoring. In W. P. Dickson (Ed.), *Children's oral communication skills.* New York: Academic Press.

Flavell, J. (1981b). Monitoring social cognitive enterprises: Something else that may develop in the area of social cognition. In J. Flavell & L. Ross (Eds.), *Social cognitive development.* (pp. 272–287) Cambridge, England: Cambridge University Press.

Forbes, D., & Lubin, D. (1981). *The development of applied strategies in children's social behavior.* Paper presented at the Society for Research and Child Development, Boston.

Gelman, R., & Spelke, E. (1981). The development of thoughts about animate and inanimate objects: Implications for research on social cognition. In J. Flavell & L. Ross (Eds.), *Social cognitive development.* (pp. 43–66) Cambridge, England: Cambridge University Press.

Goodwin, M. (1982). Processes of dispute management among urban Blacks. *American Ethnologist, 9,* 76–96.

Gottman, J. (1986). The world of coordinate play: Same- and cross-sex friendship in young children. In J. Gottman & J. Parker (Eds.) *Conversations of friends.* Cambridge, England: Cambridge University Press.

Gottman, J., & Parker, J. (1986). *Conversations of friends.* Cambridge, England: Cambridge University Press.

Gumperz, J., & Herasimchuk, E. (1973). Conversational analysis of social meaning. In R. Shuy (Ed.), *Sociolinguistics: Current trends and prospects.* Georgetown: GURT.

Haslett, B. (1983a). Communicative functions and strategies in children's conversations. *Human Communication Research, 9,* 115–124.

Haslett, B. (1983b). Preschoolers' communicative strategies in gaining compliance from peers: A developmental study. *Quarterly Journal of Speech, 69,* 84–99.

Haslett, B. (1984). Communicative development: The state of the art. In R. Bostrom (Ed.), *Communication Yearbook, vol. 8.* (pp. 198–267). Beverly Hills, CA: Sage.

Haslett, B., & Alexander, A. (1988). Acquiring communication skills. In R. Hawkins, J. Wiemann, & S. Pingree (Eds.), *Advancing communication science: Merging mass and interpersonal processes* (pp. 224–252). Beverly Hills, CA: Sage.

Higgins, E. (1981). Role taking and social judgment: Alternative developmental perspectives and processes. In J. Flavell & L. Ross (Eds.), *Social cognitive development.* Cambridge, England: Cambridge University Press.

Izard, C. (1986). Infant's development of emotional expression [Public lecture]. University of Delaware.

Kline, S. (n.d.). Developing rhetorical skill. Unpublished paper, University of Washington, Seattle.

Liss, M. (1983). *Social and cognitive skills.* New York: Academic Press.

Lloyd, P., & Beveridge, M. (1981). *Information and meaning in child communication.* London: Academic Press.

Maynard, D. (1985). How children start arguments. *Language in Society, 14,* 1–30.

Maynard, D. (1986). The development of argumentative skills among children. In *Sociological Studies of Child Development, 1,* 233–258.

Mitchell-Kernan, C., & Kernan, K. (1977). Pragmatics of directive choice among children. In S. Ervin-Tripp & C. Mitchell-Kernan (Eds.), *Child discourse.* (pp. 189–208). New York: Academic Press.

Nelson, K. (1981). Social cognition in a script framework. In J. Flavell & L. Ross (Eds.), *Social cognitive development* (pp. 97–118). Cambridge, England: Cambridge University Press.

Nelson, K. (1986). *Event knowledge.* Hillsdale, NJ: Lawrence Erlbaum.

O'Keefe, B., & Benoit, P. (1984). Children's arguments. In J.Cox & C. Willard (Eds.), *Advances in argumentation theory and research.* Carbondale: Southern Illinois University Press.

O'Keefe, B., & Delia, J. (1979). Construct comprehensiveness and cognitive complexity as predictors of the number and strategic adaptation of arguments and appeals in a persuasive message. *Communication Monographs, 46,* 221–240.

O'Keefe, B., & Delia, J. (1982). Impression formation and message production. In M. E. Roloff & C. Berger (Eds.), *Social cognition and communication.* (pp. 41–85). Beverly Hills, CA: Sage.

O'Keefe, B., & Delia, J. (1986). Psychological and interactional dimensions of communicative development. In H. Giles & R. St. Clair (Eds.), *Advances in language, communication, and social psychology.* London: Lawrence Erlbaum.

Olson, D., & Hilyard, A. (1981). Assent and compliance in children's language. In W. P. Dickson (Ed.),

Children's Oral Communication Skills. New York: Academic Press.

Pingree, S. (1983). Children's cognitive processes in constructing social reality. *Journalism Quarterly, 60,* 415–422.

Reich, R. (1986). *Language development.* New York: Prentice-Hall.

Rice, M., & Wartella, E. (1981). Television as a medium of communication: Implications for how to regard the child viewer. *Journal of Broadcasting, 26,* 365–372.

Robinson, E.J., & Robinson, W.P. (1977). Development in the understanding of causes of success and failure in verbal communication. *Cognition, 5,* 363–378.

Robinson, E.J., & Robinson, W.P. (1978a). Explanations of communication failure and ability to give bad messages. *British Journal of Social and Clinical Psychology, 17,* 219–225.

Robinson, E.J., & Robinson, W.P. (1978b). Development of understanding about communication: Message inadequacy and its role in causing communication failure. *Genetic Psychological Monographs, 98,* 233–279.

Ross, L. (1981). The "intuitive scientist" formulation and its developmental implications. In J. Flavell & L. Ross (Eds.), *Social cognitive development* (pp. 1–42). Cambridge, England: Cambridge University Press.

Scarlett, H., Press, A., & Crockett, W. (1971). Children's descriptions of peers: A Wernerian developmental analysis. *Child Development, 42,* 439–453.

Schieffelin, B., & Ochs, E. (1986). *Language socialization across cultures.* Cambridge, England: Cambridge University Press.

Shotter, J. (1984). *Self-hood and social accountability.* Oxford: Blackwell.

Stern, D. (1977). *The first relationship.* Cambridge, MA: Harvard University Press.

Trevarthen, C. (1977). Descriptive analyses of infant communication behavior. In H. Schaffer (Ed.), *Studies in mother-infant interaction.* London: Academic Press.

Trevarthen, C. (1979a). Communication and co-operation in early infancy. A description of primary intersubjectivity. In M. Bullowa (Ed.), *Before speech: The beginnings of human communication.* London: Cambridge University Press.

Trevarthen, C. (1979b). Instincts for human understanding and for cultural co-operation: Their development in infancy. In M. von Cranach, K. Foppa, W. Lepenies, & D. Ploog (Eds.), *Human ethology.* Cambridge, England: Cambridge University Press.

Trevarthen, C. (1982). The primary motives for cooperative understanding. In G. Butterworth & P. Light (Eds.), *Social cognition* (pp. 77–109). Chicago: University of Chicago Press.

Watzlawick, P., Beavin, J., & Jackson, D. (1967). *Pragmatics of human communication: A study of interactional patterns, pathologies, and paradoxes.* New York: Norton.

Wells, G. (1985). *Language development in the pre-school years.* Cambridge, England: Cambridge University Press.

Wolf, D. (1982). Understanding others: A longitudinal case study of the concept of independent agency. In G. Forman (Ed.), *Action and thought* (pp. 297–328). New York: Academic Press.

Compliance-Gaining and Health Care

Michael H. Burgoon and Judee K. Burgoon
University of Arizona

C oncern for determining the most efficacious compliance-gaining strategies in the health care context predates the concerns of social psychologists (e.g., Marwell & Schmitt, 1967) and the spate of communication research efforts that are thoroughly reviewed and documented in this volume. Eraker, Kirscht, and Becker (1984) suggest that physicians traditionally have had to face several difficult questions, "the answers to which will depend largely on the magnitude of the problem; the ability of the physician to understand, detect, and enhance compliance; and on various ethical questions" (p. 258). Among the questions they claim to be of most importance to practicing physicians are: Should a physician actively encourage patient compliance with treatment? Can a physician successfully intervene to modify patients' behavior? and, Is the enhancement of compliance, often involving attempts to modify lifestyle, in the patient's best interests?

While those questions have interested medical professionals, different concerns have dominated the research interests of social scien-

Authors' Note: Portions of this research were supported by National Cancer Institute funds made available to Michael Burgoon.

161

tists. Such differences in locus of concern undoubtedly are explained by the overwhelming amount of data in the social science research literature supporting claims that communication strategies can be used successfully to gain compliance and alter lifestyles in a variety of contexts. Moreover, most social scientists view compliance-gaining strategies aimed at treating specific problems, promoting disease prevention and control, and modifying lifestyles to promote wellness as prosocial outcomes that raise few, if any, ethical concerns. Thus, social science research in the health care context has focused on two separate but related areas of inquiry. First, research efforts have attempted to determine systematically what kinds of compliance-gaining strategies are used by medical professionals. This message-production orientation provides the conceptual framework for this chapter as well as this entire volume. A second line of inquiry has explored the relationship between the use of specific compliance-gaining message strategies and important outcome variables such as compliance (defined as adherence to suggested changes or treatment regimen), patient satisfaction with the quality of health care, and, probably most important, patient health status.

This chapter will provide an overview of research on verbal and nonverbal strategies used in the clinical context. An examination of verbal strategies aimed at securing compliance will provide the starting point for such an effort. In addition, we will discuss nonverbal communication strategies, too often neglected by compliance-gaining strategy researchers. The conceptualization offered in this chapter divides those approaches into direct strategies aimed at securing compliance, and indirect strategies designed to foster interpersonal relationship management (e.g., enhancing actor/physician credibility; demonstrating actor authority, dominance, and expertise; and increasing physician-patient intimacy). While the scope of this review is primarily limited to message-production concerns, we will make some attempts to delineate some of the important effects of different strategy choices.

THE HEALTH CARE CONTEXT AND COMPLIANCE

Unique Properties of the Health Care Context

The medical context is characterized by unique attributes that are unlike those in other situations in which an actor purposefully selects strategies aimed at securing the compliance of an individual or group of individuals. Among the qualities of the medical setting that distinguish it from other communication contexts are the following: In most cases, targets (patients) enter into the transaction voluntarily and are free to choose whether or not to comply with the suggestions and directives of the actor/physician; patients enter into an economic contract with the physician in which they pay to receive compliance-gaining directives; compliance can almost always be viewed as benefiting the patient or significant others and is rarely viewed as a benefit to the actor/physician; significant differences usually exist in the perceived normative status and expertise of the actor/physician vis-à-vis the patient/target; well-defined expectations at a sociological level provide physicians with the freedom to use a variety of means to gain compliance; neither surveillance of noncompliance nor sanctions by the physician for nonadherence is standard; and the effects of noncompliance vary in severity from continued illness and/or discomfort to decreased quality of life or even death. All these attributes *should* combine to create a communication context in which expected and actual compliance is unusually high.

The Problem of Noncompliance

The realities are otherwise. Eraker, Kirscht, and Becker (1984) state that noncompliance may be the most significant problem facing medicine today. A vast amount of research has addressed this issue. Haynes, Taylor, and Sackett (1979), for example, published an annotated bibliography of 853 articles and 569 chapters on noncompliance with suggested preventative and therapeutic regimens. Reviews of this and other research on patient compliance rates (Becker & Maiman, 1980; 1982; Blackwell, 1973; Christensen, 1978; Cohen, 1979; Eraker, Kirscht & Becker, 1984; Kirscht & Rosenstock, 1979; Ley, 1982; Marston, 1970; Zisook & Gammon, 1981) agree that noncompliance presents a serious problem to medical practitioners. As a baseline illustration of patient behavior, noncompliance ranges from 46–62 percent with drug regimens (Robbins, 1980), 50 percent with medical appointment keeping (Haynes, Taylor & Sackett, 1979), and 4–92 percent with health-promotion acts (Marston, 1970). Even with life-threatening diseases like cancer, compliance rates are alarmingly low. Klopovich and Trueworthy (1985) reported a 59 percent noncompliance rate with oral chemotherapy treatment. Thus, the available evidence suggests that noncompliance is prevalent in both chronic and acute illness situations. It is not related, as one might intuitively expect, to the severity of the disease, but is evident in all kinds of treatment, prevention, and disease control situations.

Yet physicians are often oblivious to the problem, consistently overestimating patient compliance. Because individual patients do not usually reveal noncompliant acts, physicians tend to be unaware of the magnitude of the problem in their individual practices (Davis, 1966). Consequently, they are actually no better at predicting patients' compliance than chance alone (Norell, 1981; Roth & Caron, 1978; Rothert, 1982), and persist in expecting that compliance will be quite high.

Several researchers have mounted efforts to determine patient characteristics and/or structural characteristics of the health care delivery system that might explain and predict patient nonadherence to physicians's directives. Demographic and/or personality variables have not been consistent predictors of noncompliance (Becker, 1979; Davis, 1968; Ley, 1976; Zisook & Gammon, 1981). Lane (1983) is among those who point out that no single patient sociodemographic or personality variable has been found to consistently influence compliance. Moreover, structural characteristics of the clinical situation (such as private physician, HMO, or clinic) have not been significant predictors of adherence rates.

A Communication Focus on Compliance in the Health Care Context

Given the lack of success in isolating medical conditions, patient attributes, or structural factors in health care systems as reliable and valid predictors of compliance rates, attention has turned to the nature of the communication between physicians and patients. However, the research dealing with the relationship between communication and compliance in the medical context is confusing and often confounded with contradictory findings and varying descriptions of what occurs in clinical communication transactions. Moreover, the health communication literature is filled with unsupported prescriptions that are seemingly based more on ideological considerations than on any evidential base.

Lane (1983) claims that "most published research in communication and compliance has dealt with three basic strategies that doctors use to facilitate adherence: (a) the communication of information, (b) the communication of positive affect, and (c) the communication of fear and/or threat" (p. 777). While these three generic strategies might provide a beginning point for examining compliance-gaining strategies in the medical context, research is available that provides a more micro-level analysis of verbal and nonverbal compliance-gaining message strategies in use in the health care context. That research will be dealt with in the remainder of this chapter.

VERBAL COMPLIANCE-GAINING STRATEGIES

Physicians' Selection of Verbal Compliance-Gaining Strategies

Much of the research on message production by physicians in clinical encounters has been flawed by methodological errors, biased and nonrepresentative sampling (including overreliance on medical students as subjects), and arguments over appropriate methods of data collection. Thus, conclusions from much of this research must be viewed with caution.

M. Burgoon, Parrott, Burgoon, Birk, Pfau, & Coker (in press–a) attempted to remedy some of the problems associated with research on physicians' selection of compliance-gaining strategies by advancing a theory-based propositional framework suggesting under what clinical conditions specific kinds of strategies would be used by practicing primary care physicians. Building on Dillard and M. Burgoon's (1985) contention that underlying compliance-gaining behavior is a dimension akin to instrumental verbal aggression, M. Burgoon et al. (in press–a) developed a continuum of physician communication strategies ranging from unaggressive to very aggressive compliance-gaining attempts. They derived these strategies from a modified Marwell and Schmitt (1967) typology. Guided by earlier empirical efforts (M. Burgoon, Dillard, & Doran, 1984), they then categorized the strategies into three groups, each representing a different degree of verbal aggressiveness (aggressive, moderately aggressive, unaggressive). They recast the extant medical research and theorizing in terms of verbal aggressiveness, and advanced the following propositions about physicians' message production.

> *Proposition 1*: Physicians report that they use moderately aggressive strategies (such as expertise and direction-giving) to gain patient compliance *more* than other types of available verbal compliance-gaining strategies.

> *Proposition 2*: As patients' medical problems increase in severity, primary care physicians report that they become more verbally aggressive in attempts to gain patients' compliance.

> *Proposition 3*: Physicians use more verbally aggressive communication strategies in situations in which patients have not complied with previous recommendations or treatment regimens.

Proposition 4: Severity of illness and past noncompliance interact, so physicians use the most verbally aggressive strategies in clinical situations in which the patient has a severe medical problem and a past history of noncompliance.

Proposition 5: Physicians are more verbally aggressive with patients they have known for less time and are less verbally aggressive with patients they have known for longer periods of time.

To test these propositions, primary care physicians were provided with a description of seventeen compliance-gaining strategies and asked to estimate how likely they would be to use each one, given information about the seriousness of a hypothetical patient's illness and the patient's prior compliance. The first proposition, which was based upon self-reports, observational analysis of clinical encounters, and a number of other methodological techniques, suggests that differential expert power between the physician/actor and the patient/target prompts the use of expert power in the form of simple direction giving and appeals to the authority, knowledge, and expertise of the attending physician. Table 9 provides rather unambiguous support for Proposition 1. Physicians tend to eschew threatening and/or antisocial strategies and more prosocial reinforcing strategies, and instead opt for expertise strategies to gain compliance.

The second proposition is based upon the notion that personal benefits are associated with compliance or noncompliance (Boster & Stiff, 1984; Cody & McLaughlin, 1980; Dillard & M. Burgoon, 1985). Simply stated, the greater the perception that compliance will be in the patient's own best interest, the greater the number of verbal strategies, including highly aggressive communication acts, that physicians will use to gain compliance. Proposition 3 is based upon the argument advanced by Dillard and M. Burgoon (1985) that, other things being equal, greater anticipated resistance should produce greater effort and selection of more verbally aggressive strategies (see also Lim, 1988). Thus, a history of past noncompliance when known by the physician should increase the probability of physicians using more aggressive language in the clinical context. The interaction effect posited in the fourth proposition is based upon the reasoning leading to Propositions 2 and 3. The results, shown in Table 10, offer strong empirical support for Propositions 1 through 4.

The fifth proposition is based on a logic less intuitively obvious than those advanced above. M. Burgoon et al. reasoned that as physicians gained more interpersonal information on a patient, they would respond by tailoring their messages to that individual, would

Table 9   Mean Likelihood of Use Estimates for the
Compliance-Gaining Strategies

Strategies	Mean Likelihood
Expertise Positive	79.13
Expertise Negative	74.15
Self-Feeling Positive	72.75
Liking	71.60
Altercasting Positive	39.20
Esteem Positive	34.92
Self-Feeling Negative	31.73
Pre-Giving	19.78
Threat	19.05
Promise	18.26
Esteem Negative	16.23
Debt	11.83
Altruism	11.81
Aversive Stimulation	11.66
Altercasting Negative	10.50
Moral Appeal Positive	9.63
Moral Appeal Negative	5.37

Note: Scale range = 0% (Not Used) to 100% (Certain to Use).

be able to avoid the more verbally aggressive strategies, and would use more positive strategies in their compliance-gaining attempts with a long-term patient. Physicians did use more positive (unaggressive strategies) as the length of the relationship with the patient increased, but expertise strategies were still the predominant form of compliance-gaining attempts regardless of the length of relationship with the patient.

Table 10   Likelihood of Verbal Aggression by Physician Based on Illness Severity and Time of Visit

Visit	Illness Severity		
	Low	Moderate	Severe
Initial	14.58	20.65	22.50
Subsequent (following noncompliance)	15.50	25.06	45.15

Note: Scale range = 0% to 100% probability of use.

The most surprising finding in this research effort was how seldom physicians report using positive or reinforcing strategies in the medical context. As medicine evolves from a traditional focus on curative regimens to disease prevention and control, providers may need to expand their repertoire to be more attentive to a patient's performance of desired behaviors. Although beyond the scope of this chapter, an abundance of research on learning theory points to the importance of contingent reinforcement to obtain and maintain socially important behaviors. Given the relative dearth of such positive compliance-gaining strategies in the practice of medicine, lower than desirable compliance rates are more easily understandable.

Patients' Perceptions of Compliance-Gaining Strategy Use by Physicians

In a follow-up survey research project, M. Burgoon, Parrott, Burgoon, Coker, Pfau, & Birk (in press–b) explored physicians' verbal compliance-gaining strategy selection as reported by their patients. There was a great deal of similarity in detail between patients' reports of compliance-gaining strategies used by physicians and the research findings reported above. Patients also report that health care providers rely on expertise strategies as their primary means of gaining compliance. Consistent with other investigations, it appears that patients perceive that physicians exert minimal effort to motivate or persuade them to comply with prescribed treatment regimens or suggested alterations in lifestyles. Moreover, patients do not perceive that physicians become more aggressive when they (the patients) have been noncompliant, even when the medical condition being treated is potentially severe. This is one departure from the self-report data provided by physicians.

A number of other issues addressed in this field research allowed propositional conclusions to be formulated that describe patients' perceptions.

Proposition 6: No significant relationships exist among patient characteristics, structural variables in the health care delivery system, and perceived physician compliance-gaining message strategy selection.

Proposition 7: Patients report that physicians are actually *less* verbally aggressive in clinical encounters in which patients have been noncompliant.

Proposition 8: Severity of illness is unrelated to increased use of verbally aggressive communication strategies by physicians.

Proposition 9: Altruism and negative esteem appear to be effective in increasing compliance, even though neither strategy is used often by physicians.

Proposition 10: In general, it appears that in most clinical encounters physicians can obtain more compliance by relying less on simple direction giving and expertise strategies and more on use of aggressive verbal strategies.

Proposition 11: Use of a greater number of unaggressive compliance-gaining strategies by physicians enhances patient satisfaction; use of aggressive communication, however, does not negatively impact satisfaction with the quality of health care received.

Propositions 10 and 11 run counter to many prevailing beliefs and much of the prescriptive injunctions offered by those interested in health communication. The empirical findings of M. Burgoon et al. (in press–b) have not been well received by those who believe that physicians must make every attempt to be warm and friendly in all aspects of the clinical encounter. Although the next section will deal with aspects of relational management and nonverbal communication in medical communication and will offer conclusions about how compliance might be enhanced by specific direct and indirect strategies to enhance intimacy, liking, and so forth, it is apparent from this research that doctors can combine such relational management strategies with more aggressive verbal communication strategies that will increase the likelihood of subsequent compliance, and will not significantly decrease levels of patient satisfaction. Finding the optimal combination of all available compliance-gaining strategies, direct and indirect and verbal and nonverbal, is the challenge facing people interested in the medical context.

Actor-Observer Differences in Perceptions of Compliance-Gaining Strategy Selection

M. Burgoon, Parrott, and Facciola (1988) report some interesting findings that highlight potential differences in perceptions of actors (oncologists) and observers (oncology nurses) in one medical context. Since the subspecialty of oncology involves the treatment of people with potentially severe life-threatening problems, M. Burgoon et al.

expected that clinical encounters between oncologists and their patients might provide instances of increased-reported usage of more verbally aggressive compliance-gaining strategies than that reported by primary care physicians. However, oncologists reported almost identical compliance-gaining strategy selection patterns as did the primary care physicians on the use of expertise and other moderately aggressive to unaggressive communication strategies. Contrary to expectations, oncologists reported even less use of aggressive compliance-gaining tactics than did the sample of primary care physicians. Oncology nurses, who can be more appropriately characterized as observers rather than actors or targets in such compliance-gaining attempts, differed significantly from the cancer specialists in their assessment of the frequency of aggressive compliance-gaining message use in clinical treatment and prevention situations. Specifically, the oncology nurses reported that physicians tend to be significantly more likely to use the most aggressive strategies (e.g., threat, debt, moral appeal, negative altercasting, and negative esteem) than the oncologists themselves reported.

The question of whose perceptions are more accurate within this context is an interesting twist on past communication research that has examined actor-observer differences. The issue of accuracy does not appear to be related to dispositional or situational influences. Rather, it is possible that such specialists are relatively poor self-monitors of their own behaviors and/or are unaware or unwilling to admit that they must abandon "ideal types" of communication to gain compliance of people who are gravely ill. The nature of this particular specialty may induce specialists to be especially immune to notions that they engage or should engage in persuasion or other motivational techniques to gain compliance of people who are so obviously receiving self-benefit from this specialized medical treatment. The addition of this observer dimension to the previously reported research gives additional insight into the problems of dealing with interpretations of actors, targets, and observers in this complex communication situation.

The Effects of Violations of Expectations in Health Communication

Birk and M. Burgoon (1989) sought to apply the explanatory calculus of *expectancy theory* (M. Burgoon & Miller, 1985; M. Burgoon, 1989) in an experimental study of compliance-gaining strategy use in the medical context. They reasoned that regardless of whether expectations are a function of cultural norms, social roles, or exposure to the enacted behaviors of male and female physicians, patients expect female physicians to be unaggressive, caring, friendly, and socially supportive while at the same time expecting male physicians to use aggressive verbal strategies. The most interesting, albeit complex and somewhat counterintuitive, proposition advanced in this research follows.

> *Proposition 12*: There is interaction between physician gender and efficacy of compliance-gaining message strategies such that male physicians who utilize less aggressive verbal strategies and male physicians who use more aggressive verbal strategies are more persuasive than male physicians who use moderately aggressive strategies, and there is a linear trend such that female physicians who use less aggressive verbal strategies are more persuasive than females who utilize increasingly aggressive verbal strategies.

This proposition requires a detailed explanation. It was reasoned that even though female physicians occupy a position of high credibility in this society, they still have a restricted range of acceptable communication behaviors. Any deviation from the use of unaggressive strategies was posited to decrease their persuasiveness with patients. Given all of the data that suggest that male physicians rely almost exclusively on expertise and authority appeals (moderately aggressive communication strategies), however, the use of more aggressive strategies such as threat and moral appeals might signal more personal concern on the part of the male physician and might be seen as a positive violation of expectations, leading to enhanced levels of compliance. Conversely, male physicians who adopt unaggressive and pro-social communication strategies deviate from the more standard neutral posture now enacted by most male physicians. Since such deviations should have unequivocally positive relational meaning in this society, the use of unaggressive strategies by males should also be a positive violation of expectations and result in higher compliance rates. In summary, male physicians occupy a position in this society in which they have a great deal of freedom in their selection of compliance-gaining strategies; female physicians do not have the same degree of freedom of expression, even in their area of expertise.

Data from 561 randomly sampled adults, who participated in several phases of survey and experimental research in which female or male physicians used aggressive, moderately aggressive, or unaggressive compliance-gaining strategies, provide compelling evidence that female physicians are expected to use unaggressive strategies. By contrast, male physicians have significantly more freedom to be verbally aggressive in the clinical encounter. Moreover, the specific relationship posited in Proposition 12 received clear support from one experimental manipulation (see Table 11). Thus, expectations about appropriate compliance-gaining strategies use by physicians need to be incorporated into message-production research (Birk & M. Burgoon, 1989).

NONVERBAL STRATEGIES FOR GAINING COMPLIANCE

Beyond verbal strategies, physicians have at their disposal a host of nonverbal behaviors, ranging from body movements, facial and eye behavior, gestures, vocal patterns, and touch, to manipulation of distance, time, appearance, and artifacts, that may be used to achieve or undermine patient compliance. Few studies have addressed how nonverbal behaviors are used to bring about compliance in health care contexts. Instead, most research has focused on how nonverbal behaviors achieve such communication outcomes as doctor-patient rapport and satisfaction. Nevertheless, such research is potentially relevant to compliance if greater rapport, satisfaction, and so forth serve as indirect routes to greater compliance. Hence, it becomes useful to distinguish between direct and indirect nonverbal strategies and tactics.

J. K. Burgoon, Buller, and Woodall (1989) have attempted to delineate global nonverbal strategies that may be employed to achieve social influence. Seven of their categories appear to be applicable to the health care context and will serve as our framework for analyzing nonverbal compliance attempts. The first three focus on relatively *direct strategies*. These are strategies that should, by themselves, promote compliance by facilitating information transfer, communicating what is expected, reinforcing desired behaviors, extinguishing undesired behaviors, or reducing resistance to change. The remaining four cat-

Table 11   Likelihood of Compliance by Sex and Aggressiveness of Physician

Sex of Physician	Strategy Aggressiveness		
	Low	Moderate	High
Male	3.40	2.78	3.27
Female	3.32	3.25	2.99

Note: Scale range = 1 (noncompliance) to 5 (likely compliance).

egories are more *indirect strategies* in that they rely on establishing a positive interpersonal relationship between physician and patient, promoting the credibility and attractiveness of the physician, or increasing patient satisfaction, with these relational outcomes serving as pathways to greater patient compliance (cf., Edgar & Fitzpatrick, this volume).

Reinforcement, Reward, and Punishment

Just as physicians may verbally identify the rewarding or aversive consequences of patients' behavior, so may they use nonverbal cues to signal their approval or disapproval of various courses of action. The presentation of nonverbal approval cues after a patient has complied with a given regimen or set of instructions should serve as a *positive reinforcer*, increasing the probability that the desired behavior will recur. Presentation of disapproval cues following noncompliance should act either as a *negative reinforcer*, motivating the patient to increase the desired behavior so as to remove the aversive negative feedback from the physician, or as a *punishment* that extinguishes undesired behavior.

No research of which we are aware has examined how physicians actually enact nonverbal rewards and punishments. Research in other arenas, however, indicates that all the following are likely to signal approval: closer physical proximity, touch, forward lean, direct body and facial orientation toward the other, head nods, smiles, pleasant facial expressions, increased gaze, a "warm" voice, and vocal reinforcers such as "uh-huh." These cues all fall under the heading of *immediacy behaviors*, which are those kinesic, proxemic, haptic, and vocalic cues that create high sensory involvement and signal psychological closeness or distance between interactants. Behaviors such as those listed above signal approach and positive regard; their opposites, referred to as *nonimmediacy behaviors*, signal avoidance and dislike. (Some scholars prefer to strip the evaluative component from immediacy, leaving it to reference only an approach-avoidance dimension; we have included it here because approach is so closely linked to liking and avoidance, as well as to negative effect.)

Behaviors most likely to be aversive are excessive distance, nonimmediacy, frowns, "cold" or harsh voices, silences, and threatening behaviors such as an angry voice, a glare, or a prolonged stare (J. K. Burgoon et al., 1989; Lane, 1983). These behaviors are more likely to be effective when they are congruent with one another and with the concurrent verbal message (Greene, 1977; Edinger & Patterson, 1983).

It should be noted that, while positive reinforcement tends to be favored as a predictably successful means of altering behavior, negative reinforcement and punishment can also be effective. We have already suggested that use of moderate to highly aggressive verbal strategies may sometimes be warranted. The case may likewise be true for aversive nonverbal cues. Research is needed to determine whether combinations of verbally aggressive and nonverbally punitive behaviors are efficacious and under what circumstances. Equally important to determine is whether combining verbal aggressiveness with "warm" and "friendly" nonverbal cues results in the verbal message losing its effectiveness. Speculatively, the ideal combination may be moderate verbal aggressiveness (with its implicit show of concern) and high nonverbal conversational involvement with restrained displays of positive affect (e.g., smiling and vocal warmth). Conversational involvement is a multi-dimensional construct that includes not only immediacy but also high facial, gestural, and vocal expressiveness; high attentiveness; smooth conversational management; and the absence of anxiety indicators. Greater conversational involvement would be a way to demonstrate a physician's concern for the patient's well-being, thus placing the verbal aggressiveness in an appropriate context. For the moment, we feel justified in advancing the following propositions:

> *Proposition 13:* Physicians' use of nonverbal immediacy behaviors may serve as positive reinforcers of patient behavioral compliance.

> *Proposition 14:* Physicians' use of nonimmediacy behaviors and nonverbal threat cues may increase desirable patient behaviors by serving as negative reinforcers and may lead to discontinuance of undesirable behaviors by serving as punishments.

At a more microscopic level, a physician can also use nonverbal cues to reinforce the patient's comprehension. It is often assumed that telling patients what they need to know will translate into doing what needs to be done. To the extent that physicians rely on communicating relevant information as a primary means of securing patient cooperation (Lane, 1983), nonverbal cues become increasingly critical to successful information exchange. Language is thought to be processed in chunks called phonemic clauses. Three vocal cues—pitch, rhythm, and loudness—together delineate phonemic clauses (Boomer, 1978). Successful patient comprehension of information and instructions therefore depends on physicians using appropriate intonation, stress, and pause patterns when conveying such information and recommendations to patients. Certain types of gestures, particularly rhythmic and imagistic illustrator gestures that accompany the verbal stream, also aid not only patient decoding of complex verbal information, but also physician encoding of it (see J. K. Burgoon et al., 1989, for a review of this literature). Emblematic behaviors—such as head nods that serve as replies or that affirm a patient's understanding of instructions—likewise aid information transfer (Lane, 1983). Finally, immediacy behaviors and relaxation also play a part. Larsen and Smith (1981) found that patients had greater understanding of their medical condition and the physician's instructions when the physician was more immediate, especially through forward lean, direct body orientation, and the absence of backward lean. The physician's use of touch was associated with lower understanding, however, possibly because it was unexpected in these first-time visits. Understanding was also higher when *patients* used less touch (something one would not expect patients to do anyway), were less direct in their body orientation, and had less hand relaxation (the latter two cues probably being indicative of greater concentration). These combined findings warrant the following proposition:

> *Proposition 15:* Patient comprehension, which is a precursor to compliance, is enhanced when physicians use expressive vocalic patterns, illustrator and emblem gestures, and nonverbal immediacy behaviors.

Communicating Expectancies

Physicians and patients alike enter their encounters with expectations of how the other should and will behave. Lane (1982) contends that the best way for physicians to have their expectancies fulfilled is to communicate about them. Although physicians certainly can discuss their expectations for patients verbally, an extensive body of literature reveals that expectancies are also frequently expressed nonverbally, often within the first thirty seconds of interaction. Moreover, such nonverbal signals often result in *self-fulfilling prophecies*, that is, they produce behaviors that confirm the expectancy (Rosenthal, 1976, 1985; Rosenthal & Rubin, 1978; Snyder, 1984; Snyder & Swann, 1978).

In a series of meta-analyses, Harris and Rosenthal (1985) identified those nonverbal behaviors that are most likely to be used to signal expectancies. Those behaviors enacted by expecters (physicians) that are pertinent to physician-patient interactions include displaying "warm" rather than "cold" behaviors (e.g., warmer vocal tones), maintaining closer physical distances, engaging in longer and more frequent interactions, engaging in more eye contact, smiling more, and using more nonverbal reinforcers such as head nods and facial expressions of happiness and interest. Other nonverbal behaviors that have been found to influence outcomes, but not necessarily to be enacted by expecters, include longer response latencies (giving the other person more time to respond to questions), greater loudness, faster speech rate, and more gesturing. It should be apparent that these cues parallel those that qualify as nonverbal immediacy cues, while adding elements of greater involvement and dynamism. These findings form the basis of another proposition.

> *Proposition 16:* Physicians may signal their expectancies and attain confirmation of those expectancies by exhibiting greater conversational involvement, particularly greater immediacy, greater expressiveness, and greater altercentrism (attentiveness toward the other).

Research on the nonverbal communication patterns that physicians exhibit (Street & Buller, 1987) reveals that they commit some but not all of these behaviors. They engage in more vocal backchannels (such as "uh huh" and "I see") and social touch than do patients, both of which may be reinforcing behaviors, but they also talk far longer than patients, which may create an impression of egocentrism rather than altercentrism.

Violating Expectancies

Although communicating one's expectancies can be a very effective means of achieving influence, an alternative is to violate expectations. Nonverbal expectancy violations theory (J. K. Burgoon, 1978; J. K. Burgoon & Hale, 1988) posits that communicators hold expectations about the nonverbal behavior of others, expectations that are grounded in social norms and in any knowledge of the partner's unique communication style. Significant deviations from these expectancies are posited to prompt an alertness and orienting response that shifts greater attention to the communicator and the violative behavior. This makes communicator characteristics more salient and triggers a two-stage interpretation-evaluation process of the violation behavior. The degree to which the communicator is favorably or unfavorably regarded, labeled communicator-reward valence, is predicted to mediate the interpretation-evaluation process such that violations frequently produce more desirable communication consequences than norm-conformity for high reward communicators.

The relevance for physicians should be clear. Given their expertise, their high social status relative to most patients, their control of essential information, and their ability to dispense tangible and intangible rewards (e.g., free medicines and approval), physicians normally should qualify as high reward communicators. Consequently, it may behoove them to consider violating rather than adhering to nonverbal norms. No research has tested this hypothesis in a medical context, but research in other arenas may be generalizable. If so, physicians may be well advised to adopt very close or very far conversational distances, to use high amounts of gaze, to increase conversational involvement and immediacy, and to touch their patients during the conversational portion of an examination (but only if they are well acquainted) (see J. K. Burgoon & Hale, 1988; J. K. Burgoon & Walther, 1989).

Proposition 17: Physicians may gain greater compliance by violating some nonverbal norms than by adhering to them.

Creating an Intimate Relationship

As already noted, prevailing sentiment holds that physicians will gain greater compliance if they develop a positive, "intimate" interpersonal relationship with their patients. The ingredients of an intimate relationship are affection, involvement, trust, familiarity or depth (i.e., a nonsuperficial relationship), receptivity or rapport, and possibly perceived similarity (J. K. Burgoon & Hale, 1984). In physician-patient relationships, it is far less likely that the parties will openly discuss the nature of their interpersonal relationship and far more likely that they will rely on nonverbal signals to define and maintain it. Thus, to the extent that interpersonal rapport, trust, and liking are precursors to compliance, nonverbal communication can play a significant role in its facilitation.

One indication that this is true is that patient satisfaction is frequently associated, albeit sometimes weakly, with compliance (J. K. Burgoon, Pfau, Parrott, Birk, Coker, & Burgoon, 1987; Korsch & Aley, 1973; Korsch & Negrete, 1972). Of course, there is some evidence that satisfied patients are not necessarily compliant patients, and unhappy patients may comply despite their dissatisfaction (Speedling & Rose, 1985), but common sense instructs that dissatisfaction is an avoidable inhibitor to seeking care and following medical advice.

Some research has examined the relational messages physicians are perceived to send their patients, without specific identification of the nonverbal or verbal cues responsible for those messages. Ley (1977), Geerston, Gray, and Ward (1973), and Linimon, Manaster, and Waddell (1982) found that patients who described their physician's communication style as friendly, personal, or informal complied more than those who described their physician as "businesslike." Patients also prefer and are more satisfied with physicians who treat them in a friendly, warm, caring, and sympathetic manner (Doyle & Ware, 1977; Eisenberg, 1977; Falvo & Smith, 1983; R. H. Fletcher et al., 1983; Korsch, Gozzi, & Francis, 1968; Korsch & Negrete, 1972; Jaspers, King, & Pendleton, 1983; Smith & Occhipinti, 1984).

In a comprehensive study of the multiple relational messages physicians may send their patients, J. K. Burgoon et al. (1987) found that patients of primary care physicians reported greater compliance with physicians who expressed greater similarity to patients; they were also more satisfied with those physicians who communicated greater receptivity, immediacy/affection, composure, similarity, formality, and nondominance. These findings imply that relational messages conveying greater similarity and intimacy, less dominance, and, at most, moderate formality are probably preferable if the objective is to achieve both a satisfying interpersonal relationship and compliance. These conclusions are corroborated by Street and Buller (1987), who found that patient satisfaction was positively related to use of an affiliative nonverbal style and inversely related to use of a dominant one.

Similarity messages are likely to be conveyed nonverbally through less formal or role-identified attire (e.g., the absence of the white coat and stethoscope), postural mirroring (in which one person's trunk and limb positions are mirror images of the other's), and speech convergence (i.e., use of speaking tempo, loudness, pause patterns, and accent that match or approximate the partner's). The remaining intimacy, composure, and formality messages are most likely communicated via immediacy and positive-affect cues, vocal and kinesic relaxation, and minimization of off-task behaviors. Nondominance is expressed through the absence of such behaviors as interruptions, lengthy speaking turns, rapid speaking tempo, minimal pausing, and indirect body orientation (Street & Buller, 1987).

Interestingly, the investigation by J. K. Burgoon et al. (1987) also discovered that various verbal compliance strategies carry relational connotations. Greater use of altruism, positive moral appeals, and positive self-feeling, and less use of positive expertise conveyed greater receptivity and composure. Low use of debt strategies also conveyed receptivity and composure, as well as more immediacy. Greater use of negative self-feeling and negative altercasting conveyed more dominance. Finally, greater use of promise, negative expertise, liking, moral appeals (positive or negative), and negative altercasting all connoted greater formality. Thus, compliance strategies have implications for the definition of the relationship between doctor and patient, which in turn may influence how successful the compliance-gaining strategies are, creating a nonrecursive relationship (Matthews & Hingson, 1977).

One other investigation that examined multiple relational message themes was that which compared perceptions of oncologists with those of oncology nurses (M. Burgoon et al., 1988). Nurses rated oncologists as more formal and dominant and less similar, trustworthy, immediate, and composed with patients than the physicians perceived themselves to be. Moreover, estimated compliance was higher among patients whose physicians expressed greater similarity, composure, trust, immediacy, and informality. These findings imply that physicians may recognize what the ideal relational communication with patients should be but may be practicing it less than they think, to the detriment of patient compliance.

The foregoing studies suggest the following relationship between compliance and relational communication, be it verbal or nonverbal:

Proposition 18: Physicians may achieve compliance indirectly by sending patients relational messages of similarity, intimacy, nondominance, and moderate formality.

Fairly extensive research has explored what specific nonverbal cues are responsible for creating rapport, trust, and satisfaction in the clinical context. These studies again confirm the benefits of nonverbal immediacy, affection, similarity, and composure. Doctors who adopt closer distances with their patients, face them more directly, lean forward, nod frequently, use more touch, gaze more toward their patients but engage in less mutual gaze, use a friendly vocal tone, adopt symmetrical, open arm positions, and sit with hands resting in their laps are seen as warmer and more empathic (Harrigan, Oxman, & Rosenthal, 1985; Harrigan & Rosenthal, 1983, 1986; Parrott & LePoire, 1987; Smith-Hanen, 1977).

Complete relaxation and nonarousal, however, do not seem to be the most desirable behaviors. A series of experiments demonstrated that more self-touching, rather than the absence of it, communicates greater warmth and expressiveness (Harrigan, 1985; Harrigan, Kues, & Weber, 1986; Harrigan, Weber, & Kues, 1986). This may be partly because self-touch often accompanies difficulty in encoding or decoding speech and may be taken as a sign of intense concentration. It may also be partly due to some activity being preferable to displaying none (Harrigan & Rosenthal, 1986). Similarly, a nondominant, warm, but anxious voice is perceived more favorably (Blanck, Rosenthal, & Vannicelli, 1986); and greater anxiety expressed by physicians through the combined vocal and verbal channel results in more successful referrals of alcoholic patients, while greater vocal hostility has a negative relationship with referrals (Milmoe, Rosenthal, Blane, Chafetz,

& Wolf, 1967). These findings are consistent with the conclusion that "from the perspective of most patients, physician neutrality is undesirable and patients prefer emotional expression from their physicians" (DiMatteo, Linn, Chang, & Cope, 1985, p. 407). In fact, patients are inclined to terminate relationships with physicians who lack emotional expressivity (DiMatteo & DiNicola, 1982; Friedman, 1982; Kaestler et al., 1976; Maguire, 1981). The importance of expressivity is underscored by DiMatteo (1979; DiMatteo, Prince, & Hays, 1986), who reports that patients are more satisfied with physicians who are accurate nonverbal encoders of their emotional states.

The bulk of evidence provides a sound prescription for physicians who wish to achieve greater compliance via the indirect route of establishing a positive and satisfying interpersonal relationship.

> *Proposition 19:* Physicians communicate greater similarity, intimacy, nondominance, and concern by displaying more nonverbal immediacy behaviors (excluding high amounts of mutual gaze), more nonverbal similarity indicators (such as mirroring, speech convergence, and similar attire), moderate relaxation, and emotional expressivity.

Enhancing Credibility

Another indirect route to compliance is through increased credibility. J. K. Burgoon et al. (1989) distinguish authority, expertise, dominance, and status appeals from character, sociability, composure, and dynamism appeals. Although all of these facets of image contribute to whether a physician is regarded as believable, qualified, and trustworthy, this is a useful distinction in the medical context because the former appeals may be less necessary to stress than the latter. By the very nature of their position, physicians enter patient encounters with a high degree of legitimate status, power, and authority. In fact, the status differential between physician and patient may create a barrier to full disclosure of a patient's concerns and medical habits. Patients may be intimidated from expressing their ignorance, fears, or misunderstandings. Given that physicians already rely heavily on verbal expertise strategies, it may behoove them to use nonverbal means to reduce the distance between themselves and patients rather than further reinforce their already elevated position. Nonverbal similarity cues and submissive rather than dominant nonverbal behaviors (smiling, a head tilt, a softer and higher pitched voice, greater gaze while listening to the patient, fewer interruptions) may serve this objective.

At the same time, it may be beneficial to employ character, sociability, composure, and dynamism appeals. We have already noted that patients prefer physicians who are caring, friendly, moderately composed, and expressive. We have also noted some of the nonverbal cues that convey such messages relationally. While there is a subtle distinction between sending a relational message, which is intended for a specific target, and fostering credibility impressions, which are often designed for a more generalized audience, in reality the same nonverbal behaviors may accomplish both. Thus, nonverbal signals of immediacy, expressiveness, altercentrism, and moderate relaxation may promote more general credibility as well as create a positive interpersonal relationship.

One investigation of nonverbal credibility examined how prospective patients respond to a pediatrician's tone of voice (LePoire & Parrott, 1988). It found that a friendly voice ("warmer," with considerable pitch variety, slightly high pitch level, moderately precise enunciation, and somewhat slow tempo) elicited higher ratings on character, sociability, and composure than an authoritarian voice. Moreover, female pediatricians earned higher ratings on all credibility dimensions than did male pediatricians. Research outside the medical context spotlights kinesic and proxemic immediacy, kinesic and vocal expressiveness, vocal pleasantness (which can be added to the immediacy complex), and fluency as good prospects for simultaneously achieving credibility and compliance (J. K. Burgoon et al., 1989; J. K. Burgoon, Birk, & Pfau, 1989). It is noteworthy that some of these cues are as strongly correlated with persuasiveness as they are with credibility, implying that they may achieve compliance directly as well as indirectly through the mediation of credibility.

> *Proposition 20:* Physicians may achieve greater credibility (along dimensions of character, sociability, and composure) and hence greater compliance by displaying greater nonverbal immediacy, greater nonverbal expressiveness, and less anxiety in the form of vocal fluency.

Fostering Attractiveness

Physicians are disinclined to think that attraction plays a role in the medical context. Yet its major impact in other facets of human conduct argues for its significance in physician-patient interactions. Physically attractive, well-groomed, and conventionally attired people are more persuasive and elicit more compliance than less attractive people (Chaiken, 1979; Horai, Naccari, & Fatoullah, 1974; Mills & Aronson,

1965; Snyder & Rothbart, 1971). One exception is that similarity in dress to that of one's audience may sometimes be preferable to more formal styles (Harris, James, Chavez, Fuller, Kent, Massenari, Moore, & Walsh, 1983; Hensley, 1981). Applied to the health care context, these findings recommend that physicians attend to their appearance and use their choice of formal or informal attire strategically to emphasize either status and expertise, if they feel that is lacking, or similarity, if the objective is to create rapport.

Proposition 21: Physicians achieve greater compliance if they are physically attractive and well groomed.

Proposition 22: Formal attire may be used to promote status and expertise, while informal attire may be used to promote similarity, both of which are alternative routes to compliance.

SUMMARY

There are obvious questions raised by the review of extant research on the use of instrumental verbally aggressive compliance-gaining strategies and by the literature on nonverbal and relational management communication strategies. On the one hand, it seems that physicians can gain more compliance while not decreasing satisfaction with the use of increased verbal aggression in the clinical context. On the other hand, however, a somewhat separate body of literature strongly suggests that strategies associated with increased involvement, liking, and lack of dominance are preferred by a majority of patients. One might conclude that the two bodies of literature suggest incongruent verbal and nonverbal/relational communication strategies for physicians.

If one were to conceptualize the instrumental verbal aggression strategies and the nonverbal/relational management strategies discussed in this chapter as markers of physician involvement, then no such incongruency exists. All of the strategies discussed should enhance perceptions of physician concern and involvement with the health of patients. Moreover, a more episodic analysis of the clinical situation would lead to the conclusion that physicians who use only direction-giving and cues associated with lack of involvement will be seen as indifferent, and compliance will be less than optimal. Physicians who use verbally aggressive strategies, who appear very dominant, and who make no attempt to signal involvement or some degree of concern will be seen as hostile, again leading to decreased levels of satisfaction and compliance. Thus, some combination of more verbally aggressive strategies accompanied by nonverbal and verbal strategies that express involvement and concern must punctuate the entire clinical encounter, if compliance and satisfaction are to be maximized.

REFERENCES

Becker, M. H. (1979). Understanding patient compliance: The contributions of attitudes and other psychosocial factors. In S. J. Cohen (Ed.), *New directions in patient compliance*. Lexington, MA: Lexington Books.

Becker, M. H., & Maiman, L. A. (1980). Strategies for enhancing patient compliance. *Journal of Community Health, 6,* 113–135.

Becker, M. H., & Maiman, L. A. (1982). Patient compliance. In K. L. Melmon (Ed.), *Drug therapeutics 1982. Concepts for physicians* (pp.65–79). New York: Elsevier.

Birk, T., & Burgoon, M. (1989). *The effects of instrumental verbal aggression and physician gender on compliance in the medical context.* Unpublished manuscript, University of Arizona, Tucson.

Blackwell, B. (1973). Drug therapy: Patient compliance. *New England Journal of Medicine, 289,* 249–253.

Blanck, P. D., Rosenthal, R., & Vannicelli, M. (1986). Talking to and about patients: The therapist's tone of voice. In P. D. Blanck, R. Buck, & R. Rosenthal (Eds.), *Nonverbal communication in the clinical context* (99–143). University Park: Pennsylvania State University Press.

Boomer, D. S. (1978). The phonemic clause: Speech unit in human communication. In A. W. Siegman & S. Feldstein (Eds.), *Nonverbal behavior and communication* (245–262). Hillsdale, NJ: Lawrence Erlbaum.

Boster, F. J., & Stiff, J. B. (1984). Compliance gaining message selection behavior. *Human Communication Research, 10,* 539–556.

Burgoon, J. K. (1978). A communication model of personal space violations: Explication and an initial test. *Human Communication Research, 4,* 129–142.

Burgoon, J. K., Birk, T., & Pfau, M. (1989). *The pattern of influence: Relationships among nonverbal behaviors, source credibility, and persuasion.* Manuscript submitted for publication.

Burgoon, J. K., Buller, D. B., & Woodall, G. W. (1989). *Nonverbal communication: The unspoken dialogue.* New York: Harper & Row.

Burgoon, J. K. & Hale, J. L. (1984). The fundamental topoi of relational communication. *Communication Monographs, 51,* 193–214.

Burgoon, J. K. & Hale, J. L. (1988). Nonverbal expectancy violations: Model elaboration and application to immediacy behaviors. *Communication Monographs, 54,* 58–79.

Burgoon, J. K., Pfau, M., Parrott, R., Birk, T., Coker, R., & Burgoon, M. (1987). Relational communication, satisfaction, compliance-gaining strategies, and compliance in communication between physicians and patients. *Communication Monographs, 54,* 307–324.

Burgoon, J. K. & Walther, J. (1989, May). *Nonverbal expectancies and the consequences of their violations.* Paper presented at the annual meeting of the International Communication Association, San Francisco.

Burgoon, M. (1989). Social influence. In H. Giles and P. Robinson (Eds.), *Handbook of language and social psychology.* London: Wiley.

Burgoon M., Dillard, J. P., & Doran, N. (1984). Friendly or unfriendly persuasion: The effects of violations of expectations by males and females. *Human Communication Research, 10,* 283–294.

Burgoon, M., & Miller, G. R. (1985). An expectancy interpretation of language and persuasion. In H. Giles & R. St. Clair (Eds.), *Recent advances in language, communication, and social psychology* (pp. 199–229). London: Lawrence Erlbaum.

Burgoon, M., Parrott, R., Burgoon, J., Birk, T., Pfau, M., & Coker, R. (in press–a) Primary care physicians' selection of verbal compliance-gaining strategies. *Health Communication.*

Burgoon, M., Parrott, R., Burgoon, J., Coker, R., Pfau, M., & Birk, T. (in press–b). Patients' severity of illness, noncompliance and locus of control, and physicians' compliance-gaining messages. *Health Communication.*

Burgoon, M., Parrott, R., & Facciola, P. (1988). *Actor-observer differences in perceptions of oncologists' language behavior.* Paper presented at the annual meeting of the International Communication Association, New Orleans.

Chaiken, S. (1979). Communicator physical attractiveness and persuasion. *Journal of Personality and Social Psychology, 37,* 1387–1397.

Christensen, D. B. (1978). Drug-taking compliance: A review and synthesis. *Health Services Resources, 13,* 171–187.

Cody, M. J., & McLaughlin, M. L. (1980). Perceptions of compliance-gaining situations: A dimensional analysis. *Communication Monographs, 47,* 132–148.

Cohen, S. J. (1979). *New directions in patient compliance.* Lexington, MA: Lexington Books.

Davis, M. S. (1966). Variations in patients' compliance with doctors' orders: Analysis of congruence between survey responses and results of empirical investigations. *Journal of Medical Education, 41,* 1037–1048.

Davis, M. S. (1968). Variations in patients' compliance with doctors' advice: An empirical analysis of patterns of communication. *American Journal of Public Health, 58,* 274–286.

Dillard, J. P., & Burgoon, M. (1985). Situational influences on the selection of compliance-gaining messages: Two tests of the predictive utility of the Cody-McLaughlin typology. *Communication Monographs, 52,* 289–304.

DiMatteo, M. R. (1979). Nonverbal skill and the physician-patient relationship. In R. Rosenthal (Ed.), *Skill in nonverbal communication: Individual differences* (pp. 104–134). Cambridge, MA: Oelgeschlager, Gunn, & Hain.

DiMatteo, M. R., & DiNicola, D. D. (1982). *Achieving patient compliance: The psychology of the medical practitioner's role.* New York: Pergamon.

DiMatteo, M. R., Linn, L. S., Chang, B. L., & Cope, D. W. (1985). Affect and neutrality in physician behavior: A study of patients' values and satisfaction. *Journal of Behavioral Medicine, 8,* 397–409.

DiMatteo, M. R., Prince, L. M., & Hays, R. (1986). Nonverbal communication in the medical context: The physician-patient relationship. In P. D. Blanck, R. Buck, & R. Rosenthal (Eds.), *Nonverbal communication in the clinical context* (74–98). University Park, PA: Pennsylvania State University Press.

Doyle, B. J., & Ware, J. E. (1977). Physician conduct and other factors that affect consumer satisfaction with medical care. *Journal of Medical Education, 52,* 793–801.

Edinger, J. A., & Patterson, M. L. (1983). Nonverbal involvement and social control. *Psychological Bulletin, 93,* 30–56.

Eisenberg, L. (1977). The search for care. *Daedalus, 106,* 235–246.

Eraker, S. S., Kirscht, J. P., & Becker, M. H. (1984). Understanding and improving patient compliance. *Annals of Internal Medicine, 100,* 258–268.

Falvo, D. R., & Smith, J. K. (1983). Assessing residents' behavioral science skills: Patients' views of physician-patient interaction. *Journal of Family Practice, 17,* 479–483.

Fletcher, R. H., O'Malley, M. S., Earp, J. A., Littlejohn, T. A., Fletcher, S. W., Greganti, M. A., Davidson, R. A., & Taylor, J. (1983). Patients' priorities for medical care. *Medical Care, 21,* 234–242.

Friedman, H. S. (1982). Nonverbal communication in medical interaction. In H. S. Friedman & M. R. DiMatteo (Eds.), *Interpersonal issues in health care.* New York: Academic Press.

Geerston, H. R., Gray, R. M., & Ward, R. (1973). Patient non-compliance within the context of seeking medical care for arthritis. *Journal of Chronic Disorders, 26,* 689–698.

Greene, L. R. (1977). The effects of verbal evaluative feedback and interpersonal distance on behavioral compliance. *Journal of Counseling Psychology, 24,* 10–14.

Harrigan, J. A. (1985). Self-touching as an indicator of underlying affect and language processes. *Social Science and Medicine, 20,* 1161–1168.

Harrigan, J. A., Kues, J. R., & Weber, J. G. (1986). Impressions and hand movements: Self-touching and gestures. *Perceptual and Motor Skills, 63,* 503–516.

Harrigan, J. A., Oxman, T. E., & Rosenthal, R. (1985). Rapport expressed through nonverbal behavior. *Journal of Nonverbal Behavior, 9,* 95–110.

Harrigan, J. A., & Rosenthal, R. (1983). Physicians' head and body positions as determinants of perceived rapport. *Journal of Applied Psychology, 13,* 496–509.

Harrigan, J. A., & Rosenthal, R. (1986). Nonverbal aspects of empathy and rapport in physician-patient interaction. In P. D. Blanck, R. Buck, & R. Rosenthal (Eds.), *Nonverbal communication in the clinical context* (pp. 36–73). University Park, PA: Pennsylvania State University Press.

Harrigan, J. A., Weber, J. G., & Kues, J. R. (1986). Attributions of self-touching performed in spontaneous and posed modes. *Journal of Social and Clinical Psychology, 4,* 433–446.

Harris, M. B., James, J., Chavez, J., Fuller, M. L., Kent, S., Massanari, C., Moore, C., & Walsh, F. (1983). Clothing: Communication, compliance, and choice. *Journal of Applied Psychology, 13,* 88–97.

Harris, M. J., & Rosenthal, R. (1985). Mediation of interpersonal expectancy effects: 31 meta-analyses. *Psychological Bulletin, 97,* 363–386.

Haynes, R. B., Taylor, D. W., & Sackett, D. L. (1979). *Compliance in health care.* Baltimore: Johns Hopkins University Press.

Hensley, W. E. (1981). The effects of attire, location, and sex on aiding behavior: A similarity explanation. *Journal of Nonverbal Behavior, 6,* 3–11.

Horai, J., Naccari, N., & Fatoullah, E. (1974). The effects of expertise and physical attractiveness upon opinion agreement and liking. *Sociometry, 37,* 601–606.

Jaspers, J., King, J., & Pendleton, D. (1983). The consultation: A social psychological analysis. In D. Pendleton & J. Hasler (Eds.), *Doctor-patient communication* (pp. 139–160). London: Academic Press.

Kaestler, J., Kane, R. L., Olsen, D. M., & Thetford, C. (1976). Issues underlying the prevalence of "doctor-shopping" behavior. *Journal of Health and Social Behavior, 17,* 328–339.

Kirscht, J. P., & Rosenstock, I. M. (1979). Patients' problems in following the recommendations of health experts. In G. C. Stone & F. Adler (Eds.), *Health Psychology* (pp. 189–215). San Francisco: Jossey-Bass Inc.

Klopovich, P. M., & Trueworthy, R. C. (1985). Adherence to chemotherapy regimens among children with cancer. *Topics in Clinical Nursing, 7,* 19–25.

Korsch, B. M., & Aley, E. F. (1973). Pediatric interviewing techniques. *Current Problems in Pediatrics, 3,* 3–42.

Korsch, B. M., Gozzi, E. K., & Francis, V. (1968). Gaps in doctor-patient communication, 1: Doctor-patient interaction and patient satisfaction. *Pediatrics, 42,* 855–871.

Korsch, B. M., & Negrete, V. F. (1972). Doctor-patient communication. *Scientific American, 227,* 66–74.

Lane, S. D. (1982, November). *Compliance-gaining strategies used by health practitioners: A pilot study.* Paper presented at the annual meeting of the Speech Communication Association, Boston.

Lane, S. D. (1983). Compliance, satisfaction, and physician-patient communication. In R. Bostrom (Ed.), *Communication Yearbook 7* (pp. 772–799). Beverly Hills, CA: Sage.

Larsen, K. M., & Smith, C. K. (1981). Assessment of nonverbal communication in the patient-physician interview. *Journal of Family Practice, 12,* 481–488.

LePoire, B. A., & Parrott, R. (1988, February). *Attributes of the credible pediatrician's voice.* Paper presented at the annual meeting of the Western Speech Communication Association, San Diego.

Ley, P. (1976). Towards better doctor-patient communication: Contributions from social and experimental psychology. In A. E. Bennett (Ed.), *Communication between doctors and patients* (pp. 71–98). London: Nuffield Provincial Hospital Trust.

Ley, P. (1977). Psychological studies of doctor-patient communication. In S. Rachman (Ed.), *Contributions to medical psychology, Vol. 1* (pp. 9–42). New York: Pergamon.

Ley P. (1982). Satisfaction, compliance and communication. *British Journal of Clinical Psychology, 21,* 241–254.

Lim, T. S. (1988, May). *Influences of receiver's resistance on persuader's verbal aggressiveness.* Paper presented at the annual meeting of the International Communication Association, New Orleans.

Linimon, D., Manaster, G., & Waddell, K. (1982). *Patient-physician relationships in older adulthood: Older adults' preferences for physician contact.* Paper presented to the annual meeting of the Southern Psychological Association, Dallas.

Maguire, P. (1981). Doctor-patient skills. In M. Argyle (Ed.), *Social skills and health* (pp. 55–81). London: Matheun.

Marston, M. V. (1970). Compliance with medical regimens: A review of the literature. *Nursing Research, 19,* 312–323.

Marwell, G., & Schmitt, D. R. (1967). Dimensions of compliance-gaining behavior: An empirical analysis. *Sociometry, 30,* 350–364.

Matthews, D., & Hingson, R. (1977). Improving patient compliance: A guide for physicians. *Medical Clinics of North America, 61,* 879–889.

Mills, J., & Aronson, E. (1965). Opinion change as a function of the communicator's attractiveness and desire to influence. *Journal of Personality and Social Psychology, 1,* 73–77.

Milmoe, S., Rosenthal, R., Blane, H. T., Chafetz, M. E., & Wolf, I. (1967). The doctor's voice: Postdictor of successful referral of alcoholic patients. *Journal of Abnormal Psychology, 72,* 78–84.

Norell, S. E. (1981). Accuracy of patient interviews and estimates by clinical staff in determining medication compliance. *Social Science Medicine, 15,* 57–61.

Parrott, R., & LePoire, B. (1987, November). *The pediatrician's voice: Impact on the pediatrician-parent relationship.* Paper presented to the annual meeting of the Speech Communication Association, Boston.

Robbins, J. A. (1980). Patient compliance. *Primary Care, 7,* 703–711.

Rosenthal, R. (1976). *Experimenter effects in behavioral research: Enlarged edition.* New York: Irvington Publishers, Halsted Press Division of Wiley.

Rosenthal, R. (1985). Nonverbal cues in the mediation of interpersonal expectancy effects. In A. W. Siegman & S. Feldstein (Eds.), *Multichannel integrations of nonverbal behavior* (pp. 105–128). Hillsdale, NJ: Lawrence Erlbaum.

Rosenthal, R., & Rubin, D. B. (1978). Interpersonal expectancy effects: The first 345 studies. *The Behavioral and Brain Sciences, 3,* 377–386.

Roth, H. P., & Caron, H. S. (1978). Accuracy of doctors' estimates and patients' statements on adherence to a drug regimen. *Clinical Pharmacology and Therapeutics, 23,* 361–370.

Rothert, M. L. (1982). Physicians' and patients' judgments of compliance with a hypertensive regimen. *Medical Decision Making, 2,* 179–195.

Smith, D. H., & Occhipinti, S. L. (1984, May). *Patient reactions to physician interviews.* Paper presented at the annual meeting of the International Communication Association, San Francisco.

Smith-Hanen, S. S. (1977). Effects of nonverbal behaviors on judged levels of counselor warmth and empathy. *Journal of Counseling Psychology, 24,* 87–91.

Snyder, M. (1984). When belief creates reality. In L. Berkowitz (Ed.), *Advances in experimental social psychology,* Vol. 18 (pp. 248–305). New York: Academic Press.

Snyder, M. & Rothbart, M. (1971). Communicator attractiveness and opinion change. *Canadian Journal of Behavioral Science, 3,* 377–387.

Snyder, M. & Swann, W. B., Jr. (1978). Behavioral confirmation in social interaction: From social perception to social reality. *Journal of Experimental Social Psychology, 14,* 148–162.

Speedling, E. J., & Rose, D. N. (1985). Building an effective doctor-patient relationship: From patient satisfaction to patient participation. *Social Science and Medicine, 21,* 115–120.

Street, R. L., Jr., & Buller, D. B. (1987). Nonverbal response patterns in physician-patient interactions: A functional analysis. *Journal of Nonverbal Behavior, 11,* 234–253.

Zisook, S., & Gammon, E. (1981). Medical noncompliance. *International Journal of Psychiatry in Medicine, 10,* 291–303.

Final Considerations

Gerald R. Miller
Michigan State University

As Frank Boster has chronicled briefly in pages 7–13 of this volume, the summer of 1974 was for me one of those rare professional and personal high points that make teaching and research fun. Five excellent graduate students enrolled in my seminar on interpersonal communication. Two of them, John Hocking and Barbara Walker, focused their attention on Ekman and Friesen's (1974) recently published study dealing with detecting deception from bodily and facial cues. Their efforts eventually culminated in research for Hocking's (1976) dissertation as well as several studies on deceptive communication carried out in concert with my NSF-sponsored research on the effects of using videotaped trial materials (e.g., Hocking, Bauchner, Kaminski & Miller, 1979; Miller, et al., 1981). To the best of my knowledge, this work, along with the pioneering efforts of Mark Knapp and his colleagues (e.g., Knapp, Hart & Dennis, 1974), signalled the communication field's interest in a problem area that was destined to receive widespread attention during the rest of the seventies and the decade of the eighties.

The remaining three seminar participants, Frank Boster, Michael Roloff, and David Seibold, turned their energies to the area of compliance-gaining message strategies. As Boster has recounted, this decision was reached largely because of some things Mark Steinberg and I had written about patterns of communicative control in the soon-to-be published interpersonal text, *Between People* (Miller &

Steinberg, 1975), and was reinforced by Boster's reading of Marwell and Schmitt's (1967) seminal article detailing a typology of compliance-gaining strategies. Our joint efforts produced what we have since labeled the "MBRS" study (Miller, Boster, Roloff & Seibold, 1977), a collaborative undertaking that spawned a substantial literature concerning the problem of compliance gaining—a literature, by the way, to which Boster, Roloff, and Seibold have all made substantial subsequent contributions. The present volume testifies that interest in the problem has not waned as we approach the nineties.

In the best scholarly tradition, several writers have offered criticisms of the paths pursued by researchers interested in expanding knowledge and understanding about the symbolic process of compliance gaining (e.g., Boster, pp. 7–13; Miller, 1983; Miller, Boster, Roloff & Seibold, 1987; Seibold, Cantrill & Meyers, 1985; Wheeless, Baraclough & Stewart, 1983). These criticisms include the charges that the area is in a state of terminological and typological confusion, that the research lacks theoretical substance and coherence, and that the procedures used to operationalize the selection and use of compliance-gaining message strategies are seriously wanting in ecological validity. Although I have no desire to detract from either the validity or the seriousness of these charges, it seems to me that the pattern in which research on compliance gaining has unfolded typifies most of the work conducted by communication researchers and other social scientists: an initial study examines one or two broad questions or hypotheses; concern quickly surfaces about the way variables should be conceptualized, manipulated, and measured; competing theoretical views are invoked to explain the processes of interest; and numerous studies seek to determine how various communicative, situational, and individual difference variables affect the claims advanced in the initial study. Examples of this consistent investigational pattern are numerous; they include such problems as communicator credibility, the effectiveness of fear-arousing message appeals, and the impact of prior audience attitudes on persuasive outcomes.

To say investigational events have transpired typically does not, of course, imply they have followed the scientifically optimal course; it suggests only that as we approach the nineties, the history of research on compliance gaining has not departed markedly from the beaten paths of communication scholarship. Unquestionably, steps can be taken to improve our collective efforts at understanding compliance gaining. In this brief conclusion, I will center on two steps that strike me as particularly important, occasionally using the chapters in this volume to illustrate my points. I harbor no illusion that I will bring any startling new observations to the ongoing dialogue; rather, I will be largely echoing my own prior thoughts as well as those of some of the other writers mentioned earlier. My modest goal is to outline my own priorities for future work in compliance gaining—priorities I know to be shared by some colleagues but with which other thoughtful students of communication may reasonably disagree.

STIFLING OUR HUMPTY-DUMPTY IMPULSES

If queried about the readings that have most strongly influenced my thinking about the process of communication inquiry, I would be forced to declare a dead heat between Hans Reichenbach's (1951) vintage volume, *The Rise of Scientific Philosophy*, and Donald Campbell's (1963) classic article, "Attitudes and Other Acquired Behavioral Dispositions." My vote for Reichenbach stems from his ability to strike a responsive chord regarding the crux of the eternal dispute between advocates of the rationalist and empiricist schools of philosophy. My admiration for the Campbell essay rests on my perception that he disposes effectively of one of the most hearty pseudo-problems permeating the persuasion literature, the misleadingly labeled "attitudes versus behavior" problem. In disposing of it, he offers a thought-provoking aside of particular relevance to my present remarks, asserting that the growth of twentieth-century social psychology is best marked by its proliferation of neologisms (Campbell, 1963, p. 98), and invoking such pejorative descriptive phrases as "the terminological fads and feuds in an undisciplined area such as social psychology" (p. 127).

This same charge can certainly be leveled at communication research. Are we to characterize an individual's reluctance and uneasiness to engage in symbolic transactions as *communication apprehension, reticence, shyness, social anxiety, unwillingness to communicate, speech fright*, or by yet some other term? Are certain communicators *dogmatic, authoritarian, rigid*, or short on *tolerance for ambiguity*? Do persuaders use *fear appeals, fear-arousing appeals*, or *anxiety-arousing appeals*? Do the terms *primacy/recency* and *climax/anti-climax* describe the same message phenomena or different ones? Without further flogging of the proverbial dead horse, the gist of my concern can be stated thusly: We are all often victims of our Humpty-Dumpty impulses, assuming that when we use a word or phrase it means exactly what we want, nothing more or less.

But what gloomy foreboding leads to my belief that Humpty Dumpty is sure to suffer a great scholarly fall? Unlike the novelist and poet, who cultivate rich, varied, and unique vocabularies, scientists should seek to hone an economical, publicly shared symbol system; in a word, scientists seek *parsimony* of expression. If the varied terms mentioned above, as well as others like them, are to be scientifically useful, it must be possible to draw clear theoretical, conceptual, and observational distinctions between them. And if such distinctions are not or cannot be drawn, researchers are trapped in "blooming, buzzing" terminological confusion. For these skeptics who feel that economy and consistency of word and phrase produce a drab linguistic landscape, the communication scientist has but to harken back to the venerable caveat, "Euclid alone has gazed on beauty bare."

The Humpty-Dumpty impulse problem is manifest in at least two terminological domains of the research on compliance giving. The first, most general domain concerns the term *compliance gaining* itself. What, if any, are the conceptual distinctions to be drawn between this label and terms such as *social influence* and *persuasion*? Are different processes denoted or signified by the three labels? Are the processes denoted coordinate, in the sense of functioning at the same level of abstraction, or are some processes subordinate to others—e.g., is *social influence* a more general label that encompasses those symbolic processes called *compliance gaining* and other symbolic and/or nonsymbolic processes as well? For that matter, is the term *compliance gaining* restricted to symbolic processes or does it also embrace nonsymbolic processes? Perhaps a good scientific case can be made for all three terms, as well as other similar labels, but one is hard pressed to discover much careful conceptual and definitional spade work aimed at unearthing crisp, useful distinctions between these terminological usages. In the absence of such work, it does not seem unduly pessimistic to suggest that terminological profusion results primarily from the idiosyncratic preferences of various writers and that the terms that trip most lightly off some researchers' word processors do not ring with the same scientific and rhetorical force for others.

As regards the issue of achieving parsimony, it is worth noting that the excellent chapter by O'Keefe unveils yet another terminological candidate, *regulative communication*, which she defines as communication occurring in a situation "in which one person is faced with the need to control or correct the behavior of another" (p. 87). Once again, the conceptual and definitional issues raised by the introduction of this label are fairly obvious: What, if any, are the differences between a *regulative situation*, a *persuasive situation*, a *compliance-gaining situation*, and a situation calling for a *social influence* attempt? Can clear and useful conceptual and ostensive distinctions be drawn between *regulative* messages, *compliance-gaining* messages, *persuasive* messages, and messages aimed at exerting *social influence*? O'Keefe does make the point, buttressed by an extended quotation from her work with McCornack (O'Keefe & McCornack, 1987, p. 68), that "one might think of and characterize a regulative situation in various ways including a conflict situation, a compliance-gaining situation, or a situation calling for a complain-and-remedy sequence." One can only hope, however, that the "one" referred to is a social actor and not a social scientist, for it is difficult to imagine that such terminological ambiguity will prove scientifically fruitful.

I must stress that my remarks are not meant to imply that the stipulation of clear, useful distinctions between all or some of the terms mentioned above is an impossibility, nor am I arguing for the making of distinctions for distinctions' sake. My major concern relates to the careless proliferation of terms in our research literature, a practice likely to prove scientifically counterproductive. As a colleague recently pointed out, some distinctions are probably not worth making, but when this is the case, it hardly seems necessary to coin more than one term to label the phenomena or processes of interest.

A second, less general example of the Humpty-Dumpty impulse problem surfaces in our terminological efforts to label the message elements or units used in compliance-gaining exchanges. In their original influential paper, Marwell and Schmitt (1967) referred to the 16 message alternatives found in their typology as *strategies*. Subsequent writers (e.g., Berger, 1985; Miller, 1983; Miller et al., 1987) have questioned this label, contending that *tactics* represents a more useful term, with the term *strategy* being reserved for more abstract alternatives, each of which subsumes several of the appeals found in Marwell and Schmitt's typology. For example, Miller and Parks (1982) suggest a fourfold typology of strategies, with each of the strategies encompassing four of the Marwell and Schmitt appeals.

Harkness's chapter provides a convenient vehicle for exploring some of the potential pitfalls of the Humpty-Dumpty impulse. So there can be no mistake about my overall assessment, I should first emphasize my enthusiasm for the investigational voyage she has charted and her examination of the origin and development of manipulative language. Moreover, the work reported in the chapter is generally well crafted and provides a number of valuable insights about the symbolic processes involved in children's attempts to influence their peers. Notwithstanding these plaudits, however, I sense the potential for conceptual and definitional ambiguity in her use of the term *directive*.

A *directive*, according to Harkness (p. 23), "generally refers to a word or a string of words used to influence a listener to give or to do something." Directives take several forms, including commands, questions, and statements. Harkness indicates that a crucial psychological dimension of directives is the extent of their explicitness, i.e., the degree to which they actually specify what the speaker wants the listener to do.

Is the term *directive* virtually synonymous with such terms as *compliance-gaining message strategy* and *compliance-gaining message tactic* (ignoring for the moment questions about the relative synonymy/nonsynonymy of the latter two terms), or does its meaning differ significantly? At first glance, Harkness's kernel definition seems to support the former interpretation, for compliance-gaining message appeals (whether labeled strategies or tactics) are also strings of words used to influence others. On further reflection, however, this interpretation becomes problematic. Because compliance-gaining appeals are usually conceived of as explicit symbolic warrants and/or justifications for *behavior*—e.g., "If you do *x*, I will reward you with *y*" or "If you do not do *x*, you will be derogated by significant other(s) *y*"—most of the directives listed by Harkness—e.g., "Let me see It!" "I wanna do that," "Can I push the button?"—do not qualify as compliance-gaining appeals because they specify no warrant and/or justification for complying. As directives become less explicit, one might make a case for labeling them as compliance-gaining appeals—e.g., "I won't be your friend anymore" might be conceived of as an instance of *threat* or a veiled attempt at triggering *negative esteem*, and "It's my turn to do it" might be viewed as an attempt to invoke a *moral appeal*—but such an interpretation relies on considerable "mind reading" by the intended influencee. Thus, it seems preferable to conclude that directives differ syntactically and psychologically from compliance-gaining appeals.

Some skeptical readers may dismiss my preceding remarks as mere "logic-chopping." For such skeptics, I should summarize the crux of my concern about terminological confusion. I have not meant to be unduly critical of Harkness for her use of the term *directive*, nor even sought to imply that she bears the responsibility for carefully distinguishing its meaning from its possible synonyms. After all, Harkness has adopted a perfectly acceptable theoretical framework from sociolinguistics and has used the vocabulary associated with it. What does bother me is that the term is now a part of the compliance-gaining literature *along with* numerous similar labels that remain largely unexplicated. If history has any predictive utility, it is only a matter of time before some other researcher will appropriate the term *directive*, for whatever whim or reason, and use it, a la Humpty Dumpty, in some way that obfuscates its relationship to other related labels. Although reasonable persons may differ about the gravity of such a situation, I continue to view it with alarm. While the full grandeur of a Euclidean-like vista is doubtless unattainable, some terminological tidying up would go far in remedying the conceptual and definitional clutter that characterizes the present state of compliance-gaining research.

EXCUSE ME, HAVE I BEEN PERSUADING YOU?

Some readers will recognize that the title for this section is adapted from an excellent chapter by Berger and Douglas (1982). These authors caution against the prevailing tendency to view most communicative exchanges as highly "mindful"; i.e., to assume that message production is usually characterized by considerable deliberation and rehearsal on the part of the communicators. To the contrary, they suggest, many messages are probably relatively "mindless"; i.e., they are encoded and transmitted with little accompanying thought and reflection. Rather than weighing the likely success of alternative strategies, the communicators rely on habitual, "wired in" appeals that may or may not prove to be effective.

Despite the fact that the literature on communication reveals numerous laments about the hegemony of logical positivism and radical behaviorism as guiding paradigms for research, it has always seemed to me that the prevailing theoretical and metatheoretical preferences of researchers are well calculated to drive radical behaviorists such as Watson and Skinner to paradigmatic despair—simply put, the notion that communication research is a hotbed of positivism is a red herring (see Miller & Berger, 1978). Most theories and models that attract the attention of communication researchers are replete with mediating processes and assumptions about highly mindful cognitive activity. If a cadre of committed radical behaviorists exists in our midst, I have yet to stumble upon them.

Not surprisingly, this bias towards the highly mindful communicator prevails in the literature dealing with compliance-gaining message strategies. The very term *strategy* smacks of conscious awareness and deliberate choice, a claim buttressed by the six "givens" that Seibold et al. (1985, p. 567) list as underlying the body of research on compliance-gaining message strategy selection:

1. conscious awareness of the influence "situation," including all embedded role relationships, salient sociocultural characteristics of the setting, and a clearly identifiable instrumental/interpersonal task;
2. sufficient time to rationally assess the situation and consider options;

3. the intention to formulate a plan designed to accomplish a well-defined outcome;
4. a diverse, complex, and differentiated repertoire of strategies and tactics to draw upon;
5. sufficient awareness and individual perspective-taking ability to weigh the consequences of enacting each strategic alternative; and
6. an ability to choose some strategies and forego others (that is, all strategies considered acceptable are personally accessible and can be competently enacted, and some strategies—perhaps judged by the actors to be unacceptable or inappropriate under the circumstances—can be enschewed even when they may be habitual modes of response for that actor).

Taken together, these six givens clearly imply the predominance of communicators who "think (a great deal) before they speak."

The prevailing bias toward mindfulness also manifests itself in the procedures most commonly used to study message strategy selection and use. These procedures share a common feature: *Each imposes "demands" upon communicators to reflect consciously on the persuasive task at hand, despite the fact that they may not always exert this same degree of reflectiveness in many real-world persuasive settings.* Thus, it is fair to contend that these procedures *force* communicators to behave consistently with the assumptions of cognitive, mindful models of strategy selection, even though the ecological validity of such models can reasonably be called into question.

The most obvious example of such procedural coerciveness is found in the checklist approach employed in the majority of compliance-gaining studies. Respondents receive descriptions of hypothetical scenarios requiring them to seek compliance from another. They are also presented with the investigator's pet typology of message strategies—most often, the 16 strategies identified by Marwell and Schmitt (1967)—and asked to indicate how likely they would be to use each of the strategies in attempting to achieve persuasive success. Laying aside the thorny issue of whether respondents can meaningfully discriminate among the various strategies on the checklist—e.g., whether or not respondents grasp the difference between the strategies of *positive altercasting, positive esteem,* and *positive self-feeling*—it remains crystal clear that the procedural demands require them to ponder the relative merits of numerous symbolic choices that might never occur to them in the spontaneous ebb and flow of actual persuasive exchanges.

Similar, albeit more subtle demands exist when respondents are provided with a hypothetical scenario and requested to write down the various things they might say in seeking to gain another's compliance. Although this approach is less complex and less cluttered with strategy labels than the checklist procedure, it still requires respondents to reflect consciously about the scenario and to purposefully weigh strategic alternatives. Whether such reflection would occur in real life settings involving the same circumstances described in the scenarios remains a moot issue.

The pervasive influence of mindful models of compliance gaining quickly surfaces in the present volume. The well-crafted chapters by Dillard, Meyer, and O'Keefe describe orientations based on considerable cognitive awareness and activity, and the chapter by Haslett explores the development of compliance-gaining message skills in children from a decidedly cognitive perspective. Lest I am misunderstood, I do not mean to minimize the value of these authors' contributions nor to challenge the scientific utility of highly mindful approaches for a number of compliance-gaining situations. Communicators often reflect carefully and rehearse conscientiously before undertaking compliance-gaining attempts, as important job interviews, doctoral oral examinations, and invitations to an initial date or a lifetime of marriage remind us. What does concern me is the possibility that unbridled emphasis on matters cognitive leaves us with an incomplete, inadequate picture of many persuasive exchanges occurring in everyday symbolic commerce. Perhaps I can best illustrate the reason for my concern by sketching a somewhat different way of conceiving of the process of compliance-gaining message strategy selection and use.

Start with two observations that I suspect will square with most readers' experiences: First, many communicators rely on a narrow range of strategies (indeed, as few as one or two alternatives), habitually invoking these strategies across various compliance-gaining situations; second, communicators often use ineffective strategies, hewing stubbornly to the same message alternative or alternatives even in the face of persuasive failure. Neither of these observations is consistent with a highly cognitive, mindful model of strategy selection; rather, each suggests that a number of compliance-gaining attempts occur with little accompanying deliberation.

To the extent that the two preceding observations are factually on target, they can be accounted for nicely by the venerable behaviorist dictum that *behavior is a function of its consequences*. Such a reinforcement learning approach to strategy selection and use posits the following scenario: Early attempts at compliance gaining are followed by positive or negative consequences—in terms of the present discussion they are either reinforced positively by acquiescence to message demands or they are not. If reinforced positively, the strategy is more likely to be employed in future compliance-gaining situations; if not, the probability of its occurrence in future exchanges is diminished. Moreover, if the strategy is positively reinforced in a number of compliance-gaining situations, it becomes increasingly resistant to extinction; i.e., use of the strategy persists even though it is not followed by positive consequences.

A whimsical illustration of this reinforcement learning theory approach surfaced while this epilogue was being written. In the comic strip "Calvin and Hobbes," Calvin was assailed by a burly classmate, Moe, who demanded that Calvin surrender his toy truck. Clearly, the operant strategy was threat; if Calvin did not comply with Moe's symbolic inducements, dire physical consequences would follow. Indeed, some of the threatening aspects of the exchange were treated humorously by the strip's artist, as witnessed by the following exchange between Calvin and Moe:

Moe: "You had better hand that truck over."
Calvin: "Why?"
Moe: "Because both of us will be a lot happier if you do."

Although besieged by much soul-searching and self-recrimination, Calvin complied with Moe's demand. Moreover, anyone familiar with the realities of boyhood need only look at Moe to realize that his use of the threat strategy had probably been positively reinforced in numerous compliance-gaining situations, and that he would probably continue to rely on it in future exchanges. Moreover, in light of its repeated reinforcement, the strategy would probably continue to be employed for some time even if changing circumstances rendered it ineffective. Finally, nothing about the transactions between Calvin and Moe suggested that Moe's use of threat was accompanied by a high level of awareness and cognitive activity.

My claim, simply stated, is that the world is inhabited by many Moes; in fact, I would venture to suggest that all of us behave like Moe in numerous compliance-gaining situations, even though our learned strategy preferences may not rely on threat. This claim can best be redeemed by studying the compliance-gaining process in natural settings unfettered by cognitive demands placed on the communicators by the investigator. At the outset, much of the work should be descriptive and should be at least partially devoted to assessing the validity of several assumptions underlying mindful models of strategy selection and use. For example, it would be useful to determine whether most communicators actually employ the rich repertoire of strategies that are anticipated by highly mindful models. In addition, it would be instructive to ascertain whether reliance on particular strategies persists, even when it is abundantly clear that the strategies are not yielding successful outcomes. If the results of such descriptive work should support the above possibilities, students of compliance gaining might be forced to conclude that many compliance-gaining exchanges are considerably less mindful than prevailing models imply.

To be sure, such natural-setting research will demand more effort and ingenuity than continued reliance on verbal reports regarding possible message choices in hypothetical compliance-gaining situations. But if we are interested in knowing *how communicators behave*, rather than seeking to buttress our metatheoretical biases about *how they ought to behave*, the investigational game is certainly worth the candle. Should my expectations prove to be dead wrong, it would add theoretical credence to the highly mindful models in scientific vogue; should they prove to possess some merit, it would provide a more complete explanatory picture of the compliance-gaining process. In either event, the research community would profit from the venture.

REFERENCES

Berger, C. R. (1985). Social power and interpersonal communication. In M. L. Knapp and G. R. Miller (Eds.), *Handbook of interpersonal communication* (pp. 439–499). Newbury Park, CA: Sage.

Berger, C. R., & Douglas, W. (1982). "Excuse me, but have I been talking to myself?" In F. E. X. Dance (Ed.), *Human communication theory* (pp. 42–60). New York: Harper & Row.

Campbell, D. R. (1963). Attitudes and other acquired behavioral dispositions. In S. Koch (Ed.), *Psychology: A study of a science* (Vol. 6, pp. 94–172). New York: McGraw-Hill.

Ekman, P., & Friesen, W. V. (1974). Detecting deception from the body or face. *Journal of Personality and Social Psychology, 29,* 288–298.

Hocking, J. E. (1976). *Detecting deceptive communication from verbal, visual and paralinguistic cues: An exploratory ex-periment.* Unpublished doctoral dissertation, Michigan State University.

Hocking, J. E., Bauchner, J. E., Kaminski, E. P., & Miller, G. R. (1979). Detecting deceptive communication from verbal, visual and paralinguistic cues. *Human Communication Research, 6,* 33–46.

Knapp, M. L., Hart, R. P., & Dennis, H. S. (1974). An exploration of deception as a communication construct. *Human Communication Research, 1,* 15–29.

Marwell, G., & Schmitt, D. R. (1967). Dimensions of compliance-gaining behavior: An empirical analysis. *Sociometry, 30,* 350–364.

Miller, G. R. (1983). On various ways of skinning symbolic cats: Recent research on persuasive message strategies. *Journal of Language and Social Psychology, 2,* 123–140.

Miller, G. R., Bauchner, J. E., Hocking, J. E., Fontes, N. E., Kaminski, E. P.,

200   *Contexts*

& Brandt, D. R. (1981). ". . . and nothing but the truth": How well can observers detect deceptive testimony? In B. D. Sales (Ed.), *The trial process* (pp. 145–179). New York: Plenum Press.

Miller, G. R., & Berger, C. R. (1978). On keeping the faith in matters scientific. *Western Journal of Speech Communication, 42,* 44–57.

Miller, G. R., Boster, F. J., Roloff, M. E., & Seibold, D. R. (1977). Compliance-gaining message strategies: A typology and some findings concerning effects of situational differences. *Communication Monographs, 44,* 37–51.

Miller, G. R., Boster, F. J., Roloff, M. E., & Seibold, D. R. (1987). MBRS rekindled: Some thoughts on compliance gaining in interpersonal settings. In M. E. Roloff & G. R. Miller (Eds.), *Interpersonal processes: New directions in communication research* (pp. 89–116). Newbury Park, CA: Sage.

Miller, G. R., & Parks, M. R. (1982). Communication in dissolving relationships. In S. Duck (Ed.), *Personal relationships 4: Dissolving personal relationships* (pp. 127–154). Orlando, FL: Academic Press.

Miller, G. R., & Steinberg, M. (1975). *Between people: A new analysis of interpersonal communication.* Chicago: Science Research Associates.

O'Keefe, B. J., & McCornack, S. A. (1987). Message design logic and message goal structure: Effects on perceptions of message quality in regulative communication situations. *Human Communication Research, 14,* pp. 68–92.

Reichenbach, H. (1951). *The rise of scientific philosophy.* Berkeley, CA: University of California Press.

Seibold, D. R., Cantrill, J. G., & Meyers, R. A. (1985). Communication and interpersonal influence. In M. L. Knapp & G. R. Miller (Eds.), *Handbook of interpersonal communication* (pp. 551–611). Newbury Park, CA: Sage.

Wheeless, L. R., Barraclough, R., & Stewart, R. (1983). Compliance-gaining and power in persuasion. In R. N. Bostrom (Ed.), *Communication yearbook 7* (pp. 105–145). Newbury Park, CA: Sage.

Author Index

Note: Page numbers in italic indicate that the appearance of the author's name is in a reference list.

Subject Index

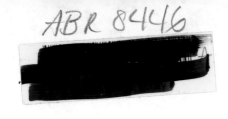